Jeanne Jones'

HEALTHY COOKING

FOR PEOPLE WHO DON'T HAVE TIME TO COOK

Jeanne Jones'
HEALTHY COOKING

FOR PEOPLE WHO DON'T HAVE TIME TO COOK

by
Jeanne Jones

Nationally
syndicated
columnist
"Cook It Light"

Rodale Press, Inc.
Emmaus, Pennsylvania

Printed in the United States of America on acid-free ∞, recycled paper ♲

Cover Design: Cecile Schoberle
Interior Design: Tad Ware & Company, Inc.

Front Cover: Scallops with Sage and Corn (page 161)
Back Cover: Chocolate Mocha Cheesecake (page 302), Chuck Wagon Stew (page 257), and Cinnamon Waffles (page 214)

Cover and Interior Photography: Tad Ware & Company, Inc.
Photograph of Jeanne Jones: Jim Coit

Library of Congress Cataloging-in-Publication Data

Jones, Jeanne.
    Jeanne Jones' healthy cooking for people who don't have time to cook / by Jeanne Jones.
        p.   cm.
    Previous edition published in 1997 under title: Healthy cooking for people who don't have time to cook.
    Includes index.
    ISBN 1–57954–092–9 paperback
    1. Quick and easy cookery.   2. Low-fat diet—Recipes.   3. Low-cholesterol diet—Recipes.   4. Low-calorie diet—Recipes.   I. Title.
TX833.5.J68   1999
641.5'63—dc21   98–31307

    ISBN 0–87596–349–8 hardcover

Distributed in the book trade by St. Martin's Press

4 6 8 10 9 7 5   hardcover
2 4 6 8 10 9 7 5 3 1 paperback

OUR PURPOSE

"We inspire and enable people to improve their lives and the world around them."

To my mother, who taught me that eating well
simply takes more planning—not more time!

 In all Rodale Press cookbooks, our mission is to provide
delicious and nutritious low-fat recipes. Our recipes also
meet the standards of the Rodale Test Kitchen for
dependability, ease, practicality, and, most of all, great
taste. To give us your comments, call 1-800-848-4735.

Contents

Acknowledgments

I would like to thank all of the people
who have helped in making
this book possible, including:

William Hansen
Tracy DeMas
Donna Burtch
Vicky Holly
My editor, Jean Rogers
My agent, Margret McBride
My husband, Don Breitenberg

You Do Have Time to Cook!

People are always telling me they wished they had more time to cook so they could prepare healthier meals for themselves and their families. The good news is—you *do* have the time!

In fact, the healthier the cooking, the less time it takes. One of the main reasons is that cleanup is so much faster. There are no greasy pots and pans to wash and no oil-spattered stove to clean.

Another real time-saver is learning to take advantage of the hundreds of convenient and healthy products we now have available in our supermarkets, such as prewashed greens and ready-cut fresh fruits and vegetables (even onions) in the produce section. In addition, there's precooked seafood, poultry and meat in the delicatessen and meat departments as well as ready-to-bake breads, rolls and pizza crusts and a wide variety of pasta sauces, salad dressings and fat-free canned broths. There are also many popular, old-fashioned soups like cream of mushroom, cream of celery and cream of chicken that now have much-improved nutritional profiles and make wonderful quick and easy sauces and gravies.

Healthy cooking also costs you less money. That is because you will be buying fewer expensive cuts of meat and more inexpensive lower-fat, higher-fiber ingredients like pasta, beans, grains, vegetables and fruits.

Healthy cooking is not about giving up your favorite recipes but rather about learning to revise them to be lower in calories, fat, cholesterol and sodium.

It is not always possible to just eliminate fat completely from a recipe without losing the desired texture and the taste of the original dish. The reason is that fat is used in cooking for two very important purposes: One is to provide texture, or "mouth feel," and the other is to carry flavor or aroma. When you eliminate fat or even lower it dramatically, you must replace it with something else in order to preserve the texture and the flavor.

To retain the texture in baked goods, for example, you can often replace some of the fat with either applesauce or pureed prunes. The cellulose in apples and the pectin in prunes traps moisture in much the same way fat does and produces a moist and tender texture. The most time-efficient way of making this substitution is to buy jars of pureed and strained baby food.

Maximize Taste by Increasing Aroma

The aroma of food is essential for our perception of flavor. Our tongues taste only four things: sweetness, saltiness, sourness and bitterness. Everything else that we call "taste" is actually "smell." Unless you are using a flavored oil or a naturally aromatic oil—such as walnut, dark sesame or extra-virgin olive—as a key ingredient in a sauce, marinade or dressing, the oil (fat) imparts no flavor of its own. It merely helps to carry the aroma of every other ingredient. Taking all the fat out of a recipe without replacing it with intensely aromatic ingredients leaves the dish tasting flat and lacking balance.

To achieve more flavor in low-fat recipes, you need to get the maximum amount of "smell" out of every ingredient you use. When adding herbs and spices, for instance, always chop fresh ones and crush dried ones with a mortar and pestle to release their aroma. Toast all nuts and seeds to enhance their flavor—as a bonus, you'll need fewer of them.

Most of the fat-free cheeses lack flavor, won't melt properly and have the texture of plastic. However, many of the reduced-fat cheeses work well as a substitute for a higher-fat cheese. When you are looking for maximum flavor from a cheese, use only the highest quality, most aromatic cheeses available, such as Parmigiano-Reggiano, Pecorino Romano or a very sharp Cheddar. Whenever possible, sprinkle both nuts and cheese over the top of a dish to stimulate the senses of both sight and smell. By doing this, the perception is always that you have used more.

Items such as nonfat sour cream, cream cheese, cottage cheese and mayonnaise work well as ingredients in recipes. However, when you are using them on their own as a topping or a spread, I recommend choosing the light or low-fat version rather than the fat free.

Balancing the flavors in a recipe can often be achieved by adding something acidic like citrus juice or vinegar. Buttermilk or yogurt can be used to replace other dairy ingredients. Also helpful for stimulating the taste buds and brightening flavor with a kind of "pleasing pain" are all of the super-hot additives such as chili oil, cayenne pepper, red-pepper flakes and Tabasco sauce.

Understand Dietary Guidelines

Every dish you prepare does not have to meet the dietary guidelines of the American Heart Association and have less than 30 percent of the calories coming from fat. By balancing higher-fat dishes with low-fat or nonfat ones, you can still easily keep your calories in line and your daily allotment of fat grams at or below the recommended levels. Remember, the guidelines are for each day or even each week, not every single meal.

Since cholesterol is found only in foods of animal origin, its consumption can easily be lowered by decreasing the portion sizes of fish, poultry, meat, high-fat dairy products and egg yolks. Conversely, fiber is found only in foods of plant origin. Therefore, it can be increased just by increasing the amounts of grains, vegetables and fruits you eat. This is certainly a simple formula for creating a lower-cholesterol, higher-fiber diet.

Many of the canned, bottled and boxed convenience foods that are so helpful in shortening cooking time are higher in sodium than their fresh counterparts. Remember, however, that the recommended maximum of 2,400-milligrams per day is for just that—an entire day. If one of your meals is particularly high in sodium, eat other meals that day that are not.

Great-Tasting Food in Record Time

This book is dedicated to achieving great-tasting dishes in a minimum amount of time. It's for people who don't have much time to cook but who are never going to be satisfied with either ordinary or unhealthy food. Interestingly enough, my favorite ways of developing the maximum amount of flavor from the healthiest, lowest-fat ingredients range from almost-instant sautéing and "oven frying" to very slow, all-day cooking in a Crock-Pot or at a very low oven temperature. In between these two techniques is rapid roasting—cooking uncovered in a very hot oven.

The recipes in this book are designed to help you meet your individual needs for cooking healthier meals in less time. For some people, that means a recipe that can be prepared, start to finish, in less than 15 minutes. For others, under 30 minutes is fast enough. Still others aren't as concerned about the start-to-finish aspect of a recipe but don't want to spend more than 30 minutes in total working time on a dish.

I have included some recipes for rapid roasting to dispel the myth that roasting is out of reach when you're in a hurry. And, of course, no cookbook would be complete without desserts. In this book, I call this section "Fast Desserts for a Fabulous Finish."

For those of you who ask the inevitable question, "Can I cut even more time from this recipe?" I've included a note with each dish entitled "In a Flash!" It provides substitutions or other ideas for making the recipe as quickly as humanly possible.

And for those who like the idea of leftovers but still want something different to eat the next day, my "Spin Off" notes give suggestions for ways to give leftovers a new taste and appearance.

Always remember, your only limitation in cooking is your own imagination. A recipe is to cooking what a blueprint is to building—it is a guideline or a plan to follow, and subject to changes and modifications wherever necessary or desired. Use these recipes as your guidelines and let your imagination run wild!

The Quick
Cook's Kitchen

Most people who think they don't have time to cook healthy meals experience some degree of frustration whenever they even enter the kitchen. Fortunately, there is a relatively simple solution for this problem. Just by properly organizing, equipping and stocking your kitchen for healthier cooking, you can go a long way toward getting get rid of this frustration forever. It's easy! In fact, a convenient kitchen will not only save you time but actually make cooking fun and exciting.

Let's start out by organizing the space you have available. Assuming that your cabinets, stove top, oven, refrigerator and sink cannot be moved, we'll begin with the countertops.

The most common mistake made in kitchen design is not

having enough counter space. In other words, there just isn't anyplace to put anything down. In fact, I have friends who have every small appliance you can think of sitting on their countertops and no room to put even a small cutting board needed to cut vegetables for a salad or slice a loaf of bread.

Counter space is of primary importance in every phase of cooking. Starting with step one in meal preparation, which is shopping, you need to have space available to put the bags down when you get home from the market. (Having to put them on the floor is not a positive first step in pursuit of the joy of cooking!)

A Place for Everything

If, like my friends, you have enough counter space but have it filled up with blenders, toasters, coffee-bean grinders, coffee makers, food processors, bread makers, waffle irons and the like, find someplace else to put the appliances you don't use daily. On the other hand, if you have a small kitchen that literally does not have counter space at all, get a folding table of some type that you can open when you need it and put away when you don't.

If you are planning on designing a new kitchen or if you're redoing the one you have, I strongly suggest having a center island in the middle of the room. The counter space on the top of it is wonderful for unloading groceries, for setting out the ingredients necessary for any dish you are making and for plating cooked food before taking it to the table. The sides of the island can be lined with drawers.

I would recommend having drawers, rather than cupboards, for all of your lower cabinet areas. You can pull out the drawers to find what you want—it sure beats getting down on your hands and knees and unloading the entire cupboard to find the pan or baking dish you want to use. Slide-out shelves behind cupboard doors are not as handy as drawers; you first have to open the doors before you can pull out the shelf—a drawer only needs to be pulled out.

Conversely, doors are more practical in upper cabinets where you can't see into drawers.

On the subject of drawers, I like to have lots of small ones, rather than a few large ones, for small items like measuring cups and spoons, rolling pins, scissors, peelers and melon ballers. An ideal place to have these small drawers is on the sides of a center island.

A real time (and frustration) saver is a wide, shallow drawer for storing dry herbs and spices in alphabetical order so that they can be found instantly. Also, by keeping herbs and spices in a cool place and out of the sunlight, they will last longer.

Another very useful kitchen feature is a trash drawer. This is a tall drawer that can house a large trash container. Any waste material you have on the countertop can be wiped off the counter directly into the drawer, rather than collected and thrown away in some other area of the kitchen. To further simplify this process, you can line the trash container with a drawstring trash liner and easily remove it when it's full. If you separate your trash into glass, metal and paper, you may want to consider a divided drawer with three separate trash containers in it.

Customize the Layout

Having the things you use most readily available is another important factor in organizing your kitchen. Believe it or not, the most common problem I see is having too much stuff in the kitchen that you don't use and not enough room to store the things you really need. Of course, the necessary basics will vary from one person to another, depending on the type of cooking you do most frequently.

If possible, install a hanging rack above the island where you can hang the utensils you use most. Just reaching up for them when you need them is a real time-saver. If an overhead rack isn't a possibility, then I suggest placing a tall round pot on top of the counter nearest the stove for long-handled spoons, scrapers, whisks and such that you use every time you cook.

Storing silverware, plates, bowls, glasses and the like near the sink makes sense. Whether you are unloading a dishwasher or washing dishes in the sink, this is the area closest to you at the time.

Pots and pans should be kept near the stove. Put baking dishes, casseroles and bowls near the countertop used most frequently to assemble ingredients.

You might not be able to choose whether your stove top is gas or electric. In many areas, only one or the other is available. When the choice is yours, I much prefer gas. When you turn it off, it is off. You don't have to move the pan to get it away from the heat, and delicate foods like fish fillets and creamy sauces can't overcook. With an electric burner, you do have to move the pan because the burner cools down slowly. Also, with gas, you can actually see exactly how much heat you are getting just by looking at the flame. With many of the fancier new electric stove tops, you can't possibly tell the exact temperature you're getting because the element is discreetly concealed under a flat opaque top for a more streamlined appearance.

A double oven is wonderful if you have the space. You can bake at two different temperatures at the same time or use the broiler in one oven while baking in the other. However, two ovens are certainly not essential. In fact, I have friends with small apartments who get along nicely with just a toaster oven.

No matter what kind of oven you're using, keep a thermometer in it that you can see easily so you know exactly what the temperature is. Don't just hope the built-in thermostat is correct. If you find it is not properly calibrated, call your gas or electric company and they will send someone out to adjust it—usually free of charge.

A microwave is a valuable timesaving appliance for thawing things quickly, reheating leftovers and, of course, heating frozen microwave dinners. However, it will never replace a stove top and a conventional oven for real cooking and baking.

Equip the Kitchen

Now let's talk about taking the Zen approach to equipping the kitchen for healthy cooking. By the Zen approach, I mean the bare essentials that you need, that you have room to store and that you always know where they are. This alone is a truly timesaving step in cooking.

Good knives are essential, but you don't need a whole set of them. In fact, for most people who don't have much time to cook, three really good knives are enough.

A **chef's knife** that has a wide, triangular-shaped blade about 8″ to 10″ long has enough leverage for chopping and can be used for other purposes as well.

A **paring knife** shaped much like a chef's knife with a blade 3″ to 4″ long is used for peeling, slicing, trimming, coring and any variety of other tasks.

A **knife with a serrated blade** about 10″ long is ideal for slicing bread, cake and fruits and vegetables that have a tough outer skin and a soft center, like tomatoes and some melons.

If you occasionally do boning, a utility or boning knife is also nice to have. It has a narrow, flexible blade about 5″ to 8″ long.

The best knives have forged blades, rather than stamped blades, of high-carbon stainless steel. They sharpen well, hold their edge, resist rust and bend without breaking.

Knife handles can be made of wood, plastic or metal, but the end of the blade, or tang, as it is called, should extend completely into the handle and be attached with rivets. The handle should be comfortable to hold and have finger grips to prevent your hand from slipping. Handle sizes do vary, so you should always "try on" a knife before buying it.

Always wash and carefully dry knives after using them and never put them in the dishwasher. Also, you should always sharpen your non-serrated knives after using them. A sharp knife is much safer to use than a dull one because it makes a cleaner cut with less pressure.

To protect your knives, store them in a wooden block (counter space permitting), in a divided drawer or on a wall-mounted rack.

To further protect your knives, use good cutting boards that won't damage the cutting edges. Polyethylene, plastic and hardwood boards all provide hygienic work surfaces. Store cutting boards near the sink, because they should always be washed before being stored. After using them for any animal product such as fish, poultry or meat, always wash them especially well with soap to prevent bacteria and germs from growing.

Kitchen scissors are another useful kitchen tool, and they are better and faster for some tasks than any knife. For example, I much prefer to cut leathery-textured things like dried tomatoes and beef jerky with scissors than with a knife.

Now let's talk pots and pans. As with knives, you don't need many of them, but the ones you have should be of high quality. For basic low-fat cooking, I recommend a large 10″ or 12″ nonstick skillet; a large 10″ or 12″ nonstick wok, sauté pan or deep skillet; small and medium saucepans; a large stock pot for cooking pasta and making stew plus a steamer basket to put in it for steaming vegetables; and a double boiler. All pots and pans should have lids.

I'm including a Crock-Pot here because it can actually substitute for any other pot for slow cooking. And the convenience of being able to start your meal in the morning in a Crock-Pot and have it ready and waiting for you when you return home is certainly an excellent way to save time.

For baking, you need a 13″ × 9″ baking dish, an 11″ × 7″ or 8″ × 8″ baking dish, at least two baking sheets or jelly-roll pans (a jelly-roll pan is a baking sheet with a rim around it), a standard-size (9″ × 5″) loaf pan, a 3-quart casserole dish, two round or square cake pans, a muffin tin (providing you ever make muffins), a 9″ or 10″ pie plate and a wire cooling rack.

You may also want a 5-quart Dutch oven, an 8-quart stock pot with a lid and a roasting pan with a rack in it for that occasional roast or turkey, if you have room for it. A meat loaf pan with a separated inner liner for the fat to drip through is also great if you make meat loaf.

Basic utensils and kitchen accessories include hot pads (which should be within reach of the stove top and the oven), dish towels, a timer if you don't have one on your oven, a can opener, a bottle opener and a corkscrew. You also need a large stirring spoon, which can be used for skimming fat, plus a slotted spoon, whisk, soup ladle, tongs, spatula, scraper, strainer and meat mallet.

Essential (must-have) gadgets include a mortar and pestle and a pepper mill. You will notice that *all* my recipes call for dried herbs to be crushed, which requires a mortar and pestle, and I always call for freshly ground black pepper.

Great (and often very useful) gadgets include a peeler, corer, zester, garlic press, meat thermometer, cheese slicer, grater, funnel, baster and ice cream scoop.

My favorite set of mixing bowls is the nest of stainless-steel bowls available in all department stores. It gives you all the needed sizes, and they are heat-proof and easily washed and stored. You will also need a colander (a bowl with holes in it) for draining pasta, fruits and vegetables. If you use many green leafy vegetables, a salad spinner is also nice to have.

Measuring equipment is essential for accurately following recipes. A set of stainless-steel dry-measure scoops, a set of glass liquid measuring cups and a set or two of measuring spoons are essential for healthy cooking. You will also need a large 8-cup glass measuring pitcher for larger amounts of ingredients.

A kitchen scale is a very useful piece of equipment. It is so much easier—and faster—to weigh many ingredients before cutting them to make sure you have the right amount.

Serious kitchen helpers include all of the marvelous electronic appliances we now have available. In the indispensable category, I would include a blender, a food processor, a hand-held mixer, a juicer and a toaster. Both a blender and a food processor are more accessible on the counter, and a toaster is messy stored in a drawer. However, both a mixer and a juicer can easily be kept in drawers or on a shelf.

In the "if you use it" category, I include a coffeemaker, coffee-bean grinder, waffle iron, standing mixer, meat slicer, hot-air popper, frozen-dessert maker and juice extractor. They can all be stored elsewhere, like in the garage, unless used frequently.

Other nonfood stuff needed in a kitchen includes all of the things we have to replace often, such as skewers, toothpicks, paper towels, paper napkins, plastic wrap, plastic bags, aluminum foil, wax paper, parchment paper, trash bags, coffee filters, cheesecloth, hand soap, dish soap, dishwasher detergent, sink cleanser, oven cleaner, sponges, dish brush, rubber gloves, scrubbing pads, Band-Aids, matches and a fire extinguisher.

Paper towels should be on a holder positioned off the counter and near the sink. Hand soap should be in a dish by the sink, because it is important to always wash your hands before handling food. Store cleaning products under the sink. Keep a fire extinguisher in perfect working condition and stored where it is easy to get to.

Dressing the Cook

Now that we have the kitchen ready for cooking in a hurry, it's time to outfit the cook. Always cook in tight-fitting clothes. Tight jeans are ideal. If you cook wearing loose-fitting clothes, you will eventually grow into them!

The tighter your clothes are, the more aware of your body you will be. And you'll be more able to control the kitchen malady I call hand-to-mouth disease, which is constantly tasting while you're cooking. Of course, a little bit of tasting is necessary. But taking in more calories tasting than you would during a meal isn't!

The Shopping List

Stocking your kitchen starts with shopping, and shopping starts with a list. Keep a shopping list out and available in your kitchen at all times. Every time you notice you're running out of anything, write it on the list. In fact, the best way to manage your kitchen inventory is by establishing a "par" stock level for everything you use often, just as they do in all restaurant kitchens. Par is the number they never drop below. For example, if par on canned tomatoes is one case, a new case will be ordered when only one case is left.

This is a good system for running your home pantry. Let's say you frequently use canned clams and it would be frustrating to run out of them. You could make two cans your par on clams. When you had only two cans left, you would put two more cans on your shopping list.

Never go to the market without a shopping list. Not only does having a list save you time, it saves you money. You are less likely to be seduced into buying all those heavily advertised, cleverly displayed and usually overpriced goodies.

Learning to be a smart shopper is the key to success. So many fantasy cookbooks out there suggest shopping every day for the freshest and best of everything. But they're simply not written for people who have trouble finding the time to shop at all, let alone every day. So I've come up with an alternate plan that works very well, particularly if you learn how to properly store what you buy.

First, you determine what day of the week is the least hectic for you. Then you decide what time during that day you can work in an hour of shopping. Plan your meals for that week using the most perishable items first. Use fish the day you buy it and freeze any poultry and meat you're not using within the first couple of days after purchase. Also, by planning your pantry carefully, you can always delay a trip to the market for several days and still have quick, easy, healthy and delicious meals in minutes.

Shopping Strategies

When making your shopping list, divide it into categories that reflect the layout of your market. Always start shopping in the middle of the market, where all the dry pantry items are located. You don't want to pile heavy cans, bottles and boxes on your fresh fruits and vegetables, and you don't want to have fresh fish, poultry, meat and dairy products off refrigeration for any longer than necessary. Nor do you want ice cream melting.

If you have enough storage space, you can save a great deal of money buying the items you use most frequently at warehouse-type stores that offer huge discounts on cases. Also, if you have a large family, you can save money buying the giant sizes of both boxed and canned goods at discount markets and shopping clubs.

Bigger is not always better, however—even when it's cheaper. If you're planning meals for just one or two people, don't buy the large economy size of things like crackers or breakfast cereal because they will often become stale and have to be thrown away.

Regardless of the size of your family, you can take advantage of weekend and seasonal specials to stock up on price-reduced staples. And don't forget to watch for sales on the nonfood pantry supplies you need as well, such as cleaning products, foil, plastic bags, paper products and the like.

Obvious but critical: Always check the expiration date on packaged goods of all types so you don't waste money on outdated products.

Purchasing for Your Pantry

The goal of a well-stocked pantry should be to have enough food stored to prepare delicious and satisfying meals without a trip to the market. I consider the refrigerator and freezer, as well as the cupboards, to be part of the total pantry system. The dry pantry contains all of the foods that are shelf stable without refrigeration. However, many items in this category, such as Worcestershire sauce, mayonnaise and ketchup, do need to be refrigerated after opening.

Start stocking your pantry by buying the things you know you like and use most frequently. Slowly add to your herb and spice inventory. If you don't have the exact type of pasta, rice or beans called for in a recipe,

(continued on page 17)

Label Reading
Made Easy

Nutrition Facts

Serving Size 1 slice (28g)
Servings Per Container 24

Amount Per Serving	
Calories 60	Calories from Fat 5

	% Daily Value*
Total Fat 0.5g	1%
Saturated Fat 0g	0%
Cholesterol 0mg	0%
Sodium 120mg	5%
Total Carbohydrate 12g	4%
Dietary Fiber 2g	6%
Sugars 2g	
Protein 3g	

Vitamin A 0%	•	Vitamin C 0%	
Calcium 10%	•	Iron 10%	
Thiamine 10%	•	Riboflavin 10%	
Niacin 10%	•	Magnesium 4%	
Phosphorus 4%	•	Zinc 2%	
Copper 2%			

*Percent Daily Values are based on a 2,000 calorie diet. Your daily values may be higher or lower depending on your calorie needs:

		Calories:	2,000	2,500
Total Fat	Less than		65g	80g
Sat Fat	Less than		20g	25g
Cholesterol	Less than		300mg	300mg
Sodium	Less than		2,400mg	2,400mg
Total Carbohydrate			300g	375g
Dietary Fiber			25g	30g

Calories per gram:
Fat 9 • Carbohydrate 4 • Protein 4

Even though labels giving all of the nutrition facts are now mandatory, there are still label-reading pitfalls that can be overcome just by knowing what they are.

- All nutritional information is given for one serving, not the entire package. So the first thing to look for is the number of servings per container. Often, buyers assume very small packages of high-calorie items contain only a single serving. But rather than eating only 100 calories' worth of a spread or dip, for example, they may be consuming a whopping 400 calories of it.

- If you want to compute the percentage of calories from fat, a simplified way is to multiply the number of fat grams by 10. Even though there are actually 9 calories in a gram of fat, it is so much easier to round them off to 10. And then divide this number by the total number of calories.

- When you're looking for whole-grain bread, make sure that the first ingredient listed *is*, in fact, a whole-grain flour. If it is simply wheat flour, it's not what you want to buy.

- To avoid products filled with preservatives, don't buy anything with too many words on the label that you can't pronounce.

- When it comes to choosing between brand names and generics, there is no hard-and-fast rule. (By generic brands, I mean those with store labels, which are usually less expensive than their nationally advertised counterparts.) The only real test is to buy both and compare the quality. It simply comes down to a cost-versus-value situation.

Pantry Basics

Dry Pantry

These items can all be stored in your kitchen pantry or cupboards. In fact, if you don't have room for them in your kitchen, they can be kept on shelves elsewhere in the house or even in the garage, if they're sealed well.

Baking powder

Baking soda

Biscuit and pancake mix, reduced fat

Clam juice

Cocoa powder, unsweetened

Cornstarch

Egg whites, powdered, such as Just Whites

Extracts, such as vanilla, almond, coconut and rum

Flour

Gelatin, unflavored

Graham cracker crumbs

Graham cracker pie crust, ready to use

Nonstick vegetable cooking spray

Oils, including canola, extra-virgin olive, dark sesame and walnut

Salt

Sugar, brown and white

Syrups, such as honey, maple syrup and molasses

Vegetables, dried, such as mushrooms and sun-dried tomatoes

Vinegars, such as balsamic, cider, distilled white, fruit flavored, red wine, rice and white wine

Beans, dried

Cereals, cooked, such as oatmeal

Cereals, ready to eat, such as All-Bran, corn flakes, Grape-Nuts, Kashi, low-fat granola, puffed rice, puffed wheat and shredded wheat

Fruit, dried, such as unsulphured apples, apricots, dates, prunes and raisins*

Grains, such as bulgur, corn grits, cornmeal, quinoa and rye berries

Jams and jellies, especially all-fruit varieties

Pasta, dry, such as spaghetti, linguine, lasagna noodles and couscous

Peanut butter, unhomogenized or old-fashioned*

Rice, regular and quick-cooking white and brown

Tofu, shelf stable*

Vegetables, such as garlic, onions and potatoes

Coffee, regular and instant

Liquors and liqueurs, such as brandy and Grand Marnier (or other orange-flavored liqueur)

Milk, nonfat instant powdered

Tea

Water, sparkling and still

Wines, such as dry red and white, sherry and Port

Condiments, seasonings, sauces and salad dressings (to be collected as needed)

• Angostura bitters

• Bacon bits, imitation

• Barbecue sauce*

- Capers*
- Chili sauce*
- Hoisin sauce*
- Horseradish*
- Ketchup*
- Liquid smoke
- Mayonnaise, low fat and fat free*
- Mustard, regular, Dijon and spicy brown*
- Olives*
- Pasta and pizza sauces*
- Pesto sauce*
- Pickle relish*
- Pickles*
- Pimientos*
- Roasted red peppers*
- Salad dressings, low fat and fat free*
- Salsa*
- Soy sauce, reduced sodium
- Tabasco sauce
- Teriyaki sauce, reduced sodium
- Worcestershire sauce*

Herbs and spices (to be collected as needed)
- Allspice berries, whole and ground
- Anise seeds, whole and ground
- Basil
- Bay leaves
- Caraway seeds
- Cardamom, ground
- Cayenne pepper
- Celery seeds, whole and ground
- Chili powder
- Cinnamon, whole sticks and ground
- Cloves, whole and ground
- Coriander, ground
- Cumin seeds, whole and ground

- Curry powder
- Dill seeds
- Dill weed
- Fennel seeds, whole and ground
- Garlic, powder and flakes
- Ginger, ground
- Juniper berries
- Mace, ground
- Marjoram
- Mustard seeds, whole and ground
- Nutmeg, whole and ground
- Onion flakes
- Oregano
- Paprika
- Peppercorns, black and white
- Poppy seeds
- Red-pepper flakes
- Rosemary
- Saffron threads
- Sage
- Sesame seeds
- Tarragon
- Thyme
- Turmeric

Herb blends
- Cajun
- Italian
- Southwestern
- Thai

Canned Goods

Beans, such as black, cannellini, chickpeas (garbanzos) and fat-free refried*
Broth, such as fat-free, reduced-sodium beef, chicken and vegetable*

Should be refrigerated after opening.

(continued)

Fruits, packed in water or juice, such as mandarin oranges and pineapple*

Juices, such as apple, pineapple, tomato and V-8*

Meat, such as ham and corned beef*

Milk, evaporated skim*

Nuts, such as peanuts, pecans, pine nuts, raw almonds and walnuts (also available in bags and in bulk)*

Poultry, such as water-packed white chicken and turkey*

Seafood, such as clams (whole, chopped or minced), crab, salmon and tuna packed in water*

Soups, such as reduced-fat, reduced-sodium cream of celery, cream of chicken, cream of mushroom, pea, tomato and vegetarian chili*

Vegetables, packed in water or juice, such as artichoke hearts, creamed corn, green chilies (diced and whole), hearts of palm, mushrooms, pumpkin, tomatoes and water chestnuts*

Refrigerated Pantry

This list includes only items that should always be stored in the refrigerator, opened or not. In all other categories, items likely to have leftovers that should be refrigerated after they are opened are marked with an asterisk.

Apples

Bread (if you don't use it quickly)

Bread dough, such as pizza and biscuit

Butter and margarine

Cabbage and cole slaw mix

Cheese

Citrus fruit

Egg substitute, liquid

Eggs

Herbs, fresh

Lemon grass (if you don't use it often, keep it in the freezer)

Milk, nonfat, low fat and buttermilk

Sour cream

Tofu, fresh

Yogurt, nonfat and low fat

Frozen Pantry

This list includes only items that should always be stored in the freezer.

Bread dough

Frozen yogurt, low fat or fat free

Fruit, unsweetened, such as blueberries, cherries, cranberries, raspberries, strawberries and sliced peaches

Ice cream, light

Ice milk, low fat or fat free

Juice concentrates, such as orange and apple

Leftovers, well-wrapped so that they are airtight

Meat, such as very lean ground beef and cubed stew meat

Phyllo pastry

Poultry, such as skinless, boneless chicken breasts and ground turkey

Seafood, such as crab and shrimp

Vegetables, such as chopped onions, chopped spinach, corn, peas and stir-fry and stew mixes

Whipped toppings, light

Should be refrigerated after opening.

substitute another type. If you don't have fresh or frozen chicken breasts called for in a recipe, you can always use canned tuna and vice versa. If you don't have the particular herb or spice called for, have fun experimenting with what you do have.

Never use dried parsley, cilantro or lemon grass, because they all taste much more like dried alfalfa than their flavorful fresh counterparts. If you don't have fresh lemon grass, substitute grated lemon rind to taste. Also, never buy the pregrated Parmesan, Romano and Cheddar cheeses that come in those round boxes—their fresh counterparts last for months in the refrigerator. Just a little freshly grated Parmigiano-Reggiano, Pecorino Romano or high-quality aged Cheddar can make a simple pantry dish seem truly gourmet, while a bit of the boxed stuff can ruin the taste of an otherwise excellent, totally fresh culinary creation. Canned stocks, broths and consommés are a much more viable alternative for homemade stocks than bouillon cubes, which are also much too salty.

Picking Produce

Fresh food is almost always everyone's first choice from a standpoint of both taste and price. However, it is not always an option if you are shopping only once a week. Also, many frozen fruits and vegetables, if properly prepared, are viable substitutes. The only produce items for which there are no stand-ins are the fresh lettuces, greens and herbs—you simply can't make a satisfactory salad out of frozen and thawed lettuce or spinach. Fortunately, the most popular varieties of whole fruits for which there are also no substitutes, like apples, bananas and oranges, all keep well in the refrigerator.

When planning your menus, always allow room for change in the selection of fresh fruits and vegetables. Wait to choose them at the market, selecting the best available at the time. In-season produce is always the best buy. It is better looking, more flavorful and less expensive. Also, check out the salad-bar section. It is a real time-saver to buy fruits and vegetables already cleaned and cut up.

Frozen Favorites

There are also many timesaving frozen ingredients available, such as chopped onions and spinach, mixed vegetables specifically for stews and stir-fries, and chopped or shredded potatoes. Frozen juice concentrates are wonderful for making sauces as well as beverages. And you can't make my famous Secret Sauce (page 278) in the dessert section of this book without vanilla ice milk.

Take advantage of the fabulous frozen fruits such as cherries, sliced peaches and berries of all types. In fact, I prefer frozen blueberries to fresh for muffins because I put them in the batter still frozen. They thaw and plump up during baking and make muffins that are much more moist than the fresh, unfrozen berries.

Even though there are some wonderful canned seafoods, such as tuna, clams and crab, when it comes to shrimp and scallops, a frozen product is far superior.

Items in the Dairy Case

Dairy products such as milk, yogurt, cottage cheese and sour cream were among the first foods to have nutritional information on their labels about their fat content. These products are generally divided into three groups: whole, low fat and nonfat. Whole milk contains about 3.5 percent butter fat; low fat contains between 2 percent and 0.5 percent; and nonfat is fat free.

To select the best dairy product with the best nutritional profile, you must always keep in mind how you are going to be using it. For example, if you are buying sour cream to put on a baked potato, I would recommend the low-fat or light sour cream because its taste and texture are more like that of regular sour cream. If you are going to be using it as an ingredient in a salad dressing, however, I would suggest getting the fat-free version because you are using it mostly as a flavor carrier.

Buttermilk is now available in both low-fat and nonfat forms. Its tangy taste is refreshing and thirst quenching. It works well as a substitute for cream in many recipes and is wonderful in baked goods from biscuits, muffins and quick breads to pancakes and waffles.

Yogurt, once considered a "foreign food," is now totally mainstream. It is a popular snack food available in a variety of flavors, and it is a good substitute for sour cream in sauces and salad dressings. When cooking with yogurt, add one tablespoon of flour to each cupful to prevent it from separating under heat.

When buying margarine, always choose one containing pure corn oil or safflower oil. Diet margarines contain water, which will make toast soggy. They are also not good for cooking. Always buy tub margarine instead of the sticks because they are less hydrogenated. Remember that, although margarine can contain saturated fat, it has no cholesterol.

Butter does contain cholesterol but not enough to affect most people when used in moderation. There are two types of butter: sweet and lightly salted. The "sweet" does not mean it contains sugar but that it contains no salt. Sweet butter is often found in the freezer section of supermarkets because it does not keep as long as the salted variety.

Eggs are usually found in the dairy case. Never buy eggs that are cracked. Always open the carton to check them before purchasing. Whether an egg is brown or white has no bearing on its nutritional value, taste or cooking time. Egg size is determined by the weight of a dozen eggs. Most recipes calling for eggs are based on large eggs, which weigh 24 ounces per dozen or 2 ounces each.

Each egg yolk contains 213 milligrams of cholesterol, but the white contains none. That is why many healthful recipes call for egg whites rather than the yolks. However, for many types of recipes, the amount of cholesterol you get per serving from whole eggs is not very high, and the yolk adds to the appeal of the dish. Also, eggs are an excellent source of moderately priced high-quality protein and are a good source of vitamin A. Even though many refrigerators have special egg holders built into them, eggs keep better when left in the carton.

Choosing Your Cheeses

Cheese is so popular that many markets have completely separate sections devoted exclusively to it. But no matter where you find it, there are now an abundance of fat-free and reduced-fat cheeses available. Fat-free cheese is not a good substitute for regular cheese because it lacks both the taste and texture of the original and does not melt properly. However, many of the reduced-fat cheeses are excellent substitutes for their higher-fat counterparts. These include ricotta, mozzarella, Monterey Jack, Cheddar, Swiss and Jarlsberg.

Generally speaking, I recommend using smaller amounts of truly fabulous higher-fat cheeses to achieve the most flavor.

Soft, moist, white cheeses such as cottage cheese, ricotta and cream cheese have a rather bland flavor that can develop an off-taste quickly. Always check the dates on the packages and use them within a week.

Soft cheeses such as Brie and Camembert should always be served at room temperature. They have a distinctive flavor that's good for both hors d'oeuvres and dessert. As with all cheeses, they should be stored in the refrigerator, tightly wrapped. They will keep for about two weeks if you change the wrap every other day.

Semisoft cheeses such as Monterey Jack, Muenster, Gouda, Havarti and Port-Salut melt well and are wonderful in casseroles. They will keep for up to three weeks if you change the wrap every few days.

Firm cheeses such as Cheddar, Jarlsberg, Edam and fontina also melt well and make wonderful melted cheese sandwiches. They will keep for up to six weeks if you change the wrapping every few days. If they develop small mold spots, just cut off the moldy area.

Hard cheeses such as Parmesan and Romano should be firm but not dry and cracked. They keep for months if you change the wrap every few days. The best Parmesan cheese is called Parmigiano-Reggiano, and the best Romano is Pecorino-Romano. Grate only as much as you plan to use immediately because these cheeses keep much better in a chunk than when grated.

Blue-veined cheeses such as bleu, Roquefort, Stilton and Gorgonzola have textures that range from creamy to hard, and they all crumble well. They will keep for well over a month if you change the wrapping every few days.

Goat cheese has been enjoying a rapid increase in popularity. Goat's milk is generally lower in butterfat than cow's milk. And because fresh goat cheeses are higher in moisture, they are typically lower in fat. Many types of goat cheese can be used interchangeably in recipes. Chèvre (pronounced *shev*) is fresh goat cheese that's somewhat similar in consistency to cream cheese. Fromage blanc, which usually comes in a tub, is somewhat higher in moisture than the goat cheeses that come in logs. Other types include feta (which is also often made from cow's milk or sheep's milk), Jack, Cheddar and mold-ripened varieties similar to Brie and Camembert. Most goat cheese keeps for up to two weeks if you change the wrapping every other day.

Fresh mozzarella is becoming popular in this country. In addition to regular mozzarella, there is now buffalo mozzarella, which has a tangier taste than that made from cow's milk. It has a delicate, spongy texture and tastes somewhat like solidified milk. Store it immersed in cold water and covered with plastic wrap. It will keep for several days if you change the water every day.

Packaged mozzarella lasts much longer than fresh mozzarella. Store it for up to two weeks, changing the wrap every few days, or freeze it for up to six months.

Selecting Seafood

Fish and other seafood are generally lower in fat than either poultry or meat and are an excellent source of protein. The rise in popularity of seafood in recent years is nothing short of amazing. In fact, the biggest-selling appetizer item throughout this country is the traditional shrimp cocktail.

Fresh fish should smell fresh, with only a mild odor. Never buy fish with a fishy smell. Whole fish should have clear, shiny eyes and shimmering scales. Fish fillets should look moist and lie flat; they should never be dry or curling up on the ends. When buying shellfish, make sure the shells are tightly closed.

Generally speaking, for quick cooking, you should buy fish and shellfish that are already cleaned and ready to cook. You can also buy shellfish such as shrimp and crab that is precooked, shelled and ready to add to salads, soups or stir-fries.

Different people divide fish into different categories, such as freshwater and saltwater, and lean and oily. Freshwater fish, such as trout, catfish and perch, tend to have more tender flesh and many more tiny bones. Saltwater fish, such as tuna, snapper and halibut, have a more solid flesh and larger bones, which are easier to remove.

Lean fish, such as sole and halibut, are more delicate and dry out easily; therefore, they are better cooked with additional fat or liquid. Oilier fish like salmon and swordfish, on the other hand, can be grilled or broiled.

All fresh seafood is extremely perishable and should be used the same day it is purchased. If you must keep it for more than a day, wash it under cold running water, pat it dry and wrap it tightly in plastic wrap. Place it on a pan of crushed ice in the coldest part of your refrigerator. If you have to keep it longer, freeze it.

When using frozen fish, always thaw it in the refrigerator. Force-thawing fish, as in a microwave, causes the texture to become mushy. Remember that fish should never be refrozen.

Purchasing Poultry

Chicken is by far the most popular poultry in this country. It provides high-quality protein and, when eaten without the skin, is low in calories, fat and cholesterol. Look for chicken with moist skin that's free of blemishes. If it is wrapped, there should not be any red liquid in the bottom of the package. That is a sign the poultry has been frozen and defrosted.

All poultry is extremely perishable and should be refrigerated as soon after purchase as possible. You can leave it in its original package if you will be using it within 24 hours. Otherwise, rewrap it well in new plastic.

Before cooking poultry, rinse it under cold running water. If washing a whole chicken, be sure to rinse inside the cavity and remove any excess fat. Also, remove any packages of giblets from inside the bird (check the neck area in larger birds) before cooking. You can rinse the giblets separately and cook them with the bird if you wish to use them for dressing or gravy.

Salmonella is a serious problem often associated with poultry; therefore, you should be careful to wash your hands both before and after handling raw poultry. And you should wash the cutting board, knife and any other utensils used with poultry in lots of hot, soapy water (plastic, acrylic and Lucite boards can go into the dishwasher).

Never defrost poultry at room temperature because bacteria multiply rapidly under those conditions. Instead, let it thaw in the refrigerator or in several changes of cold water. It is safer to cook any dressing or stuffing separately, in a baking dish, rather than in the bird, because the stuffing's moisture can encourage bacterial growth.

Broilers, or fryers, are the most popular type of chickens and weigh from 2½ to 4 pounds. You can buy them whole or cut into various-size pieces.

For quick cooking, skinless, boneless chicken breasts and chicken tenders are ideal.

Stewing hens are older and tougher chickens that require slower cooking in a liquid to tenderize them and bring out their flavor. Stewing hens are excellent for making stock.

Capons are castrated male chickens. The meat is both tender and sweet. Capons are large enough to serve as a roast when you don't want a turkey.

Rock Cornish hens are very small chickens that cook more quickly than larger birds. They can be served whole or halved, depending on their size.

Turkey used to be served primarily for Thanksgiving and Christmas. Now you can buy small turkeys and turkey parts for everyday meals. The most convenient forms for quick cooking are ground turkey and boneless breasts. You can also buy smoked and plain precooked turkey, which is wonderful for salads and casseroles.

Best Buys in Meat

Although red meat is generally higher in calories because of its fat content, it is not all bad. Red meat is supplies protein and is abundant in minerals like zinc that are often difficult to find in other foods. Meat is also packed with many of the B vitamins.

Red meat is actually not much higher in cholesterol than poultry and some fish. The problem is more that the fat of meat is primarily saturated. Worse is that the fat in meat runs throughout it, so even after you have removed all visible fat, plenty remains. It is impossible to get it all out the way you can by removing the skin and visible fat from poultry.

Beef is divided into three grades—select, choice and prime—which depend upon the amount of marbling it contains. The marbling consists of the streaks of fat running through the meat. Select contains the least amount of fat and prime the most. The leanest cuts of beef include flank steak and round steak.

(continued on page 31)

North African Stew (page 82) and Harissa (page 40)   23

Hummus (page 41)

Black Bean Dip (page 42)

Sparkling Papaya Soup (page 44)

Instant Cream of Tomato Soup (page 47)

Mexican Corn and Shrimp Chowder (page 50)

Pickled Asparagus with Herbed Lemon Dressing   29
(page 53)

Watercress and Bean Salad (page 55)

Interestingly enough, while veal is lower in fat content, it is higher in cholesterol than beef. That's because, being baby beef, it is milk fed during its short life.

According to the National Pork Producers Council, today's pork contains an average of 31 percent less fat, 14 percent fewer calories and 10 percent less cholesterol than the pork of 10 years ago. A 3-ounce serving of roasted pork tenderloin (one of the leanest cuts of pork) contains 4.1 grams of fat. That's the same amount as a 3-ounce serving of skinless roasted chicken breast.

According to the American Lamb Council, one loin chop, one shoulder chop, two rib chops and four spareribs or riblets each contain approximately 3 ounces of cooked lamb and from 8 grams to 10 grams of fat. On the higher end of the scale is roasted rack of lamb, with approximately 11 grams of fat. Your best low-fat lamb choice is cubes of leg or shoulder. Thread them onto skewers for lamb kabobs—you'll get about 6 grams of fat per 3-ounce serving.

Organ meats, such as liver, are also low in fat but extremely high in cholesterol. All organ meats are very high in vitamins and minerals but should be limited in the diet because of their high cholesterol. Cured and processed meats, such as ham, bacon, bologna, lunch meats and hot dogs, should be limited or avoided because they contain nitrates. (Nitrates give cured meats their pinkish color instead of the unappealing brown color they would otherwise have.) Also, these meats are often extremely high in saturated fat and sodium.

When buying meat, always look for the leanest cuts available. Check (or ask about) the grade of beef and avoid cuts with a lot of fat marbling. Fortunately, you really don't have to concern yourself about prime beef, which has the highest fat content, because it is not often found in ordinary stores. It is usually sold only to restaurants and specialty meat markets.

Wild game such as venison, elk and the like are also good low-fat choices but are not readily available. They are leaner because they have been allowed to run wild rather than being confined in small spaces to prevent them from losing weight.

If possible, grind your own meat for things like hamburgers and meat loaf because you can then better control the fat content.

When preparing meat, always carefully remove all visible fat. Use cooking methods that allow the fat to drain off the meat rather than being held in. For example, when you are baking or broiling meat, always put it on a rack above the pan so the fat won't be served with it. When making stews or soups, try to always make them the day before you plan to serve them so you can remove the fat that rises to the top and solidifies. This gives you not only a healthier dish but also a more appetizing-looking entrée because it will not have fat globules floating around on the top. An interesting aside is that the pictures you see in magazines for recipes containing lots of fat are always taken of defatted versions in order to avoid the congealed fat that would show in the photographs.

The one thing about meat that is much easier than fish or seafood is that cooking time is not so crucial. Even though there are many cuts of meats that are much better served very rare rather than well done, there are also many others that can be cooked for long periods of time—and the time only improves both the taste and the texture.

The single most important tip for preparing and serving meat is to use less of it. I have been in restaurants where a steak weighing at least a pound was served to a single person and arrived looking like a roast for the whole table. Remember that animal protein should never be more than one-fifth the volume of your meal. So think in terms of a small steak, a large baked potato, lots of vegetables and a wonderful salad. Or make a vegetable stir-fry with only a little beef, pork or lamb to add flavor and texture. Treat all meat as a condiment rather than the focus or main part of the meal.

All about Storing

Storing everything you purchase as soon as you return home is essential for both the organization of your kitchen and the freshness of your food. You'll save both time and money!

Always keep adequate supplies of material needed for proper storage, such as plastic bags, plastic wrap, plastic containers, aluminum foil and jars with tight-fitting lids. When storing anything in the refrigerator or the freezer, seal it tightly so air cannot get to it. That prevents dehydration, which causes loss of taste and texture. Also, unless dairy products are tightly covered in the refrigerator, they will pick up the taste of other foods.

Wash and store all your leafy vegetables and fresh herbs properly and promptly, which saves time later. It also saves money because there is less spoilage and less likelihood of contamination by bugs and bacteria.

All leafy greens, such as lettuce, spinach, parsley, basil and dill, should be torn apart and dunked in cold water until completely free of dirt and grit. Drain the leaves thoroughly and then roll them up in paper or cotton toweling to dry them well. Put them into bags before refrigerating them. When you are ready to prepare a salad, your lettuce is clean, crisp and dry. Dryness is very important because wet lettuce dilutes the salad dressing so that you need more of it.

From Start to
Finish in 15 Minutes

The recipes in this section of the book can literally be·made in 15 minutes—or less. That means that, from the time you walk into your kitchen until you have a dish ready to serve, no more than 15 minutes has elapsed.

When creating this group of recipes, I had to discipline my own thinking dramatically in order to organize all the ingredients and plan their preparation in such a way that I could stay within the allotted time. In fact, this chapter has truly changed my approach to quick cooking.

I have also included a number of sauces and dressings in this chapter. Any of these simple sauces can turn a piece of grilled fish or chicken, or even a hamburger patty, into a truly special dish.

From Start to Finish in 15 Minutes

Fresh Peach Salsa

This delightfully different fresh fruit salsa is a refreshing change from the more usual tomato salsas. It is also a wonderful accompaniment for plain grilled fish and poultry.

Each ¼-cup serving contains approximately:

Calories: 20
Fat: 0 g.
Cholesterol: 0 mg.
Sodium: 11 mg.

6   **fresh peaches, peeled and diced**
¼   **cup finely chopped fresh cilantro**
1   **jalapeño pepper, seeded and finely chopped (wear plastic gloves when handling)**
1   **shallot, finely chopped**
1   **garlic clove, pressed or minced**
1   **tablespoon rice vinegar**
1   **teaspoon fresh lemon or lime juice**

1.   In a large bowl, combine the peaches, cilantro, peppers, shallots, garlic, vinegar and lemon or lime juice; mix well. Store, tightly covered, in the refrigerator.

Makes 3 cups

↔ In a Flash!

The easiest way to peel a peach is to dip it into boiling water for 30 seconds. It will literally slip out of its skin!

↔ Spin Off

Leftover salsa adds a nice bite to fruit salads and is good served over green salads as well.

Savory Apricot Sauce

This sauce has a variety of uses. I particularly like it on pork chops, but it is also good on poultry and other meats.

Each ⅓-cup serving contains approximately:

Calories: 107
Fat: 0 g.
Cholesterol: 0 mg.
Sodium: 271 mg.

6 **ounces dried apricot halves**
1 **can (14½ ounces) defatted chicken stock**
¼ **cup water**
2 **teaspoons dried Italian herb seasoning**
1 **teaspoon balsamic vinegar**
½ **teaspoon salt**
¼ **teaspoon ground nutmeg**

1. In a medium saucepan, combine the apricots, stock and water. Bring to a boil over high heat. Reduce the heat to medium and boil for 5 minutes. Transfer to a blender or a food processor.

2. Add the Italian seasoning, vinegar, salt and nutmeg. Puree. (If a thinner consistency is desired, add a little more water.)

3. Pour the mixture back into the same saucepan and reheat briefly over medium heat.

Makes 2 cups

↔ In a Flash!

There is no faster way to make this sauce!

↔ Spin Off

Add ½ tablespoon extra-virgin olive oil to ½ cup of leftover sauce for a delicious salad dressing or an unusual pasta sauce.

Herbed Mustard Sauce

Tofu (soybean curd) is a wonderful flavor carrier and can be used to extend the volume of sauces and salad dressings. Silken soft tofu is a form of soft tofu that is really creamy when blended.

1	cup silken soft tofu
2	tablespoons Dijon mustard
1	tablespoon fresh lemon juice
1½	teaspoons extra-virgin olive oil
1	garlic clove, pressed or minced
¼	teaspoon dried thyme, crushed
¼	teaspoon dried rosemary, crushed
¼	teaspoon salt
¼	teaspoon freshly ground black pepper

1. Place the tofu, mustard, lemon juice, oil, garlic, thyme, rosemary, salt and pepper in a blender container. Blend until satin smooth.

Each 1-tablespoon serving contains approximately:

Calories: 14
Fat: 1 g.
Cholesterol: 0 mg.
Sodium: 51 mg.

Makes 1 cup

↦ In a Flash!
Use ¼ teaspoon garlic powder instead of the fresh garlic clove.

↦ Spin Off
Add to soups, stews and other sauces and salad dressings for added flavor and nutrition.

Honeyed Yogurt Sauce

If you prefer a sweeter sauce, add more honey. You can also add a little cinnamon or nutmeg.

1	cup fat-free plain yogurt
1	tablespoon honey
½	teaspoon vanilla extract

1. In a small bowl, combine the yogurt, honey and vanilla. Mix well. Store, tightly covered, in the refrigerator.

Each ¼-cup serving contains approximately:

Calories: 43
Fat: 0 g.
Cholesterol: 1 mg.
Sodium: 38 mg.

Makes 1 cup

↦ In a Flash!
Use vanilla yogurt and eliminate the vanilla extract.

↦ Spin Off
Add leftover sauce to blender drinks, other sauces and salad dressings

Creamy Chilean Kiwi Dressing

This is a recipe I developed for the Chilean Fresh Fruit Association. Since our winter is their summer, we get fabulous fresh fruits from Chile during the months that we cannot grow them ourselves. This dressing has become such a popular recipe with my family that I now make it all year around, using Chilean kiwis in the winter and California kiwis in the summer. It can be used as a dressing on salads of all types or as a sauce on cold fish, poultry or meat. When time permits, refrigerate until cold before serving.

Each ¼-cup serving contains approximately:

Calories: 42
Fat: 0 g.
Cholesterol: 0 mg.
Sodium: 18 mg.

3   **kiwifruit, finely diced**
1   **banana, mashed**
¾   **cup fat-free vanilla yogurt**
2   **tablespoons rice vinegar**
½   **teaspoon coconut extract**

1. In a large bowl, combine the kiwis, bananas, yogurt, vinegar and coconut extract. Mix well.

Makes 2 cups

↪ In a Flash!

The easiest way to peel a kiwi is to first cut off both ends, then insert a small spoon up under the peel. Carefully run it all the way around the fruit just under the peel. Then just slip the peel off. You can also buy kiwis already peeled in the salad bar section of your supermarket.

↪ Spin Off

Substitute white wine or pineapple juice for the rice vinegar in the recipe; serve as a dessert or a chilled fruit soup.

This is my favorite blue cheese dressing. It is a revision I did for a reader in San Diego. She had gotten the original recipe from a restaurant called the Hob Nob. She wanted it revised to be both lower in fat and cholesterol and greatly reduced in volume. I decided that 2 cups was a good amount to make because this dressing is so rich tasting that you need only a very small amount of it on a salad. Even though this dressing can easily be made in less than 15 minutes, it is better if refrigerated for at least 1 hour before serving.

Each 2-tablespoon serving contains approximately:

Calories: 32
Fat: 1 g.
Cholesterol: 4 mg.
Sodium: 324 mg.

Blue Cheese Dressing

1½	**teaspoons cider vinegar**
1	**teaspoon steak sauce**
1	**teaspoon Worcestershire sauce**
½	**teaspoon sugar**
½	**teaspoon salt**
2	**tablespoons minced onions**
1	**garlic clove, pressed or minced**
½	**teaspoon freshly ground black pepper**
2	**ounces blue cheese, crumbled**
½	**cup low-fat cottage cheese**
½	**cup buttermilk**
¾	**cup fat-free mayonnaise**

1. Combine the vinegar, steak sauce, Worcestershire sauce, sugar and salt in a medium bowl and stir until the sugar and salt have completely dissolved.

2. Add the onions, garlic and pepper; mix well. Stir in the blue cheese, cottage cheese and buttermilk. Add the mayonnaise and stir until completely blended. Store, tightly covered, in the refrigerator.

Makes 2 cups

↦ **In a Flash!**

Buy blue cheese that's already crumbled. You'll need ½ cup.

↦ **Spin Off**

This is a great sauce for poultry and meat.

Creamy Italian Dressing

Try to make the dressing the day before you plan to use it so the flavors can blend. You can alter the character of this dressing dramatically by changing the herbs.

Each 1-tablespoon serving contains approximately:

Calories: 10
Fat: 0 g.
Cholesterol: 1 mg.
Sodium: 94 mg.

½ **cup fat-free sour cream**
⅓ **cup buttermilk**
2 **tablespoons shredded fresh Parmesan cheese**
1 **teaspoon dried basil, crushed**
1 **garlic clove, pressed or minced**
½ **teaspoon salt**
¼ **teaspoon freshly ground black pepper**

1. In a small bowl, mix the sour cream and buttermilk until smooth. Stir in the Parmesan, basil, garlic, salt and pepper. Mix well.

Makes 1 cup

↔ **In a Flash!**

Use ⅛ teaspoon garlic powder (or less) instead of fresh garlic.

↔ **Spin Off**

This dressing is also a good sauce for fish, poultry and meat.

Harissa

Harissa is a hot and spicy condiment frequently served in North Africa with couscous dishes of all types. In Tunisia, you can buy it in the markets already prepared. Some versions of this popular condiment are very hot.

3 **garlic cloves, pressed or minced**
1 **tablespoon crushed red-pepper flakes**
1 **can (6 ounces) tomato paste**
3 **tablespoons fresh lemon juice**

Pictured on page 23

1. Combine the garlic and red-pepper flakes in a small bowl and mix well. Add the tomato paste and lemon juice. Blend to make a smooth paste.

Makes about 1 cup

Each 1-tablespoon serving contains approximately:

Calories: 11
Fat: 0 g.
Cholesterol: 0 mg.
Sodium: 85 mg.

↔ In a Flash!

Use ½ teaspoon garlic powder instead of fresh garlic. Place all the ingredients in a bowl and mix.

↔ Spin Off

This condiment keeps well for over a week in the refrigerator and can be used in or on virtually any dish of your choice.

Hummus

This is a low-fat version of the popular Middle Eastern dip. It is traditionally served with pita bread, but it is also good with raw vegetables.

Each 2-tablespoon serving contains approximately:

Calories: 49
Fat: 1 g.
Cholesterol: 0 mg.
Sodium: 39 mg.

1 **can (15 ounces) chick-peas, undrained**
2 **tablespoons fresh lemon juice**
4 **garlic cloves, pressed or minced**
1 **teaspoon extra-virgin olive oil or dark sesame oil**
1 **teaspoon ground cumin (optional)**

Pictured on page 24

1. Place the chick-peas in a blender or food processor. Add the lemon juice, garlic, oil and cumin (if using). Blend until smooth.

Makes 1½ cups

↔ In a Flash!

Use ½ teaspoon garlic powder in place of fresh garlic.

↔ Spin Off

Thin any leftover dip with broth or stock and use as a sauce on couscous.

Black Bean Dip

This bean dip can be served with baked tortilla chips as an appetizer. Or you can serve it as a side dish with quesadillas or other Mexican entrées.

Each serving contains approximately:

Calories: 71
Fat: 1 g.
Cholesterol: 0 mg.
Sodium: 544 mg.

Pictured on page 25

1   can (15 ounces) black beans, undrained
1   teaspoon chili powder
¼   teaspoon salt
¼   teaspoon freshly ground black pepper
¼   teaspoon ground cumin
2   drops Tabasco sauce (or to taste)
½   medium onion, chopped
2   garlic cloves, pressed or minced
1   can (4 ounces) diced green chili peppers

1.   Drain the beans and reserve 2 tablespoons of the liquid. Place the beans and liquid in a blender container. Add the chili powder, salt, black pepper, cumin and Tabasco sauce. Blend until smooth.

2.   Combine the onions and garlic in a large nonstick skillet. Cover and cook over low heat until the onions are soft and translucent. Uncover and cook, stirring often, until slightly browned. Add the chili peppers and cook for 3 minutes. Add the bean puree and mix well. Serve hot or cold.

Makes 6 servings

⇥ In a Flash!

Replace the garlic cloves with ½ teaspoon garlic powder. Or use ¾ cup prechopped onions and ¼ teaspoon garlic powder.

⇥ Spin Off

Use leftover dip as a filling for burritos; spread it on tortillas and roll up.

Herbed Grilled Cheese Sandwiches

This recipe is for open-faced sand- wiches. However, for a heartier sandwich, just put two of the slices together for a traditional sandwich and double the nutritional figures.

Each serving contains approximately:

Calories: 145
Fat: 3 g.
Cholesterol: 6 mg.
Sodium: 308 mg.

4   **slices bread, toasted**
1   **cup shredded reduced-fat Monterey Jack cheese**
1   **teaspoon dried oregano, crushed**
1   **teaspoon freshly ground black pepper**

1.   Preheat the broiler. Place the bread in a single layer on a baking sheet. Sprinkle evenly with the Monterey Jack, oregano and pepper. Broil for about 2 minutes, or until the cheese is melted and starts to bubble.

Makes 4 servings

↣ In a Flash!
Buy the cheese already shredded.

↣ Spin Off
Cube leftover sandwiches to use in salads and soups.

Sparkling Papaya Soup

Pictured on
page 26

This refreshing tropical-fruit soup is one of my favorite first courses for brunch or lunch. Also, I have never served it to anyone who didn't ask me for the recipe! Note that the recipe calls for low-fat yogurt; fat-free doesn't work well.

Each serving contains approximately:

Calories: 193
Fat: 1 g.
Cholesterol: 2 mg.
Sodium: 37 mg.

2	**large ripe papayas, peeled and cut into large cubes**
¼	**cup fresh lime juice**
¼	**cup mild-flavored honey, such as clover**
¾	**cup plain low-fat yogurt, divided**
1	**cup sparkling water, divided**
	Mint sprigs (optional)

1. Reserve a few cubes of the papaya for a garnish. Place the remainder in the bowl of a food processor. Add the lime juice, honey and ½ cup of the yogurt. Process until smooth.

2. Add ½ cup of the water and process until blended. Transfer to a large bowl.

3. Mix in the remaining ½ cup water. Serve immediately, garnished with the reserved papaya, dollops of the remaining ¼ cup yogurt and the mint sprigs (if using).

Makes 4 servings

⇥ In a Flash!

Make the soup ahead through step 2. Chill until serving time. Add the remaining sparkling water just before serving.

⇥ Spin Off

Blend leftover soup with crushed ice for a great drink.

Herbed Melon Soup

This delightfully refreshing cold soup also makes an unusual and very light summer dessert. To serve the soup immediately, start with cold cantaloupe. Otherwise, chill the soup before serving for the best flavor.

Each serving contains approximately:

Calories: 57
Fat: 0 g.
Cholesterol: 0 mg.
Sodium: 15 mg.

6 cups diced cantaloupe
1½ tablespoons fresh lemon juice
1 tablespoon chopped fresh basil
Basil sprigs (optional)

1. Place the cantaloupe, lemon juice and chopped basil in a blender container. Blend until smooth. Serve garnished with the basil sprigs (if using).

Makes 6 servings

⇥ In a Flash!

Buy already-cut cantaloupe in the salad-bar section of the market.

⇥ Spin Off

Thicken the soup with gelatin and use it as a dressing on fruit salad. One envelope of unflavored gelatin, which is 1 scant tablespoon, will jell 2 cups of liquid firmly. To simply thicken liquid, you need only about 1 teaspoon of gelatin for 2 cups. Soften the gelatin first in 2 tablespoons of cold water, then add ¼ cup of boiling water and stir until completely dissolved. Add enough of the liquid you want thickened to equal 2 cups.

Egg Drop Soup

This traditional soup is served in all Chinese restaurants. It is so quick and easy to make that it is also a great first course to serve at home. For an interesting variation, try making it with clam juice instead of chicken stock. For a vegetarian Asian menu, use vegetable stock.

Each serving contains approximately:

Calories: 42
Fat: 1 g.
Cholesterol: 0 mg.
Sodium: 157 mg.

2 **cans (14½ ounces each) defatted chicken stock**
3 **egg whites, lightly beaten**
1 **teaspoon reduced-sodium soy sauce**
¼ **cup chopped scallion tops**

1. In a medium saucepan, bring the stock to a boil over high heat. Cook, uncovered, for 5 minutes to reduce the volume.

2. Add the egg whites all at once and cook, stirring constantly, until they're white and stringy. Remove from the heat and stir in the soy sauce and scallion tops.

Makes 4 servings

↬ In a Flash!

Buy scallions already chopped in the salad-bar section of the market.

↬ Spin Off

Add leftover pasta, rice, vegetables, fish, poultry or meat to this soup for a hearty main-course soup.

Instant Cream of Tomato Soup

Pictured on
page 27

This recipe is from my friend Leni Reed, who publishes the newsletter Supermarket Savvy. *When I told her that I was working on a book for people who don't have time to cook, she said I should try this recipe. I made it immediately and found it so tasty that I have made it many times since.*

1   **jar (26 ounces) low-fat pasta sauce**
1   **cup defatted chicken stock**
6   **ounces silken soft tofu**
    Chopped fresh basil (optional)

1. Combine the pasta sauce, stock and tofu in a blender or food processor and blend until creamy.

2. Pour the mixture into a medium saucepan and warm over medium heat. (Or pour into a medium bowl and microwave on high power until warmed through.) Serve garnished with the basil (if using).

Makes 6 servings

↔ In a Flash!

This is already truly "instant"! There's literally no way to make it faster.

↔ Spin Off

Leftover soup is a perfect pasta sauce, delicious and nutritious.

Each serving contains approximately:

Calories: 100
Fat: 5 g.
Cholesterol: 0 mg.
Sodium: 480 mg.

Chick-Pea Soup for the Soul

This recipe was sent to me by a reader who is a vegetarian. He said that it is every bit as healing and soothing to the soul as the more traditional chicken soup.

Each serving contains approximately:

Calories: 301
Fat: 6 g.
Cholesterol: 0 mg.
Sodium: 753 mg.

1	tablespoon extra-virgin olive oil
3	garlic cloves, pressed or minced
1	medium onion, finely chopped
2	tablespoons chili powder
1	teaspoon dried thyme, crushed
¼	teaspoon salt
¼	teaspoon freshly ground black pepper
3	medium zucchini, cut into ½" rounds
1	can (16 ounces) chick-peas, rinsed and drained
1	can (14½ ounces) ready-cut tomatoes, undrained
6	cups vegetable stock or water
2	ounces dry angel hair, broken into 2" pieces

1. Heat the oil and garlic in a large heavy saucepan over medium heat for about 1 minute, or just until the garlic starts to sizzle. Add the onions and cook, stirring frequently, for 4 minutes, or until the onions are soft and translucent. Add the chili powder, thyme, salt and pepper; mix well.

2. Add the zucchini and turn the heat to high. Continue to cook, stirring frequently, for 5 minutes, or until the zucchini is soft. Add the chick-peas, tomatoes and stock or water. Bring to a boil.

3. Add the pasta and cook for 2 minutes, or until the pasta is tender but still firm to the bite.

Makes 4 servings

↣ In a Flash!

Use ½ teaspoon garlic powder and buy the zucchini already sliced in the salad-bar section of the market.

↣ Spin Off

Add more pasta to leftover soup and create a pasta main dish.

Sherried Pea Soup

If you prefer not to use the sherry in this recipe, you can substitute apple juice and add 1 tablespoon wine vinegar and ½ teaspoon sherry extract. If you're using salted stock, omit the salt. The easiest way to quick-thaw the frozen peas in this recipe—and other vegetables throughout the book—is in the microwave.

Each serving contains approximately:

Calories: 71
Fat: 1 g.
Cholesterol: 1 mg.
Sodium: 171 mg.

2	cups defatted chicken stock
3	cups frozen peas, thawed
½	teaspoon sugar
¼	teaspoon salt
¼	teaspoon freshly ground black pepper
1	cup skim milk
⅓	cup dry sherry

1. Combine the stock, peas, sugar, salt and pepper in a blender container and blend until pureed. Pour the mixture into a medium saucepan and bring to a boil over medium heat. Reduce heat to low and simmer for 5 minutes.

2. Stir in the milk and sherry.

Makes 8 servings

↝ In a Flash!
Use 1 can (14½ ounces) defatted chicken stock plus ¼ cup water.

↝ Spin Off
Leftover soup is excellent served cold.

Mexican Corn and Shrimp Chowder

Pictured on page 28

This hearty soup can be served as either an appetizer or an entrée. The recipe makes about 6½ cups, so you can decide how large you want each serving to be. The figures below are for servings of about ¾ cup.

Each serving contains approximately:

Calories: 175
Fat: 3 g.
Cholesterol: 66 mg.
Sodium: 302 mg.

1	tablespoon canola oil
1	medium onion, finely chopped
1	medium red bell pepper, seeded and finely chopped
1	can (4 ounces) diced green chili peppers
3	cups frozen corn kernels, thawed, divided
1½	cups defatted chicken stock, divided
1	can (12 ounces) evaporated skim milk
12	ounces frozen shelled uncooked small shrimp, thawed
¼	cup chopped fresh cilantro leaves
	Freshly ground black pepper (to taste)
	Cilantro sprigs (optional)

1. In a large soup pot over medium-high heat, warm the oil. Add the onions, red peppers and chili peppers. Sauté until the onions are transparent but do not brown.

2. Place 2 cups of the corn and ½ cup of the stock in a food processor and blend until pureed. Add to the pot.

3. Stir in the milk, the remaining 1 cup corn and the remaining 1 cup stock. Simmer for 3 minutes.

4. Add the shrimp and simmer gently for 1 to 2 minutes, or until the shrimp turn opaque. Stir in the chopped cilantro and black pepper. Serve garnished with the cilantro sprigs (if using).

Makes 8 servings

⤙ In a Flash!
Use about 1½ cups prechopped onions.

⤙ Spin Off
Serve leftover soup as a sauce for rice or pasta.

Cool Coleslaw

This quick and easy coleslaw is sure to be a hit with the whole family. It is great served with a cold sandwich, with bar-becue fare of all types or with grilled fish, poultry or meat.

Each ½-cup serving contains approximately:

Calories: 47
Fat: 3 g.
Cholesterol: 3 mg.
Sodium: 94 mg.

2   **tablespoons sugar**
1   **tablespoon fresh lemon juice**
1   **tablespoon white vinegar**
¼   **teaspoon freshly ground black pepper**
⅛   **teaspoon salt**
¼   **cup reduced-fat mayonnaise**
2   **tablespoons low-fat milk**
2   **tablespoons buttermilk**
1   **package (8 ounces) coleslaw mix**

1.   Combine the sugar, lemon juice, vinegar, pepper and salt in a large bowl and stir until the sugar and salt have dissolved. Mix in the mayonnaise, milk and buttermilk.

2.   Stir in the coleslaw mix. If not serving immediately, cover tightly and refrigerate.

Makes 4 cups

↔ In a Flash!

Instead of using a mixture of milk and buttermilk, substitute ¼ cup fat-free or light sour cream.

↔ Spin Off

Add chopped cooked fish, poultry or meat to leftover salad to turn it into a main dish. If desired, use the mixture as a filling for tacos or sand-wiches.

Baby Lima Appetizer

These tasty tidbits can be served as a vegetable side dish, a salad or hors d'oeuvres (use tooth-picks for serving). The lima beans will absorb more sesame oil flavor if you allow them to stand for a while before serving.

Each ¼-cup serving contains approximately:

Calories: 61
Fat: 1 g.
Cholesterol: 0 mg.
Sodium: 31 mg.

1   **can (14½ ounces) defatted chicken stock**
1   **package (16 ounces) frozen baby lima beans, thawed**
2   **teaspoons dark sesame oil**

1.   Bring the stock to a boil in a medium saucepan over high heat. Add the lima beans and bring back to a boil. Reduce the heat to low, cover and simmer for 12 minutes, or until the limas are tender but not starting to split. Drain thoroughly; if desired, reserve the liquid for another use.

2.   Transfer the limas to a medium bowl and add the oil. Mix well.

Makes 3 cups

↔ In a Flash!
Make the beans a day or two before you plan to serve them.

↔ Spin Off
The drained cooking liquid may be served as a soup on its own or added to other soups. You could also use it to cook other vegetables. Any left-over beans can be added to other hot or cold dishes.

Pickled Asparagus
with Herbed Lemon Dressing

The cholesterol-free dressing on these asparagus is amazingly rich tasting. You may use it immediately or chill it first. For added flavor, serve the asparagus garnished with chives and their edible flowers. To pickle your own asparagus, blanch spears and marinate them in ¼ cup vinegar. Refrigerate and let stand for 2 to 4 hours.

Each serving contains approximately:

Calories: 35
Fat: 1 g.
Cholesterol: 0 mg.
Sodium: 780 mg.

¼   **cup fat-free mayonnaise**
½   **teaspoon dried thyme, crushed**
½   **teaspoon grated lemon rind, yellow part only**
⅛   **teaspoon cayenne pepper**
1   **jar (16 ounces) pickled asparagus spears, chilled**

Pictured on page 29

1. In a small bowl, combine the mayonnaise, thyme, lemon rind and cayenne. Spoon out 1 tablespoon of the liquid from the asparagus and add to the bowl; mix well.

2. To serve, divide the asparagus among serving plates and drizzle with the dressing.

Makes 4 servings

↔ In a Flash!
Use ¼ teaspoon pure lemon extract in place of the grated lemon rind.

↔ Spin Off
These zesty asparagus are good chopped up in salads or added to pasta.

Creamy Cucumber Salad

This salad is wonderful served with cold fish or chicken. Although it's very good served at room temperature, sometimes I make it the day before to give the flavors time to marry in the refrigerator.

Each serving contains approximately:

Calories: 70
Fat: 0 g.
Cholesterol: 0 mg.
Sodium: 532 mg.

1 **cup fat-free mayonnaise**
¼ **cup sugar**
4 **teaspoons white vinegar**
½ **teaspoon dried dill weed, crushed**
½ **teaspoon salt**
4 **medium cucumbers, peeled and thinly sliced**
3 **scallions, chopped**

1. Combine mayonnaise, sugar, vinegar, dill and salt in a large bowl and mix well. Add the cucumbers and scallions and again mix well.

Makes 8 servings

↔ In a Flash!
Have all of the ingredients chilled before making the salad.

↔ Spin Off
Add cold cooked fish or poultry to leftover salad.

Watercress and Bean Sprout Salad

This is a quick and easy salad that is a nice accompaniment to almost any entrée. You can also add fish, poultry or meat to this salad and serve it as a main course.

Each serving contains approximately:

Calories: 68
Fat: 4 g.
Cholesterol: 2 mg.
Sodium: 137 mg.

Pictured on page 30

1	bunch watercress
1½	cups fresh bean sprouts
1	tablespoon extra-virgin olive oil
1	tablespoon red wine vinegar
⅛	teaspoon salt
⅛	teaspoon freshly ground black pepper
3	ripe tomatoes, sliced
2	tablespoons shredded or grated fresh Parmesan cheese

1. Clean the watercress and bean sprouts. Place in a bowl. Add the oil, vinegar, salt and pepper. Mix well.

2. Place the tomatoes on individual plates. Top with the watercress mixture. Serve sprinkled with the Parmesan.

Makes 4 servings

↣ In a Flash!

Buy the watercress, bean sprouts and tomatoes in the salad-bar section of the supermarket already washed and ready to use.

↣ Spin Off

Salt tends to wilt all types of salad greens. If you want to store this salad in the refrigerator for a couple of days, prepare it without the salt. Add salt just before serving.

Pear and Blue Cheese Salad

The various tastes and textures in this recipe combine to create a distinctively different and truly delicious salad that is ideal for entertaining. It takes only about 15 minutes to make, and you can prepare it hours before your guests arrive. Arrange the greens, pears and blue cheese on individual plates, cover with plastic wrap and refrigerate until serving time. Add the dressing and walnuts at the last minute. I always toast walnuts before using them in any dish because that greatly enhances their flavor.

Each serving contains approximately:

Calories: 223
Fat: 13 g.
Cholesterol: 8 mg.
Sodium: 209 mg.

Pictured on page 63

½   cup chopped walnuts
1½   cups port wine, apple cider or grape juice
6   cups assorted young greens, torn into bite-size pieces
2   pears, peeled, cored and sliced
6   tablespoons crumbled blue cheese
2   shallots, sliced
1   garlic clove, halved
1   tablespoon Dijon mustard
2   tablespoons balsamic vinegar

1. Put the walnuts in a medium saucepan and place over medium heat. Cook, stirring frequently, until nicely toasted; watch carefully as they burn easily. Transfer the walnuts to a bowl and set aside.

2. Pour the port, cider or grape juice into the same pan. Bring to a boil over medium-high heat. Continue to boil until reduced in volume by half. Remove from the heat and allow to cool while you prepare the salads.

3. Divide the greens among serving plates. Arrange the pear slices evenly over the top of the greens. Sprinkle with the blue cheese.

4. Pour the reduced liquid into a blender container. Add the shallots, garlic, mustard and vinegar; puree. Drizzle over the salads and sprinkle with the walnuts.

Makes 4 servings

➳ In a Flash!
Use canned pears packed in juice; they're already peeled and cored.

➳ Spin Off
Make more of the dressing than you need for this recipe and use it on other salads. Or serve it as a hot or cold sauce on poultry or meat.

Warm Southwestern Couscous Salad

1½ **cups water**
 1 **cup dry whole-wheat couscous**
 1 **can (15 ounces) black beans, rinsed and drained**
 1 **cup frozen corn kernels, thawed**
¾ **cup salsa**
 1 **can (4 ounces) diced green chili peppers**
 1 **tablespoon chopped fresh cilantro**
½ **teaspoon salt**
¼ **teaspoon freshly ground black pepper**

1. Bring the water to a boil in a medium saucepan over high heat. Stir in the couscous and bring to a boil again. Reduce the heat to low, cover the pan and cook for 2 minutes, or until all the water has been absorbed. Remove from the heat. Fluff with a fork. Cover and allow to stand for 5 minutes.

2. In a large bowl, mix the beans, corn, salsa, peppers, cilantro, salt and pepper. Add the couscous and mix well. Serve warm.

Makes 4 servings

⟿ In a Flash!

Prepare the recipe with leftover couscous or any other grain for a cold salad.

⟿ Spin Off

Refrigerate leftovers and stuff into a pita pocket lined with lettuce for a handy brown bag lunch.

Savory Chicken Salad

This salad offers a delightful combination of tastes and textures. It can be prepared in advance and stored, tightly covered, in the refrigerator. If you do that, do not add the almonds until serving time or they will lose much of their crispness.

Each serving contains approximately:

Calories: 252
Fat: 8 g.
Cholesterol: 72 mg.
Sodium: 436 mg.

¼ **cup fat-free mayonnaise**
¼ **cup fat-free sour cream**
1 **tablespoon honey mustard**
¼ **teaspoon celery salt**
¼ **teaspoon freshly ground black pepper**
¼ **teaspoon onion powder**
3 **cups diced cooked chicken**
1½ **cups seedless green grapes, halved**
1 **cup chopped celery**
¾ **cup sliced scallions, including the tops**
¼ **cup chopped almonds, toasted**

Pictured on page 64

1. In a large bowl, combine the mayonnaise, sour cream, mustard, celery salt, pepper and onion powder; mix well. Add the chicken, grapes, celery and scallions; toss until well mixed. Stir in the almonds.

Makes 4 servings

⇥ In a Flash!

Use about 12 ounces canned white chicken or water-packed white albacore tuna in place of the cooked chicken.

⇥ Spin Off

Use leftover salad as a filling for pita-pocket sandwiches.

Tasty Tuna Salad

Serve this nutrition-packed tuna mixture over greens. Or turn it into a sandwich by spreading it on your favorite whole-grain bread.

Each serving contains approximately:

Calories: 195
Fat: 1 g.
Cholesterol: 15 mg.
Sodium: 965 mg.

1	**can (12 ounces) solid-pack white albacore tuna in water, drained and flaked**
1	**can (8 ounces) water chestnuts, drained and chopped**
2	**scallions, sliced**
1	**small carrot, peeled and grated**
½	**cup fat-free mayonnaise**
¼	**cup sweet pickle relish**
1	**teaspoon Dijon mustard**
¼	**teaspoon salt**
⅛	**teaspoon freshly ground black pepper**

Pictured on page 65

1. In a medium bowl, mix the tuna, water chestnuts, scallions, carrots, mayonnaise, relish, mustard, salt and pepper.

Makes 4 servings

↔ In a Flash!

Buy carrots that are already grated or shredded and scallions that are chopped in the salad-bar section of the market. Also, if serving as a salad, buy a package of ready-to-serve greens.

↔ Spin Off

Leftovers can be added to scrambled eggs and omelets.

Tuscan Tuna Salad

This salad is ideal for picnics and tail-gate parties because it's better served at room temperature than cold. When carrying it to events such as these, take along a can opener and add the tuna just before serving. Pack along crisp vegetables to serve with the salad.

Each serving contains approximately:

Calories: 309
Fat: 6 g.
Cholesterol: 15 mg.
Sodium: 1,091 mg.

Pictured on page 66

2   cans (16 ounces each) cannellini beans, rinsed and drained

1   tablespoon extra-virgin olive oil

1   can (12 ounces) solid-pack white albacore tuna in water, drained and flaked

½   medium red onion, thinly sliced

¼   cup chopped fresh basil

1½ tablespoons fresh lemon juice

½   teaspoon freshly ground black pepper

1. Combine the beans and oil in a large bowl and mix well. Add the tuna, onions, basil, lemon juice and pepper; mix well.

Makes 4 servings

↪ In a Flash!
Use ½ cup prechopped onions.

↪ Spin Off
Heat leftover salad and serve over pasta.

Oatmeal Crème Brûlée

Here's a delightfully different way to serve your morning cereal. In fact, I like it so much I have included it on the "Sail Light" menus I have created for Windstar Cruises. And it is extremely popular with the passengers.

Each serving contains approximately:

Calories: 392
Fat: 3 g.
Cholesterol: 11 mg.
Sodium: 404 mg.

1	**can (12 ounces) evaporated skim milk**
½	**cup quick-cooking rolled oats**
⅛	**teaspoon salt**
4	**tablespoons packed dark brown sugar, divided**
½	**cup vanilla ice milk**
½	**cup fresh raspberries**

1. In a medium saucepan, combine the milk, oats, salt and 2 table-spoons of the brown sugar. Bring to a boil over medium heat. Reduce the heat to low and simmer, stirring constantly, for 1 minute.

2. Divide the mixture between 2 ovenproof bowls or gratin dishes. Top each serving with ¼ cup of the ice milk and 1 tablespoon of the remaining brown sugar. Arrange ¼ cup of the raspberries on the top of each one.

3. Place under a preheated broiler for about 1 or 2 minutes, or until the sugar starts to bubble and turn dark. Serve immediately.

Makes 2 servings

↬ In a Flash!

Prepare the recipe ahead. Assemble and broil each serving as indicated. Then cool to room temperature, cover with plastic wrap and refrigerate. At serving time, reheat in a microwave on high power for about 2 minutes. For a simplified version of the crème brûlée, cook the oatmeal as indicated in step 1 above; serve it plain or topped with fruit of your choice.

↬ Spin Off

Leftovers can be stirred together to make a sort of pudding and served hot or cold for dessert.

Herbed Green Beans

You can use this recipe for other vegetables, such as brussels sprouts, cauliflower and broccoli.

4 **cups fresh green beans**

1 **tablespoon canola oil**

½ **cup chopped fresh parsley**

½ **cup chopped fresh chives or scallion tops**

1 **teaspoon dried basil, crushed**

¼ **teaspoon dried thyme, crushed**

¼ **teaspoon salt**

Each serving contains approximately:

Calories: 36
Fat: 2 g.
Cholesterol: 0 mg.
Sodium: 79 mg.

1. Steam the beans for 5 minutes, then rinse under cold running water and drain thoroughly. (This stops the cooking process and preserves the bright color of the beans.)

2. Warm the oil in a large nonstick skillet over medium heat. Add the parsley, chives or scallion tops, basil, thyme and salt; mix well. Cook for about 1 minute, or until the mixture starts to sizzle. Stir in the beans and heat through.

Makes 8 servings

↦ In a Flash!

Use frozen green beans and thaw in the microwave before adding them to the skillet.

↦ Spin Off

Use leftover beans in cold salads.

Pear and Blue Cheese Salad (page 56)

Savory Chicken Salad (page 58)

Tasty Tuna Salad (page 59)

Tuscan Tuna Salad (page 60)

Honey-Mint Couscous (page 74)

Zesty Orange and Onion Rice (page 76)

Mixed-Tomato Marinara Sauce with Herbed Couscous   **69**
(page 80)

Tomato-Basil Fettuccine with Spinach-Cheese Sauce
(page 83)

Chinese Spinach

Water spinach (sometimes called water broccoli) is my favorite Chinese vegetable, and this is my favorite way to prepare it. This uniquely different green vegetable has very long stems and is usually available only in Asian markets. If you can't find it, you can substitute regular spinach, but both the taste and texture are quite different.

Each serving contains approximately:

Calories: 88
Fat: 3 g.
Cholesterol: 0 mg.
Sodium: 480 mg.

2 pounds Chinese water spinach
2 tablespoons reduced-sodium soy sauce
2 teaspoons dark sesame oil
2 teaspoons sugar
3 garlic cloves, pressed or minced

1. Trim the stems off the spinach and wash the leaves well to remove any grit. Drain thoroughly.

2. Combine the soy sauce, sesame oil, sugar and garlic in a small bowl and mix well.

3. Bring a large pot of water to a rapid boil. Add the spinach and stir for 30 seconds, or until it just starts to wilt and turns a brighter green. Immediately drain thoroughly in a colander. Return the spinach to the pot, add the soy sauce mixture and mix well.

Makes 4 servings

⇥ In a Flash!

Buy a bag of washed and trimmed regular spinach.

⇥ Spin Off

Leftovers are wonderful in soups. Also, you can serve the cold spinach as a side dish with fish, poultry or meat.

Sesame Stir-Fried Asparagus

The intense bright green of this asparagus is perfect for adding color to a plate, and the sesame flavor is outstanding with grilled fish, poultry or meat.

Each serving contains approximately:

Calories: 49
Fat: 4 g.
Cholesterol: 0 mg.
Sodium: 2 mg.

12 **ounces fresh asparagus**
1 **tablespoon dark sesame oil**

1. Break the tough ends off the asparagus and discard. Cut each spear diagonally into 1½″ pieces.

2. Place a large nonstick skillet over medium-high heat until drops of water sprinkled into the skillet dance on the surface. Add the oil, tilting the pan to coat the surface. Add the asparagus and cook, stirring constantly, for about 2 to 3 minutes, or until a very bright green.

Makes 4 servings

↔ In a Flash!

Buy ready-cut asparagus in the salad-bar section of the market.

↔ Spin Off

Serve cold leftover asparagus as a sensational salad on its own or add it to other salads. I sometimes make this dish just to chill for salad.

Mushroom and Pea Medley

This simple vegetable side dish is truly versatile. It is particularly good served with roasted poultry and meats.

Each serving contains approximately:

Calories: 83
Fat: 2 g.
Cholesterol: 0 mg.
Sodium: 207 mg.

1	tablespoon corn-oil margarine
2	garlic cloves, pressed or minced
2	cups chopped fresh mushrooms
¼	teaspoon onion powder
¼	teaspoon salt
¼	teaspoon freshly ground black pepper
1	bag (1 pound) frozen peas, thawed

1. Melt the margarine in a large nonstick skillet over medium heat. Add the garlic and cook for about 1 minute, or just until it sizzles. Add the mushrooms and cook, stirring frequently, for 3 minutes. Add the onion powder, salt and pepper and mix well. Stir in the peas and cook for 3 more minutes, or until thoroughly heated.

Makes 6 servings

↦ In a Flash!

Use ¼ teaspoon garlic powder and packaged ready-to-use chopped mushrooms.

↦ Spin Off

Serve leftovers cold as a salad.

Honey-Mint Couscous

This quick dish is as versatile as it is delicious. You can serve it as a side dish or mix it with fish, poultry or meat for an entrée. This recipe is fabulous enough for holidays yet easy enough to make a regular item on your everyday menus. For a vegetarian meal, prepare the couscous with vegetable stock. For a great-tasting and unusual breakfast treat, use skim milk for all of the liquid, omit the pepper, substitute canola oil for the olive oil and top the mixture with the fresh fruit of your choice.

Each serving contains approximately:

Calories: 268
Fat: 3 g.
Cholesterol: 0 mg.
Sodium: 185 mg.

Pictured on page 67

1   can (14½ ounces) defatted chicken stock
¼   cup water
¼   cup honey
2   teaspoons extra-virgin olive oil
¼   teaspoon salt
¼   teaspoon freshly ground black pepper
1   cup dry couscous
½   cup chopped fresh mint leaves
    Mint sprigs (optional)

1. Combine the stock, water, honey, oil, salt and pepper in a medium saucepan and bring to a boil over high heat. Stir in the couscous and chopped mint. Bring to a boil again. Reduce the heat to low, cover the pan and cook for 2 minutes, or until all the liquid has been absorbed. Remove from the heat. Fluff with a fork. Cover and allow to stand for 5 minutes. Serve garnished with the mint sprigs (if using).

Makes 4 servings

⇥ In a Flash!

This is as fast as it gets!

⇥ Spin Off

The cold couscous makes a wonderful salad all by itself. You can also mix it with fruit, vegetables, fish, meat or poultry.

Fiesta Corn Surprise

I named this dish "surprise" because I couldn't believe anything so easy could possibly be such a hit with my whole family. It is my sister's recipe, and she is always asked to bring it to every family gathering.

Each serving contains approximately:

Calories: 123
Fat: 6 g.
Cholesterol: 16 mg.
Sodium: 427 mg.

1	**can (16 ounces) salt-free corn kernels, undrained**
1	**package (3 ounces) reduced-fat cream cheese, softened**
1	**medium red bell pepper, seeded and diced**
1	**can (4 ounces) diced green chili peppers**
¼	**cup chopped scallions**

1. Drain the corn, reserving 2 tablespoons of the liquid. Combine the reserved liquid and the cream cheese in a medium saucepan and stir until smooth.

2. Add the corn, red peppers, chili peppers and scallions. Warm over medium heat.

Makes 4 servings

↤ In a Flash!

Buy already-chopped scallions and red bell peppers in the salad-bar section of your supermarket.

↤ Spin Off

Serve leftovers as a dip with baked tortilla chips or as a sandwich filling in pita bread. You can also add leftover chopped cooked poultry or meat to the corn and serve it as a main dish.

Zesty Orange and Onion Rice

Orange juice is fabulous in low-fat cooking because it can be used to replace fat while enhancing the dish's flavor, richness and nutritional profile. Rice, too, is an extremely versatile ingredient, and brown rice, in particular, is an excellent source of fiber. Instant brown rice takes only 10 minutes to cook, making it an ideal ingredient when you're in a hurry. For a more striking presentation, serve the rice in hollowed-out oranges.

Each ½-cup serving contains approximately:

Calories: 119
Fat: 1 g.
Cholesterol: 0 mg.
Sodium: 149 mg.

Pictured on page 68

2 teaspoons extra-virgin olive oil
2 garlic cloves, pressed or minced
1 medium onion, chopped
2 cups orange juice
1 teaspoon dried oregano, crushed
½ teaspoon salt
¼ teaspoon freshly ground black pepper
¼ teaspoon ground cinnamon
⅛ teaspoon crushed red-pepper flakes (or to taste)
1½ cups uncooked quick-cooking brown rice

1. Combine the oil and garlic in a medium saucepan and cook over medium heat for about 1 minute, or until the garlic sizzles. Add the onions and continue to cook, stirring frequently, for 3 minutes, or until the onions are translucent.

2. Add the orange juice, oregano, salt, black pepper, cinnamon and red-pepper flakes. Bring to a boil over high heat. Stir in the rice. Cover, reduce the heat to low and cook for 10 minutes, or until the liquid is absorbed. Fluff with a fork.

Makes 4 cups

↔ In a Flash!

Substitute couscous for the brown rice and save 5 minutes.

↔ Spin Off

Mix cold leftovers with assorted greens and vegetables for a salad. For a soup, thin leftovers with vegetable or chicken stock.

Stir-Fried Ginger Noodles

These spicy noodles are delicious by themselves or combined with tofu, fish, poultry or meat.

Each serving contains approximately:

Calories: 179
Fat: 4 g.
Cholesterol: 0 mg.
Sodium: 351 mg.

1 tablespoon canola oil
¼ cup chopped fresh ginger
5 garlic cloves, pressed or minced
2 tablespoons reduced-sodium soy sauce
1 teaspoon dark sesame oil
2 tablespoons Chinese rice wine, dry sherry or apple juice
8 ounces dry angel hair

1. Warm the canola oil in a wok or large nonstick skillet over medium-high heat. Add the ginger and garlic. Cook over medium heat for about 1 minute, or until they start to sizzle. Continue to cook, stirring constantly, for 1 minute. Add the soy sauce, sesame oil and the rice wine, sherry or apple juice. Mix well.

2. Cook the pasta in a large pot of boiling water for about 2 minutes, or until tender but still firm to the bite. Drain thoroughly in a colander and add to the mixture in the wok or skillet. Stir until thoroughly mixed.

Makes 6 servings

↬ In a Flash!

Omit the soy sauce and rice wine, sherry or apple juice; replace them with ¼ cup teriyaki sauce.

↬ Spin Off

Serve leftover noodles cold as a salad—either plain or mixed with leftover cold fish, poultry or meat.

Asian Pasta

I use Japanese chuka soba noodles in this recipe because I love their appearance. They are so curly they look like they have a tight perm. Also, they cook in just 2 minutes. However, if you can't find them in your market, you can substitute any thin wheat noodle, such as angel hair. You can also substitute a spicy-hot salsa for the Chinese chili paste.

Each serving contains approximately:

Calories: 182
Fat: 2 g.
Cholesterol: 0 mg.
Sodium: 204 mg.

¼   cup rice vinegar
2   tablespoons reduced-sodium soy sauce
2   tablespoons honey
1   teaspoon Chinese chili paste
2   tablespoons minced fresh ginger
2   scallions, minced
8   ounces dry chuka soba noodles
2   teaspoons dark sesame oil

1. In a small bowl, mix the vinegar, soy sauce, honey, chili paste, ginger and scallions.

2. Cook the noodles in a large pot of boiling water for about 2 minutes, or until tender but still firm to the bite. Drain thoroughly in a colander. Return to the pot, add the sesame oil and toss well. Add the sauce mixture and toss again.

Makes 6 servings

↔ In a Flash!
Replace the soba with angel hair pasta, which also takes only 2 minutes to cook.

↔ Spin Off
Serve leftover pasta cold as a salad. (This pasta is so good cold that I often make it just to have on hand as a salad.) If desired, add chopped cooked fish, poultry or meat.

Fettuccine Alfredo

This recipe offers a wonderfully delicious and nutritious alternative to the fat- and cholesterol-laden original version of this popular Roman dish.

Each serving contains approximately:

Calories: 358
Fat: 8 g.
Cholesterol: 17 mg.
Sodium: 438 mg.

2 tablespoons fat-free cream cheese, softened
2 teaspoons unbleached all-purpose flour
1 garlic clove, pressed or minced
1⅓ cups skim milk
¾ cup grated fresh Parmesan cheese
¼ teaspoon freshly ground black pepper
1 package (9 ounces) fresh fettuccine
Chopped fresh parsley (optional)

1. In a medium saucepan, mix the cream cheese, flour and garlic until well blended. Stir in the milk. Bring to a boil over high heat, whisking constantly. Reduce the heat to medium-low and simmer for 2 minutes, or until thickened. Add the Parmesan and pepper; mix well. Remove from the heat.

2. Cook the fettuccine in a large pot of boiling water for 2 minutes, or until tender but still firm to the bite. Drain thoroughly in a colander and return to the pot. Add the sauce and toss to mix well. Serve sprinkled with the parsley (if using).

Makes 4 servings

⇢ In a Flash!

Use ⅛ teaspoon garlic powder in place of the garlic clove. Buy ready-grated fresh Parmesan.

⇢ Spin Off

Combine leftover pasta and sauce with cooked vegetables for a pasta salad.

Mixed-Tomato Marinara Sauce
with Herbed Couscous

**Pictured on
page 69**

*I use couscous in this
recipe because it can
be prepared so
rapidly. However,
this sauce is equally
delicious on any
type of pasta, rice or
beans.*

Each serving contains
approximately:

Calories: 405
Fat: 4 g.
Cholesterol: 0 mg.
Sodium: 561 mg.

Sauce

2   ounces sun-dried tomatoes
    (½ cup tightly packed)

1   medium onion, coarsely chopped

2   garlic cloves, pressed or minced

2   cups sliced fresh mushrooms

1   can (14½ ounces) Italian-style stewed tomatoes

¾   teaspoon dried oregano, crushed

½   teaspoon freshly ground black pepper

¼   teaspoon ground nutmeg

⅛   teaspoon crushed red-pepper flakes

Couscous

2   cups water or defatted chicken stock

1   tablespoon extra-virgin olive oil

1   teaspoon ground coriander

¾   teaspoon ground cumin

½   teaspoon salt

¼   teaspoon freshly ground black pepper

1   cup dry whole-wheat couscous

1. *To make the sauce:* Place the sun-dried tomatoes in a heatproof
bowl, cover with boiling water and allow to stand for 5 minutes.

2. Combine the onions and garlic in a large heavy saucepan. Cover
and cook over low heat for 10 minutes, or until the onions are soft
and translucent; add a little water if necessary to prevent scorching.

3. Transfer the sun-dried tomatoes and liquid to a blender container and blend until coarsely chopped. Add to the onion mixture. Add the mushrooms, stewed tomatoes, oregano, black pepper, nutmeg and red-pepper flakes. Simmer, uncovered, for 5 minutes, or until the mushrooms are tender.

4. *To make the couscous:* While the sauce is simmering, combine the water or stock, oil, coriander, cumin, salt and pepper in a medium saucepan. Bring to a boil over high heat. Stir in the couscous and bring to a boil again. Reduce the heat to low, cover the pan and cook for 2 minutes, or until all the liquid has been absorbed. Remove from the heat. Fluff with a fork. Cover and allow to stand for 5 minutes.

5. Spoon the couscous onto serving plates. Top with the sauce.

Makes 4 servings

⇢ In a Flash!

Use 1½ cups prechopped onions, ¼ teaspoon garlic powder and an 8-ounce package of presliced mushrooms in place of their equivalents above.

⇢ Spin Off

Mix leftover sauce and couscous together and serve cold as a salad. Or serve the sauce alone as a condiment with poultry or meat.

North African Stew

**Pictured on
page 23**

*Quick and hearty is
a good description
for this spicy vege-
tarian stew. It is
almost always served
with harissa, a very
hot and spicy condi-
ment that North
Africans either make
at home or buy in
their markets
already prepared,
like ketchup. There's
a recipe for harissa
on page 40 if you
want to serve this
dish in true Tunisian
style.*

Each serving contains
approximately:

Calories: 462
Fat: 3 g.
Cholesterol: 0 mg.
Sodium: 649 mg.

2   **cups water**
1   **cup dry whole-wheat couscous**
1   **medium onion, chopped**
1   **green bell pepper, seeded and chopped**
1   **can (14½ ounces) ready-cut tomatoes, undrained**
2   **cans (15 ounces each) chick-peas, rinsed and drained**
1   **package (8 ounces) shredded carrots**
2   **cups frozen peas, thawed**
1   **cup raisins**
2   **tablespoons ground cumin**
2   **tablespoons paprika**
1   **tablespoon ground cinnamon**

1.   Bring the water to a boil in a medium saucepan over high heat.
Stir in the couscous and bring to a boil again. Reduce the heat to low,
cover the pan and cook for 2 minutes, or until all the water has been
absorbed. Remove from the heat. Fluff with a fork. Cover and allow
to stand for 5 minutes.

2.   Combine the onions, peppers and tomatoes in a large saucepan.
Cover and simmer over medium heat until the onions are soft and
translucent. Add the chick-peas, carrots, peas, raisins, cumin, paprika
and cinnamon. Mix well. Simmer for 5 minutes.

3.   Serve the vegetable mixture over the couscous.

Makes 6 servings

⤹ In a Flash!

Buy the peppers already chopped in the salad-bar section of the market.

⤹ Spin Off

*Leftovers make a wonderful cold couscous salad; combine the couscous
and the vegetable mixture.*

Tomato-Basil Fettuccine
with Spinach-Cheese Sauce

This creamy spinach and cheese sauce is also good served over other flavors of fresh pasta. For maximum visual appeal, however, the wonderful color contrast of the red tomato pasta and the green sauce can't be beat.

Each serving contains approximately:

Calories: 499
Fat: 11 g.
Cholesterol: 22 mg.
Sodium: 904 mg.

1 package (10 ounces) frozen chopped spinach, thawed and drained
1 cup shredded fresh Parmesan cheese
¾ cup low-fat cottage cheese
½ cup skim milk
1 tablespoon extra-virgin olive oil
1 garlic clove, halved
¾ teaspoon dried oregano, crushed
½ teaspoon freshly ground black pepper
¼ teaspoon ground nutmeg
¼ teaspoon salt
⅛ teaspoon crushed red-pepper flakes
12 ounces fresh tomato-basil fettuccine

Pictured on page 70

1. In a blender or food processor, combine the spinach, Parmesan, cottage cheese, milk, oil, garlic, oregano, black pepper, nutmeg, salt and red-pepper flakes. Blend until smooth and evenly green in color. Pour the sauce into a medium saucepan and warm over medium heat.

2. Cook the fettuccine in a large pot of boiling water for about 2 minutes, or until tender but still firm to the bite. Drain thoroughly in a colander. Serve topped with the sauce.

Makes 4 servings

↤ In a Flash!
Make the sauce ahead of time and store it, covered, in the refrigerator.

↤ Spin Off
Use cold leftover sauce as a salad dressing.

Parmesan Polenta

Precooked polenta is wonderful to have on hand, both for instant hors d'oeuvres and for easy entrées. It is available seasoned and unseasoned. And it does not need to be refrigerated until it is opened. This recipe calls for half of a 24-ounce package.

Each serving contains approximately:

Calories: 52
Fat: 1 g.
Cholesterol: 2 mg.
Sodium: 212 mg.

12 ounces (½ package) precooked ready-to-serve unseasoned polenta

3 tablespoons grated fresh Parmesan cheese

1. Preheat the broiler. Coat a baking sheet or a pizza pan with non-stick vegetable cooking spray. Slice the polenta into eight ½″-thick rounds and arrange them on the pan. Coat the polenta lightly with the spray. Top each round with about 1 teaspoon of the Parmesan.

2. Place the polenta under the broiler for about 3 to 4 minutes, or until the Parmesan melts and starts to brown lightly.

Makes 4 servings

↔ In a Flash!
This is as quick and easy as it gets!

↔ Spin Off
Serve leftovers for breakfast in place of toast.

Polenta with Creamy
Sun-Dried Tomato Sauce

**Pictured on
page 94**

This is a quick, easy and inexpensive vegetarian entrée that's sure to be a hit with the whole family. You can also serve the sauce over pasta or rice. To make your own dried tomatoes, halve plum tomatoes and sprinkle lightly with kosher salt. Place in a 250° oven for 10 to 12 hours, or until dried.

Each serving contains approximately:

Calories: 322
Fat: 9 g.
Cholesterol: 16 mg.
Sodium: 986 mg.

1	cup sun-dried tomatoes
1½	cups boiling water
1	package (24 ounces) precooked ready-to-serve unseasoned polenta
1	cup skim milk
1	cup low-fat cottage cheese
1	tablespoon extra-virgin olive oil
1	garlic clove, halved
½	teaspoon freshly ground black pepper
¼	teaspoon crushed red-pepper flakes
¼	teaspoon salt
¾	cup shredded fresh Parmesan cheese

1. Place the tomatoes in a medium heatproof bowl. Add the water and allow to stand for 5 minutes.

2. Coat a large nonstick skillet with nonstick vegetable cooking spray. Cut the polenta crosswise into rounds or lengthwise into quarters and arrange them in a single layer in the skillet (if necessary, cook in batches). Lightly coat them with the spray. Cook over medium heat until hot and lightly browned.

3. Drain the tomatoes and place in a blender or food processor. Add the milk, cottage cheese, oil, garlic, black pepper, red pepper flakes, salt and ½ cup of the Parmesan. Blend until smooth. Pour over the polenta and heat briefly to warm the sauce. Serve sprinkled with the remaining ¼ cup Parmesan.

Makes 4 servings

⇥ In a Flash!

Make the sauce ahead of time and store it, covered, in the refrigerator.

⇥ Spin Off

Puree leftover polenta and sauce to make a sauce for cannellini beans and diced tomatoes.

Basil-Garlic Polenta
with Marinara Sauce

This is a fast and fabulous entrée for nights when you have only 10 minutes to make dinner. It has just three ingredients, and they are already-prepared products. All you have to do is slice the polenta.

1 **package (24 ounces) precooked ready-to-serve basil-garlic polenta**
1 **jar (26 ounces) fat-free marinara sauce**
1 **cup shredded fresh Parmesan cheese**

1. Cut the polenta into 12 equal slices. Arrange them in a single layer in a large nonstick skillet. (If necessary, use 2 skillets.) Pour the marinara sauce evenly over the polenta. Bring to a simmer over medium heat. Reduce the heat to low, cover and simmer for 5 minutes.

2. Sprinkle the Parmesan evenly over the top of the sauce. Cover and cook for 2 minutes, or until the Parmesan is melted.

Makes 6 servings

Each serving contains approximately:

Calories: 193
Fat: 5 g.
Cholesterol: 13 mg.
Sodium: 813 mg.

↪ In a Flash!
Teach your children to make it!

↪ Spin Off
Combine leftover polenta and sauce in a blender or a food processor and puree. Serve over beans or greens.

Maple-Glazed Canadian Bacon (page 118)

Southwestern Snapper with Hot Salsa (page 97)

Shrimp Fettuccine (page 104)

Cantonese Sweet and Sour Chicken (page 106)

Cajun Chicken (page 110)

Spicy Poultry Sausage Patties (page 113)

Mediterranean Lamb (page 116)

Polenta with Creamy Sun-Dried Tomato Sauce
(page 85)

Quickie Chili

This chili is so quick you can literally throw the ingredients into a pan while your friends are getting out of their cars to come into your house for dinner! The down-side to using so many canned prod-ucts in a recipe is that the sodium tends to be high. So serve this chili with low-sodium side dishes.

Each serving contains approximately:

Calories: 285
Fat: 7 g.
Cholesterol: 24 mg.
Sodium: 1,500 mg.

1   **can (30 ounces) chili beans, rinsed and drained**
1   **can (14½ ounces) chili-style tomatoes, undrained**
1   **can (4 ounces) diced green chili peppers**
1   **teaspoon sugar**
1   **teaspoon ground cumin**
1   **cup shredded reduced-fat Cheddar cheese (optional)**

1. In a large saucepan, combine the beans, tomatoes, peppers, sugar and cumin. Bring to a boil over medium-high heat. Reduce the heat to medium-low and cook for 12 minutes. Serve topped with the Cheddar (if using).

Makes 4 servings

↔ In a Flash!
Reduce the cooking time; simply bring the ingredients to a boil.

↔ Spin Off
Heat leftover chili and use it as filling for burrito-size tortillas along with lettuce, tomatoes, onions and cheese.

Honey-Mustard Pecan Catfish

This easy Southern fish dish is fabulous served with rice or grits and wilted greens of any kind.

Each serving contains approximately:

Calories: 301
Fat: 22 g.
Cholesterol: 67 mg.
Sodium: 194 mg.

4 farm-raised catfish fillets (about 4 ounces each)
¼ cup Dijon mustard
2 tablespoons skim milk
2 tablespoons honey
1 cup crushed pecans

1. Preheat the oven to 450°. Coat a baking sheet with nonstick vegetable cooking spray.

2. Rinse the catfish with cold water and pat dry with paper towels.

3. Combine the mustard, milk and honey in a shallow dish and mix well. Put the pecans on a large plate. Dip the catfish into the mustard mixture and then press into the pecans to coat. Place on the baking sheet in a single layer. Bake for about 12 minutes, or until the coating is crisp and the fish flakes when tested with a fork.

Makes 4 servings

⤙ In a Flash!

The fastest way to crush the pecans is to put them in a food processor or in a self-sealing plastic bag and pound them with the flat side of a cleaver.

⤙ Spin Off

Chop up leftovers and mix with rice, grits or couscous for a cold salad or a hot entrée.

Southwestern Snapper with Hot Salsa

If you can't find red snapper, use any other firm-fleshed fish, such as bass, catfish or halibut. The secret of this recipe is "oven fry-ing" the fish, which means baking it for a very short time in a very hot oven to crisp the outside without overcooking the inside. If using salted tortilla chips, omit the salt from the recipe.

Each serving contains approximately:

Calories: 438
Fat: 22 g.
Cholesterol: 66 mg.
Sodium: 364 mg.

4	red snapper fillets (about 4 ounces each)
¼	cup fresh lime juice
2	tablespoons canola oil
1	cup finely crushed unsalted baked tortilla chips
1	teaspoon chili powder
¼	teaspoon ground cumin
¼	teaspoon salt
1	cup salsa
¼	cup chopped fresh cilantro

Pictured on page 88

1. Preheat the oven to 450°. Coat a baking sheet with nonstick vegetable cooking spray.

2. Cut each fillet in half, rinse with cold water and pat dry with paper towels.

3. Mix the lime juice and oil in a shallow dish. Mix the tortilla chips, chili powder, cumin and salt in another shallow dish.

4. Dip the snapper into the lime juice mixture and then press into the seasoned crumbs to coat. Place on the prepared baking sheet in a single layer. Sprinkle with any remaining crumbs. Bake for about 10 minutes, or until the coating is crisp and the fish flakes when tested with a fork.

5. Warm the salsa in a small saucepan over medium heat. Spoon over the snapper and sprinkle with the cilantro.

Makes 4 servings

⇥ In a Flash!

To crush the tortilla chips in a hurry, and without a mess, place them in a self-sealing plastic bag and roll them with a rolling pin.

⇥ Spin Off

Turn cold leftover snapper into taco salad: Place on a bed of shredded lettuce or cabbage and top with salsa and a dollop of sour cream. You can also heat the fillets and roll them up in hot corn tortillas with a little lettuce or cabbage, cilantro and salsa.

Cider-Poached Salmon
with Spiced Pear Sauce

I am delighted with the flavor the cider imparts to both the salmon and the couscous in this recipe—and with the subtle blending of these flavors when combined with the pear sauce.

Each serving contains approximately:

Calories: 558
Fat: 12 g.
Cholesterol: 62 mg.
Sodium: 419 mg.

Couscous

1	**can (14½ ounces) defatted chicken stock**
¼	**cup apple cider**
1	**tablespoon extra-virgin olive oil**
½	**teaspoon freshly ground black pepper**
½	**teaspoon ground allspice**
¼	**teaspoon salt**
1	**cup dry couscous**

Salmon

1	**can (14½ ounces) defatted chicken stock**
8	**ounces dried pears**
½	**teaspoon freshly ground black pepper**
½	**teaspoon ground allspice**
¼	**teaspoon salt**
¼	**cup apple cider**
1	**salmon fillet (about 1 pound), cut into 4 equal pieces**
	Coarsely ground black pepper
	Finely chopped fresh parsley (optional)

1. *To make the couscous:* Bring the stock, cider, oil, pepper, allspice and salt to a boil in a medium saucepan over high heat. Stir in the couscous and bring to a boil again. Reduce the heat to low, cover the pan and cook for 2 minutes, or until all the water has been absorbed. Remove from the heat. Fluff with a fork. Cover and allow to stand for 5 minutes.

2. *To make the salmon:* While the couscous is cooking, place the stock and pears in a large saucepan and bring to a boil over high heat. Reduce the heat to low, cover and simmer for 10 minutes. Let cool for a minute or two, then transfer to a blender or food processor. Add the black pepper, allspice and salt; blend until a chunky consistency.

3. While the pears are cooking, pour the cider into a large nonstick skillet and bring to a boil over high heat. Add the salmon to the pan, reduce the heat to low, cover and simmer for about 5 minutes, or until the salmon is the desired doneness.

4. Carefully remove the salmon from the pan with a slotted spoon and place on a plate. Add the blended pears to the pan and mix well with the pan juices. Bring to a boil and remove from the heat.

5. Divide the couscous among serving plates. Top with the salmon. Spoon the sauce evenly over the salmon and sprinkle with the coarsely ground pepper and the parsley (if using).

Makes 4 servings

↪ In a Flash!

Both the couscous and the pear sauce can be made ahead of time and reheated.

↪ Spin Off

This dish is excellent served cold and makes a wonderful lunch or brunch entrée.

Italian Halibut Steaks

For a fast meal, steam a package of ready-cut fresh vegetables while the fish is cooking and serve the fish over instant rice, fresh pasta or couscous— all of which can be prepared in minutes.

Each serving contains approximately:

Calories: 166
Fat: 5 g.
Cholesterol: 57 mg.
Sodium: 404 mg.

4 **halibut steaks (about 4 ounces each)**
1 **tablespoon fresh lemon juice**
¼ **cup plain dried bread crumbs**
1 **teaspoon dried Italian herb seasoning**
½ **teaspoon salt**
1 **tablespoon extra-virgin olive oil**

1. Rinse the halibut with cold water and pat dry using paper towels.

2. Place the lemon juice in a shallow dish. Mix the bread crumbs, Italian seasoning and salt on a plate. Dip the halibut into the lemon juice, then press into the bread crumb mixture to coat.

3. Place the oil in a large nonstick skillet over medium-high heat. Add the halibut and cook for 8 minutes, turning once, until the fish flakes when tested with a fork.

Makes 4 servings

⇢ In a Flash!
Use already-breaded fish and squeeze fresh lemon juice on it.

⇢ Spin Off
Leftover halibut steaks make great sandwiches. You can also chop them up and add to salads or soups.

Creamy Lemon Shrimp Pasta

This dish is good enough to become habit forming! I used fresh pasta because it cooks so fast. If you can't find fresh shells, use another type of fresh pasta or any kind of dried pasta, cooked according to the package directions. You can also substitute leftover cooked fish or poultry for the shrimp.

Each serving contains approximately:

Calories: 406
Fat: 9 g.
Cholesterol: 275 mg.
Sodium: 711 mg.

8	ounces fresh pasta shells
1	tablespoon extra-virgin olive oil
1	can (10¾ ounces) condensed reduced-fat cream of chicken soup, undiluted
1	cup skim milk
2	tablespoons fresh lemon juice
2	tablespoons dry sherry (optional)
2	teaspoons grated lemon rind, yellow part only
¼	teaspoon freshly ground black pepper
1	pound shelled cooked shrimp
¼	cup shredded fresh Parmesan cheese

1. Cook the shells in a large pot of boiling water for about 2 minutes, or until tender but still firm to the bite. Drain thoroughly in a colander, return to the pot and toss with the oil. Transfer to an 8″ × 8″ baking dish.

2. Preheat the broiler.

3. In a medium saucepan, combine the soup, milk, lemon juice, sherry (if using), lemon rind and pepper; mix well. Bring to a simmer over medium heat. Stir in the shrimp and heat through. Pour the mixture over the pasta in the dish. Sprinkle the Parmesan evenly over the top.

4. Broil for about 3 minutes, or until the cheese is melted and lightly browned.

Makes 4 servings

↔ In a Flash!

Use 1 teaspoon pure lemon extract in place of the grated lemon rind.

↔ Spin Off

Serve leftovers cold as a pasta salad. Or add defatted chicken stock to the leftovers, heat and serve as a soup.

Tuna Trifle

This extremely
unusual and very
tasty dish is actually
just a chopped-up
sandwich. However,
it is much less messy
to eat than a sand-
wich, and it's sure to
be a conversation
piece with your
family and friends.
In fact, they will
probably ask you for
the recipe!

Each serving contains
approximately:

Calories: 240
Fat: 9 g.
Cholesterol: 33 mg.
Sodium: 943 mg.

½	**loaf whole-grain bread, unsliced**
½	**cup reduced-fat mayonnaise**
½	**cup fat-free sour cream**
2	**tablespoons chopped pitted kalamata olives**
2	**tablespoons fresh lemon juice**
1	**teaspoon grated lemon rind, yellow part only**
1	**tablespoon capers**
1	**can (12 ounces) solid-pack white albacore tuna in water, drained and flaked**
1	**jar (7 ounces) roasted red peppers, drained**

1. Cut the bread into 1″ cubes.

2. In a medium bowl, mix the mayonnaise, sour cream, olives, lemon juice, lemon rind and capers.

3. Layer a third of the bread cubes in the bottom of a glass trifle dish or bowl. Spread a third of the mayonnaise mixture evenly over the top. Sprinkle with a third of the tuna and then a third of the peppers. Repeat the layers two more times to use all the ingredients.

4. To serve, spoon the mixture onto plates.

Makes 6 servings

↔ In a Flash!

Use ½ teaspoon pure lemon extract in place of the grated lemon rind. Combine the tuna with the mayonnaise mixture, rather than layering it; the mixture may be prepared ahead.

↔ Spin Off

Add just enough fat-free chicken stock to the leftover trifle to soften the bread; toss the mixture together and pack it in a loaf pan. Bake in a pre-heated 350° oven for about 20 minutes, or until hot. Serve as a hot tuna loaf.

Cajun Shrimp Pasta

For a vegetarian dish, omit the shrimp and substitute cooked beans.

Each serving contains approximately:

Calories: 462
Fat: 9 g.
Cholesterol: 179 mg.
Sodium: 934 mg.

8   **ounces dry linguine**
1   **tablespoon extra-virgin olive oil**
3   **garlic cloves, pressed or minced**
¼   **cup chopped scallions**
2   **teaspoons dried Cajun seasoning**
1   **can (12 ounces) evaporated skim milk**
¼   **teaspoon Worcestershire sauce**
¼   **teaspoon Tabasco sauce**
¼   **teaspoon salt**
½   **cup shredded fresh Parmesan cheese**
12 **ounces shelled cooked shrimp**

1. Cook the linguine in a large pot of boiling water for about 10 minutes, or until tender but still firm to the bite. Drain thoroughly in a colander and set aside.

2. Meanwhile, combine the oil and garlic in a large nonstick skillet and cook over medium-high heat for about 1 minute, or until the garlic sizzles. Add the scallions and Cajun seasoning; cook for 1 minute.

3. Add the milk and simmer for 5 minutes. Stir in the Worcestershire sauce, Tabasco, salt and ¼ cup of the Parmesan; simmer for 3 minutes.

4. Remove from the heat and stir in the shrimp and pasta. Serve topped with the remaining ¼ cup Parmesan.

Makes 4 servings

↔ In a Flash!

Use angel hair pasta instead of linguine because it cooks in 2 minutes. Or use leftover cooked noodles; reheat briefly in the microwave.

↔ Spin Off

Serve leftovers cold as a pasta salad.

Shrimp Fettuccine

Pictured on
page 89

You can usually find shelled raw shrimp only in the freezer section of your market. When using frozen shrimp, always thaw it completely before cooking or it will have a mushy texture. You can always buy fresh shrimp in their shells in any supermarket, but it does take time to clean them. Remember to buy a little more than a pound to compensate for the removal of the shells.

Each serving contains approximately:

Calories: 476
Fat: 13 g.
Cholesterol: 234 mg.
Sodium: 577 mg.

1	package (9 ounces) fresh fettuccine
¾	cup shredded fresh Parmesan cheese, divided
1	tablespoon extra-virgin olive oil
2	garlic cloves, pressed or minced
1	pound shelled uncooked shrimp
2	small zucchini, sliced into ¼" rounds
2	tablespoons water
2	medium tomatoes, diced
1	cup frozen peas, thawed
1	tablespoon chopped fresh basil

1. Cook the fettuccine in a large pot of boiling water for about 2 minutes, or until tender but still firm to the bite. Drain thoroughly in a colander, place in a bowl and toss with ½ cup of the Parmesan. Set aside.

2. Warm the oil in a large nonstick skillet over medium-high heat. Add the garlic and cook for about 1 minute, or just until it sizzles. Add the shrimp and cook, stirring constantly, for about 2 minutes, or until it turns opaque. Transfer the mixture to a bowl.

3. Add the zucchini and water to the same skillet and cook over medium-high heat for about 3 minutes, or until the zucchini is crisp-tender. Add the tomatoes, peas and basil; cook for 1 minute. Stir in the cooked shrimp.

4. Divide the fettuccine among serving plates and top with the shrimp mixture. Serve sprinkled with the remaining ¼ cup Parmesan.

Makes 4 servings

↔ In a Flash!

Use one bag of frozen mixed vegetables instead of the zucchini, tomatoes and peas; cook briefly to heat. Replace the fresh basil with 1 teaspoon dried.

↔ Spin Off

Add some reduced-fat or fat-free Italian dressing to the cold leftover pasta and shrimp for a salad.

Angel Hair Nests with Clam Sauce

If you want to further reduce the fat in this quick and easy 15-minute meal, just eliminate the oil and add the garlic to the clam juice and tomatoes before heating them.

Each serving contains approximately:

Calories: 403
Fat: 12 g.
Cholesterol: 39 mg.
Sodium: 1,017 mg.

8	ounces dry angel hair
2	cans (6½ ounces each) minced clams, undrained
2	tablespoons extra-virgin olive oil
2	garlic cloves, pressed or minced
1	can (14½ ounces) Italian-style stewed tomatoes, undrained
½	cup shredded fresh Parmesan cheese

1. Cook the angel hair in a large pot of boiling water for about 2 minutes, or until tender but still firm to the bite. Drain thoroughly in a colander and set aside.

2. Drain the clams, reserving the liquid; set the clams and liquid aside.

3. Combine the oil and garlic in a large nonstick skillet. Cook over medium heat for about 1 minute, or until the garlic starts to sizzle. Add the tomatoes and the reserved clam liquid. Bring to a boil. Remove from the heat and stir in the reserved clams.

4. Divide the angel hair among serving plates. Using a fork, twist each mound of pasta to form a nest. Top each nest with the clam sauce and sprinkle with the Parmesan.

Makes 4 servings

↝ In a Flash!

Use a small variety of pasta, such as shells, rotini or rotelle, and mix it with the sauce instead of making nests. Replace the garlic with ¼ teaspoon garlic powder.

↝ Spin Off

Mix leftover sauce with cold leftover pasta and serve as a pasta salad.

Cantonese Sweet and Sour Chicken

This is a very popular dish to prepare at the last minute. I use red bell pepper in this recipe for color contrast because I like to serve the chicken over rice with either steamed pea pods or Sesame Stir-Fried Asparagus (page 72) on the side.

Each serving contains approximately:

Calories: 511
Fat: 4 g.
Cholesterol: 72 mg.
Sodium: 635 mg.

Pictured on page 90

- 1   **can (20 ounces) pineapple chunks packed in juice, undrained**
- 2   **tablespoons cornstarch**
- ⅓   **cup cider vinegar**
- ½   **teaspoon salt**
- 3   **tablespoons sugar**
- 1   **tablespoon reduced-sodium soy sauce**
- 1½ **cups sliced fresh mushrooms**
- 1   **red bell pepper, seeded and thinly sliced**
- 1   **medium onion, thinly sliced**
- 1   **can (8 ounces) sliced water chestnuts**
- 4   **cooked boneless, skinless chicken breast halves (about 4 ounces each), cut into bite-size pieces**
- 2   **cups hot cooked white or brown rice**

1. Drain the juice from the pineapple and pour it into a large saucepan. Add the cornstarch and stir to dissolve it. Add the vinegar and salt. Cook, stirring constantly, over medium heat for about 5 minutes, or until the sauce has thickened. Stir in the sugar and soy sauce.

2. Add the pineapple, mushrooms, peppers, onions and water chestnuts. Cook for about 5 minutes, or until the vegetables are crisp-tender. Stir in the chicken and heat through. Serve over the rice.

Makes 4 servings

↔ In a Flash!

Buy a 6-ounce package of sliced mushrooms. Buy sliced red peppers and onions in the salad-bar section of the market.

↔ Spin Off

Mix any leftover chicken mixture with rice and serve cold as a Cantonese chicken salad.

Chicken Linguine

You can now buy cooked chicken breast in most supermarkets. (Sometimes it's even chopped.) It is more expensive than raw chicken, but it is also a real time-saver. I call for fresh linguine in this recipe because it cooks so much faster than the dry pasta. However, you can certainly substitute dry linguine or any other dry pasta.

Each serving contains approximately:

Calories: 420
Fat: 12 g.
Cholesterol: 116 mg.
Sodium: 400 mg.

9 **ounces fresh linguine**
1 **tablespoon corn-oil margarine**
½ **cup chopped red bell peppers**
2 **garlic cloves, pressed or minced**
1 **teaspoon dried oregano, crushed**
2 **cooked boneless, skinless chicken breast halves (about 4 ounces each), cut into bite-size pieces**
½ **cup evaporated skim milk**
½ **cup sliced scallions**
2 **ounces reduced-fat Jarlsberg cheese, shredded**
½ **cup shredded fresh Parmesan cheese**

1. Cook the linguine in a large pot of boiling water for about 5 minutes, or until tender but still firm to the bite. Drain thoroughly in a colander and set aside.

2. Meanwhile, melt the margarine in a large nonstick skillet over medium heat. Add the peppers, garlic and oregano. Cook, stirring occasionally, for 5 minutes.

3. Add the chicken, milk, scallions, Jarlsberg and Parmesan. Cook, stirring, until the cheeses melt. Add the linguine and mix well.

Makes 4 servings

⇥ In a Flash!

Eliminate the chicken for a vegetarian pasta meal. Buy shredded Jarlsberg; use ½ cup.

⇥ Spin Off

Serve leftovers cold as a pasta salad.

Poached Chicken Breasts with Gingered Applesauce

I like to serve these chicken breasts with rice and stir-fried vegetables. You can complete the entire meal in under 20 minutes if you use quick-cooking rice and a bag of frozen stir-fry vegetables.

Each serving contains approximately:

Calories: 199
Fat: 3 g.
Cholesterol: 66 mg.
Sodium: 486 mg.

4 boneless, skinless chicken breast halves (about 4 ounces each)
½ teaspoon garlic salt
½ teaspoon freshly ground black pepper
¼ cup dry sherry or apple juice
2 cups unsweetened applesauce
1 tablespoon finely chopped fresh ginger
1 tablespoon reduced-sodium soy sauce
1 teaspoon Chinese 5-spice blend
1 teaspoon dark sesame oil
1 teaspoon rice vinegar
   Chopped fresh cilantro (optional)

1. Sprinkle the chicken with the garlic salt and pepper. Pour the sherry or apple juice into a large nonstick skillet and bring to a boil over medium heat. Add the chicken and cook for about 5 minutes, or until the meat looks opaque.

2. In a medium bowl, mix the applesauce, ginger, soy sauce, Chinese 5-spice blend, oil and vinegar.

3. Remove the cooked chicken from the skillet and place it on serving plates. Add the applesauce mixture to the pan, mix well with the pan liquid and bring to a boil. Spoon over the chicken. Sprinkle with the cilantro (if using).

Makes 4 servings

↝ In a Flash!

Substitute 1 teaspoon ground ginger for the fresh ginger.

↝ Spin Off

Chop up leftover chicken, mix it with leftover sauce and thin with chicken stock for an unusual and delicious soup.

Country Chicken and Corn Stew

This stew is also very good made with turkey or ham. It's a wonderful recipe for using up leftovers.

Each serving contains approximately:

Calories: 290
Fat: 7 g.
Cholesterol: 49 mg.
Sodium: 410 mg.

1	tablespoon corn-oil margarine
1	medium onion, finely chopped
2	packages (10 ounces each) frozen corn kernels, thawed
1¼	cups defatted chicken stock
1½	teaspoons sugar
½	teaspoon salt
¼	teaspoon freshly ground black pepper
¼	cup skim milk
1½	teaspoons cornstarch
2	cups diced cooked chicken

1. Melt the margarine in a large saucepan over medium heat. Add the onions and cook for about 5 minutes, or until soft and translucent. Add the corn, stock, sugar, salt and pepper. Simmer for 3 minutes, or until the corn is tender.

2. Combine the milk and cornstarch in a cup and stir until the cornstarch is completely dissolved. Add to the corn mixture. Stir in the chicken. Mix well and simmer for about 3 minutes, or until slightly thickened.

Makes 4 servings

⇢ In a Flash!

Use prechopped onions (about 1 to 1½ cups).

⇢ Spin Off

Combine leftover stew with a can of undrained diced tomatoes, thin with a little more chicken stock and serve as a soup.

Cajun Chicken

This is truly a quick way to prepare a chicken dish. I like to serve it with Dirty Rice (page 144) and wilted mustard greens.

Each serving contains approximately:

Calories: 164
Fat: 5 g.
Cholesterol: 66 mg.
Sodium: 644 mg.

2	teaspoons dried Cajun seasoning
1	teaspoon lemon pepper
½	teaspoon salt
4	skinless, boneless chicken breast halves (about 4 ounces each)
1	tablespoon canola oil
	Lemon wedges (optional)

Pictured on page 91

1. Mix the Cajun seasoning, lemon pepper and salt in a small bowl. Sprinkle on both sides of the chicken.

2. Place a large nonstick skillet over high heat until drops of water sprinkled into the skillet dance on the surface. Add the oil, tilting the pan to coat the surface.

3. Add the chicken and cook for about 3 minutes per side, or until the meat looks opaque. Serve garnished with the lemon wedges (if using) to squeeze over the chicken.

Makes 4 servings

↔ In a Flash!
It doesn't get any faster!

↔ Spin Off
Cold leftovers are wonderful chopped up in soups and salads.

Creamed Chicken on Toast

This recipe is a healthier version of the old-fashioned chicken à la king, which I revised for a reader so she could serve it to her bridge club. She wrote back and told me it was a big hit with her group.

Each serving contains approximately:

Calories: 294
Fat: 7 g.
Cholesterol: 52 mg.
Sodium: 430 mg.

1 tablespoon canola oil
1 large green bell pepper, seeded and diced
¼ cup unbleached all-purpose flour
¾ teaspoon dried tarragon, crushed
¼ teaspoon salt
¼ teaspoon freshly ground black pepper
1 can (12 ounces) evaporated skim milk
2 cups diced cooked chicken
1 jar (4 ounces) sliced pimientos, drained
1 tablespoon dry sherry (optional)
4 slices whole-wheat bread, toasted
Chopped parsley (optional)

1. Place the oil in a large nonstick skillet and warm over medium heat. Add the green peppers and cook for about 3 minutes, or until tender. Add the flour, tarragon, salt and black pepper; mix well. Add the milk and bring to a simmer. Reduce the heat to low and cook, stirring frequently, for 3 minutes, or until slightly thickened.

2. Stir in the chicken, pimientos and sherry (if using). Cook just until heated through. Spoon over the toast and sprinkle with the parsley (if using).

Makes 4 servings

↝ In a Flash!

Buy already-chopped green bell peppers in the salad-bar section of the market.

↝ Spin Off

This creamed chicken is also great served in split or hollowed-out baked potatoes or over rice or pasta.

Turkey Hash

Serve this hash hot with ketchup or your favorite salsa. You can substitute ground chicken or beef for the turkey in this recipe, or you can add a can of beans for a vege-tarian hash. You can also use leftover cooked poultry or meat—add it to the skillet after cooking the other ingredients and heat thoroughly.

Each serving contains approximately:

Calories: 281
Fat: 7 g.
Cholesterol: 121 mg.
Sodium: 377 mg.

1	pound lean ground turkey breast
12	ounces (½ package) frozen hash brown potatoes, thawed
1	medium onion, finely chopped
1	medium green bell pepper, seeded and finely chopped
1	egg, lightly beaten
1	egg white, lightly beaten
¾	teaspoon dried thyme, crushed
½	teaspoon dried oregano, crushed
½	teaspoon garlic salt
½	teaspoon freshly ground black pepper
1	tablespoon extra-virgin olive oil

1. In a large bowl, thoroughly mix the turkey, hash browns, onions, green peppers, egg, egg white, thyme, oregano, garlic salt and black pepper.

2. Place a large nonstick skillet over medium-high heat until drops of water sprinkled into the skillet dance on the surface. Add the oil, tilting the pan to coat the surface.

3. Place the turkey mixture in the skillet, pressing it down with a metal spatula to form a cake-like patty. Cook without stirring until lightly browned on the bottom. Continue to cook, turning the mixture over with the spatula and breaking it up, until the turkey is well cooked but not dry.

Makes 4 servings

↔ In a Flash!

Use a food processor to chop the onions and peppers. Then add the other hash ingredients and process until well mixed.

↔ Spin Off

Leftover hash is delicious cold. Serve it as a salad or as a filling for pita-pocket sandwiches. Or heat it and use as a filling in flour tortillas with a little salsa and shredded cheese for great burritos.

Spicy Poultry Sausage Patties

These spicy patties are perfect for almost any breakfast or brunch menu.

Each 2-patty serving contains approximately:

Calories: 110
Fat: 6 g.
Cholesterol: 55 mg.
Sodium: 176 mg.

1	**pound lean ground turkey or chicken breast**
1½	**teaspoons dried sage, crushed**
½	**teaspoon ground mace**
½	**teaspoon garlic powder**
½	**teaspoon freshly ground black pepper**
¼	**teaspoon salt**
⅛	**teaspoon ground allspice**
⅛	**teaspoon ground cloves**
½	**cup defatted chicken stock**

Pictured on page 92

1. In a large bowl, thoroughly mix the turkey or chicken, sage, mace, garlic powder, pepper, salt, allspice and cloves. Divide the mixture into 12 patties.

2. Pour the stock into a large nonstick skillet and bring to a boil over medium-high heat. Add the patties, cover and cook over medium heat for about 10 minutes, or until cooked through. Remove the patties from the skillet and place them on paper towels to drain.

Makes 12 patties

⇢ In a Flash!

Form the patties and wrap them individually in freezer bags. Cook as needed.

⇢ Spin Off

Crumble up leftover patties and add them to soups and pasta sauces or sprinkle them over salads.

Ground Beef Stroganoff on Noodles

Each serving contains approximately:

Calories: 599
Fat: 16 g.
Cholesterol: 83 mg.
Sodium: 482 mg.

12	ounces dry egg-free noodles
1	cup defatted beef stock, divided
1	pound extra-lean ground round
1	tablespoon corn-oil margarine
1	medium onion, chopped
8	ounces fresh mushrooms, thinly sliced
½	teaspoon salt
½	teaspoon freshly ground black pepper
¾	cup light sour cream
	Chopped parsley (optional)

1. Cook the noodles in a large pot of boiling water for about 7 minutes, or until tender but still firm to the bite. Drain thoroughly in a colander. Return to the pot and mix in ½ cup of the stock. Cover and keep warm.

2. Meanwhile, crumble the beef into a large nonstick skillet and cook, stirring frequently, over medium-high heat for about 3 minutes, or until no longer pink. Remove from the skillet and set aside.

3. Melt the margarine in the same skillet and add the onions; cook for 3 minutes. Add the mushrooms; cover and cook for 3 minutes. Add the salt, pepper and the remaining ½ cup stock. Bring to a boil; allow to boil for 1 minute and remove from the heat.

4. Stir in the sour cream and the cooked beef. Return the skillet to the stove and cook over low heat just until heated through; do not allow to boil or the sour cream will curdle.

5. Serve over the noodles. Sprinkle with the parsley (if using).

Makes 4 servings

↔ In a Flash!

Buy the mushrooms already sliced. Use leftover chopped roast beef and eliminate step 2. (You could also substitute chopped cooked turkey or chicken.)

↔ Spin Off

Leftover stroganoff is good served in a split or hollowed-out baked potato. It is also a wonderful filling for crêpes and omelets.

Creamy Beef Hash

Traditional hash is made with leftover roast beef, leftover gravy and the seasonings of your choice. Many people also like to add onions, bell peppers, mushrooms and potatoes. When you're really hungry for hash but don't have any leftover roast beef and gravy, this easy recipe is the perfect solution. I like to serve this creamy hash over baked or mashed potatoes.

Each serving contains approximately:

Calories: 262
Fat: 11 g.
Cholesterol: 69 mg.
Sodium: 396 mg.

1	tablespoon canola oil
1	medium onion, finely chopped
1	large green or red bell pepper, seeded and finely chopped
1	pound extra-lean ground round
1	can (10¾ ounces) condensed reduced-fat cream of mushroom soup, undiluted
¼	cup skim milk
¾	teaspoon dried oregano, crushed
¼	teaspoon freshly ground black pepper

1. Warm the oil in a large nonstick skillet over medium heat. Add the onions and bell peppers; cook for 2 minutes. Add the beef and cook, stirring frequently, for 4 to 5 minutes, or until the meat is crumbly and no longer pink.

2. Add the soup, milk, oregano and black pepper; mix well. Continue cooking until the mixture is heated through.

Makes 4 servings

⤙ In a Flash!

Use prechopped onions and peppers from the salad-bar section of the market. Replace the ground round with chopped cooked roast beef; use leftover gravy in place of the soup. Add both in step 2.

⤙ Spin Off

Serve leftover hash as a sauce over pasta or rice. Or thin the hash with defatted stock and serve as a soup.

Mediterranean Lamb

This robust lamb dish is good served with crusty bread or over pasta or rice. I also like it with the Honey-Mint Couscous on page 74.

Each serving contains approximately:

Calories: 218
Fat: 7 g.
Cholesterol: 76 mg.
Sodium: 637 mg.

1   **pound leg of lamb, trimmed of all visible fat and cut into 1″ cubes**
1   **can (28 ounces) ready-cut tomatoes, drained**
3   **garlic cloves, pressed or minced**
1   **teaspoon dried rosemary, crushed**
1   **teaspoon dried oregano, crushed**
¼   **teaspoon salt**
¼   **teaspoon freshly ground black pepper**
⅛   **teaspoon crushed red-pepper flakes**

Pictured on page 93

1.   Coat a large nonstick skillet with nonstick vegetable cooking spray. Place over medium-high heat until drops of water sprinkled into the skillet dance on the surface. Add the lamb cubes and cook, stirring frequently, for 2 minutes, or until browned on all sides.

2.   Add the tomatoes, garlic, rosemary, oregano, salt, black pepper and red-pepper flakes. Reduce the heat to medium-low and cook for 5 minutes, or until the lamb is cooked as you like it.

Makes 4 servings

⤳ In a Flash!

Ask your butcher to cut the lamb into cubes for you.

⤳ Spin Off

You can add potatoes and a variety of fresh or frozen vegetables to the leftovers and serve it as a spicy lamb stew.

Pork Chops with Cherry Sauce

Pork and cherries are a wonderful flavor combination. When fresh cherries are in season, use them instead of frozen ones. The only drawback to fresh cherries is the time needed to pit them. If you don't want to use the port wine called for, substitute ½ cup red grape juice plus ½ teaspoon balsamic vinegar.

Each serving contains approximately:

Calories: 224
Fat: 4 g.
Cholesterol: 74 mg.
Sodium: 460 mg.

4   **center-cut boneless pork chops (¾" thick and about 4 ounces each), trimmed of all visible fat**
½   **teaspoon garlic salt**
½   **teaspoon freshly ground black pepper**
½   **cup port wine**
¾   **teaspoon dried oregano, crushed**
¼   **teaspoon ground nutmeg**
¼   **teaspoon salt**
1   **bag (16 ounces) frozen dark red pitted cherries, thawed and drained**

1. Coat a large nonstick skillet with nonstick vegetable cooking spray. Place over medium heat until drops of water sprinkled into the skillet dance on the surface.

2. Sprinkle both sides of the pork chops evenly with the garlic salt and pepper. Arrange in the skillet and brown the chops well on both sides.

3. In a blender container, combine the port, oregano, nutmeg, salt and half of the cherries. Puree. Pour over the chops. Sprinkle with the remaining cherries. Reduce the heat to low, cover and simmer for 10 minutes.

4. Transfer the chops to serving plates and spoon the cherries and sauce evenly over the top.

Makes 4 servings

↔ In a Flash!

Thaw the cherries in a microwave oven on high power for about 2 or 3 minutes.

↔ Spin Off

Dice the cold leftover pork and serve over fresh greens; add leftover sauce to a light vinaigrette dressing. Or dice the pork, mix with the cherries and sauce, heat and serve over wild rice.

Maple-Glazed Canadian Bacon

This method of cooking Canadian bacon gives it both a rich, satisfying flavor and an attractive appearance. I designed this recipe for a fast brunch menu for Shape *magazine a couple of years ago, and it quickly became a family favorite.*

Each serving contains approximately:

Calories: 61
Fat: 2 g.
Cholesterol: 14 mg.
Sodium: 399 mg.

6   slices Canadian bacon
2   tablespoons pure maple syrup

Pictured on page 87

1.   Coat a large nonstick skillet with nonstick vegetable cooking spray. Place over medium heat until drops of water sprinkled into the skillet dance on the surface. Arrange the Canadian bacon in the skillet and brown lightly on both sides.

2.   Add the syrup. Turn each slice to coat it with the syrup. Increase the heat to high and cook until the pan is almost dry.

Makes 6 servings

↦ In a Flash!
Prepare the Canadian bacon ahead of time and just reheat it to serve.

↦ Spin Off
Chop leftover Canadian bacon and use it in soups, salads and casseroles.

On the Table
in 30 Minutes

In many books, the "start to finish" time for recipes assumes that someone else has already done a great deal of time-consuming cleaning, paring and chopping. I assume that you are the only one in your kitchen!

In fact, many of the recipes in this section were originally designed to be made in 15 minutes or less. However, I found that—as simple as many of these recipes are—I couldn't quite pull everything together in that time allotment. Since I'm trying to be very realistic about time expenditure throughout this book, I moved those recipes to this chapter. If you're especially quick in the kitchen—and if you've done a bit of prep work in advance—you may be able to get many of these dishes on the table in a quick 15 minutes.

On the Table in 30 Minutes

Cranberry-Orange Ketchup

Even though cranberries are usually associated with holiday menus, this tasty ketchup is great served as a condiment with any kind of poultry. It is fabulous spread on turkey sandwiches. Last year, I made this ketchup for holiday gifts, and all of my friends wanted more of it. This year, I'm giving them gift-wrapped packages containing all of the ingredients and *the recipe!*

Each ¼-cup serving contains approximately:

Calories: 57
Fat: 0 g.
Cholesterol: 0 mg.
Sodium: 224 mg.

12	ounces raw cranberries
½	medium onion, chopped
⅓	cup water
½	cup frozen unsweetened orange juice concentrate, thawed
⅓	cup white vinegar
¾	teaspoon ground cinnamon
¾	teaspoon ground allspice
¾	teaspoon salt
¼	teaspoon freshly ground black pepper
⅛	teaspoon ground cloves

Pictured on page 127

1. Combine the cranberries, onions and water in a medium saucepan. Cook over medium-low heat, stirring frequently, until the onions are tender. Spoon into a food processor and puree.

2. Pour the mixture back into the saucepan and add the orange juice concentrate, vinegar, cinnamon, allspice, salt, pepper and cloves. Bring to a boil over medium heat. Reduce the heat to low and simmer for about 10 minutes, or until thickened.

Makes 2 cups

↤ In a Flash!

Use ¾ cup prechopped onions in place of fresh.

↤ Spin Off

Thin the ketchup with a little orange juice, water or oil and use it as a salad dressing. It's great on turkey salad!

Pico de Gallo Sauce

This is a wonderfully fresh-tasting salsa that is popular all over Mexico and becoming increasingly popular over the rest of the world. It is great on grilled fish, meat and poultry. And, of course, it's a fabulous accompaniment to all Southwestern-style dishes.

½ cup chopped red onions
½ cup cider vinegar
2 tomatoes, diced
2 oranges, diced
½ avocado, diced
¼ cup fresh cilantro leaves
1 serrano pepper, seeded and finely chopped (wear plastic gloves when handling)
1 garlic clove, pressed or minced
¼ teaspoon salt
¼ teaspoon freshly ground black pepper

1. In a small bowl, combine the onions and vinegar and allow to stand for 20 minutes.

2. Meanwhile, in a large bowl, combine the tomatoes, oranges, avocados, cilantro, serrano peppers, garlic, salt and black pepper. Mix well. Drain the onions and add to the bowl. Mix well.

Makes 3 cups

Each ½-cup serving contains approximately:

Calories: 76
Fat: 3 g.
Cholesterol: 0 mg.
Sodium: 149 mg.

↝ In a Flash!
Omit the serrano pepper and add Tabasco sauce to taste.

↝ Spin Off
This salsa makes a tasty ingredient in green salads as well as a great sauce on fruit salads.

Corn and Tomato Soup

Pictured on page 128

In the summertime, when both fresh corn and tomatoes are available, by all means use them in this recipe.

Each serving contains approximately:

Calories: 125
Fat: 2 g.
Cholesterol: 0 mg.
Sodium: 258 mg.

1   tablespoon corn-oil margarine
½   small onion, finely chopped
1   garlic clove, pressed or minced
1   can (12 ounces) evaporated skim milk
1   cup defatted chicken stock
1   tablespoon chopped fresh sage
¼   teaspoon freshly ground black pepper
1   cup frozen or canned corn kernels
1   tablespoon cornstarch
2   tablespoons cold water
1   can (14½ ounces) ready-cut tomatoes, undrained
     Fresh sage leaves (optional)

1. Melt the margarine in a medium saucepan. Add the onions and garlic. Cover and cook over low heat for about 5 minutes, or until the onions are soft and translucent. Add the milk, stock, chopped sage and pepper. Bring to a boil. Reduce the heat to low and simmer, uncovered, for 10 minutes.

2. Add the corn and bring back to a boil. Reduce the heat to low and simmer, uncovered, for 10 minutes.

3. In a cup, dissolve the cornstarch in the water and add to the soup, mixing thoroughly. Cook, stirring, until thickened. Remove from the heat and stir in the tomatoes. Serve garnished with the sage leaves (if using).

Makes 6 servings

↦ In a Flash!

Use ½ cup prechopped onions, 1 teaspoon dried sage and ⅛ teaspoon garlic powder.

↦ Spin Off

Add more tomatoes to leftover soup and serve over pasta, rice or beans.

Tomato and Basil Soup

This practically fat-free but absolutely fabulous-tasting soup can be served as a first course or as an entrée. I like it best with Herbed Grilled Cheese Sandwiches (page 43) for a light lunch or dinner. Remember to vent the blender whenever blending anything hot. This allows steam to escape so that it will not blow the top off of the blender.

Each serving contains approximately:

Calories: 65
Fat: 0 g.
Cholesterol: 0 mg.
Sodium: 495 mg.

5   plum tomatoes, peeled
1   medium onion, diced
6   garlic cloves
1   teaspoon dried rosemary, crushed
½   teaspoon salt
1   cup water
½   cup tomato puree
½   cup tightly packed fresh basil leaves

1.   In a medium saucepan, combine the tomatoes, onions and garlic. Cook, stirring, over medium heat for 5 minutes. Stir in the rosemary and salt. Add the water and tomato puree. Cook for 15 minutes.

2.   Add the basil and cook for 2 minutes. Remove from the heat and allow to cool for a few minutes. Transfer, 2 cups at a time, to a blender and puree.

Makes 4 servings

↔ In a Flash!

The easiest way to peel a tomato is to dip it in boiling water for 30 seconds. It will literally slip out of its skin! You can also use 5 canned tomatoes that have already been peeled. Also, you can use 1½ cups prechopped onions and buy already-peeled garlic in the produce section of your market.

↔ Spin Off

Leftover soup is good cold. Try putting it in a thermos and packing it in a picnic basket.

Italian Vegetable Soup

For variety, you can add other vegetables to this soup and serve it over pasta or rice. Most of the sodium in this soup comes from the tomatoes and beans. To reduce it, look for low-sodium versions.

Each serving contains approximately:

Calories: 275
Fat: 4 g.
Cholesterol: 5 mg.
Sodium: 1,234 mg.

2 cans (14½ ounces each) vegetable stock
3 small carrots, peeled and cut into ¼" rounds
1 garlic clove, pressed or minced
½ teaspoon freshly ground black pepper
¼ teaspoon crushed red-pepper flakes
1 can (14½ ounces) Italian-style stewed tomatoes, undrained
2 cans (15 ounces each) cannellini beans, rinsed and drained
1 medium zucchini, cut lengthwise in half and crosswise into ¼" slices
3 cups lightly packed torn spinach leaves
¼ cup grated fresh Parmesan cheese

1. In a large saucepan, combine the stock, carrots, garlic, black pepper and red-pepper flakes. Break up the tomatoes and add to the pan. Bring to a boil over high heat. Reduce the heat to low and simmer for 10 minutes.

2. Stir in the beans and zucchini. Cook for about 5 minutes, or until the zucchini is crisp-tender. Remove from the heat and stir in the spinach.

3. Serve sprinkled with the Parmesan.

Makes 4 servings

↔ In a Flash!

Buy precut carrots and a bag of prewashed and torn spinach leaves. Use ⅛ teaspoon garlic powder.

↔ Spin Off

Add leftover cooked poultry or meat to leftover soup.

Tortilla Soup

Pictured on page 129

For a vegetarian soup, substitute vegetable stock for the chicken stock.

Each serving contains approximately:

Calories: 195
Fat: 6 g.
Cholesterol: 10 mg.
Sodium: 435 mg.

1   can (14½ ounces) tomatoes, undrained
1   small onion, quartered
1   garlic clove, halved
⅛   teaspoon sugar
½   cup chopped fresh cilantro, divided
2   cans (14½ ounces each) defatted chicken stock
1   can (8 ounces) tomato puree
½   teaspoon chili powder
¼   teaspoon dried marjoram, crushed
1   bay leaf
3   corn tortillas, cut into thin strips
½   cup shredded reduced-fat Monterey Jack cheese
¼   cup fat-free sour cream
1   small avocado, diced (optional)
4   fresh lime wedges

1. Combine the tomatoes, onions, garlic, sugar and ¼ cup of the cilantro in a blender container; puree. Pour the mixture into a large saucepan. Add the stock, tomato puree, chili powder, marjoram and bay leaf. Bring to a boil over high heat. Reduce the heat to low, cover and simmer for 20 minutes. Remove and discard the bay leaf.

2. Preheat the oven to 400°. Place the tortilla strips on a baking sheet in a single layer and bake for 10 minutes, or until lightly browned.

3. Divide the tortilla strips and Monterey Jack among soup bowls. Ladle in the soup. Garnish with the sour cream, the remaining ¼ cup cilantro and the avocado (if using). Serve with the lime wedges to squeeze into the soup.

Makes 4 servings

⇸ In a Flash!

Crumble baked tortilla chips into the bowls instead of baking the tortillas.

⇸ Spin Off

Serve as a sauce over pasta or rice.

Cranberry-Orange Ketchup (page 121)

Corn and Tomato Soup (page 123)

Tortilla Soup (page 126)

Antipasto Salad (page 137)

Lemony Lamb Salad (page 139)

Hot Artichoke Dip (page 140)

Chunky Vegetarian Caponata (page 141)

Corn Casserole (page 142)

Turkey and Tortilla Soup

You can substitute ground chicken or beef for the turkey in this recipe. For a vegetarian soup, use beans and vegetable stock.

Each serving contains approximately:

Calories: 259
Fat: 6 g.
Cholesterol: 63 mg.
Sodium: 46 mg.

1	**pound lean ground turkey breast**
1	**medium onion, chopped**
1½	**teaspoons ground cumin**
¼	**teaspoon freshly ground black pepper**
1	**can (14½ ounces) defatted chicken stock**
1	**can (10 ounces) diced tomatoes with green chilies, undrained**
1	**can (8¾ ounces) salt-free corn kernels, drained**
¼	**cup water**
¼	**cup chopped fresh cilantro**
1	**cup baked tortilla chips**

1. Place a large saucepan over medium heat until drops of water sprinkled into the pan dance on the surface. Crumble the turkey into the pan. Add the onions. Cook, stirring, for 4 to 5 minutes, or until the turkey is browned and the onions are soft. Add the cumin and pepper and mix well.

2. Stir in the stock, tomatoes, corn and water. Bring to a boil. Reduce the heat to low and simmer for 8 minutes. Stir in the cilantro.

3. Divide the tortilla chips among soup bowls. Ladle in the soup.

Makes 4 servings

⇢ In a Flash!
Use 1½ cups prechopped onions.

⇢ Spin Off
Use leftover soup as a sauce for rice.

Shrimp Bisque

This is a quick version of a recipe developed by my friend Shirley Corriher of Atlanta, who teaches both food science and cooking classes all over the country. She said I wouldn't believe how thick, creamy and rich tasting this low-fat soup is. Overcooking the rice until it is almost mushy is the secret to the soup's creaminess. Although the sherry is optional, I recommend it because it acts as a flavor enhancer by dissolving and distributing the flavors of the other ingredients.

Each serving contains approximately:

Calories: 125
Fat: 3 g.
Cholesterol: 87 mg.
Sodium: 420 mg.

1	tablespoon canola oil
½	medium onion, chopped
1	piece (1″) jalapeño pepper, seeded and chopped (wear plastic gloves when handling)
1	bay leaf
2	teaspoons seafood-boil seasoning, such as Old Bay
1	teaspoon salt
½	teaspoon dried thyme, crushed
5	cups water
⅓	cup uncooked quick-cooking white rice
1	pound shelled cooked shrimp
1½	cups skim milk
2	tablespoons dry sherry (optional)

1. Place the oil in a large saucepan over medium heat. Add the onions, peppers and bay leaf. Cook, stirring frequently, for about 5 minutes, or until the onions are soft and translucent. Stir in the seafood-boil seasoning, salt and thyme; cook for 1 minute.

2. Add the water and rice. Bring to a boil, stir well and reduce the heat to low. Cover and cook for 5 minutes, or until the rice is very soft. Remove from the heat and set aside. Remove and discard the bay leaf.

3. Place the shrimp in a food processor. Using a slotted spoon, transfer 3 large spoonfuls of the rice and a little of the liquid to the food processor; puree the mixture. Add the remaining rice and cooking liquid in 2 batches, pureeing after each addition.

4. Pour the mixture back into the saucepan and add the milk. (If you want a thinner soup, add a bit more milk.) Warm through but do not boil. Stir in the sherry (if using).

Makes 8 servings

⟶ In a Flash!

Use ½ cup prechopped onions. Eliminate the jalapeño pepper and add Tabasco sauce, cayenne pepper or red-pepper flakes to taste.

⟶ Spin Off

Leftover bisque is good served cold as a soup or as a sauce over fish and other seafood. It can also be reheated and served as a sauce over pasta, rice or beans.

Antipasto Salad

This hearty Italian salad makes a wonderful lunch or dinner entrée. It can also be served as a first course by making the portion sizes smaller. I like to serve it with crusty Italian bread.

Each serving contains approximately:

Calories: 588
Fat: 17 g.
Cholesterol: 12 mg.
Sodium: 682 mg.

Dressing

Pictured on page 130

½ teaspoon balsamic vinegar
¼ teaspoon salt
1 tablespoon dry red wine
¼ teaspoon sugar
⅛ teaspoon dry mustard
⅛ teaspoon freshly ground black pepper
⅛ teaspoon dried tarragon, crushed
⅛ teaspoon dried oregano, crushed
1 tablespoon extra-virgin olive oil

Salad

1 ounce sun-dried tomatoes (¼ cup tightly packed)
1 jar or can (16 ounces) caponata (Mediterranean-style eggplant)
1 can (16 ounces) chick-peas, rinsed and drained
½ cup diced part-skim mozzarella cheese
¼ cup grated fresh Parmesan cheese

1. *To make the dressing:* In a small bowl, mix the vinegar and salt, stirring until the salt is completely dissolved. Add the wine, sugar, mustard, pepper, tarragon and oregano and mix thoroughly. Slowly add the oil, stirring constantly.

2. *To make the salad:* Cut the tomatoes into thin strips using kitchen scissors and put them in a small bowl. Cover with boiling water and allow to stand for 2 minutes. Drain and place in a large bowl.

3. Add the caponata, chick-peas, mozzarella and Parmesan. Toss to combine. Add the dressing and mix well.

Makes 4 servings

↔ In a Flash!

Use a commercial Italian dressing. Use leftovers from Chunky Vegetarian Caponata (page 141) in place of the canned caponata.

↔ Spin Off

Combine leftover salad with fresh greens.

California New Potato Salad

This salad is made without mayonnaise or eggs and can be kept without refrigeration for several hours, making it a perfect choice for picnics and tailgate parties.

Each ½-cup serving contains approximately:

Calories: 47
Fat: 2 g.
Cholesterol: 0 mg.
Sodium: 209 mg.

1	**pound small new potatoes, scrubbed and halved**
1	**tablespoon extra-virgin olive oil**
1	**garlic clove, pressed or minced**
2	**tablespoons balsamic vinegar**
2	**tablespoons fresh lemon juice or rice vinegar**
1	**tablespoon Dijon mustard**
1	**teaspoon dried rosemary, crushed**
½	**teaspoon salt**
¼	**teaspoon freshly ground black pepper**
1	**can (8 ounces) quartered artichokes, drained**
½	**cup diced red bell peppers**
½	**cup chopped scallions**

1. Put the potatoes in a large saucepan and cover with cold water. Bring to a boil over high heat. Reduce the heat to low and simmer for about 10 minutes, or until just fork tender.

2. Meanwhile, heat the oil in a large nonstick skillet. Add the garlic and cook for 1 minute, or just until the garlic sizzles. Remove from the heat and stir in the balsamic vinegar, lemon juice or rice vinegar, mustard, rosemary, salt and black pepper.

3. Drain the potatoes and add to the skillet. Toss or stir well to coat the potatoes. Transfer to a large bowl.

4. Add the artichokes, red peppers and scallions. Mix well.

Makes 4 cups

⇢ In a Flash!

Buy the peppers and scallions already chopped in the salad-bar section of your supermarket.

⇢ Spin Off

Leftover salad keeps well, tightly covered, in the refrigerator. Add it to other salads as well as soups and stews. It is even good heated and served as a hot vegetable side dish. You can also add cooked poultry or meat and serve it as an entrée.

Lemony Lamb Salad

Pictured on
page 131

*I asked my butcher,
Joe Hunnicutt,
which cut of lamb
would be the best for
this stir-fry recipe.
He suggested a steak
cut from the shank
end of the leg
because it is the
leanest part of the
lamb. It works
perfectly and is not
only lean but also
extremely tender
and very flavorful.
Because I think this
salad is so good
served with crusty
French bread, I have
included it in the
recipe. However, it is
also wonderful with
warm new potatoes.*

Each serving contains
approximately:

Calories: 400
Fat: 18 g.
Cholesterol: 81 mg.
Sodium: 520 mg.

Dressing

- 2 tablespoons extra-virgin olive oil
- 2 tablespoons fresh lemon juice
- 2 teaspoons lemon pepper
- 2 teaspoons Dijon mustard
- 2 garlic cloves, pressed or minced

Salad

- 1 pound lean boneless lamb, trimmed of all visible fat and cut into ½" strips
- 1 package (10 ounces) torn mixed salad greens
- ⅓ cup grated fresh Parmesan cheese
- 4 thick slices crusty French bread

1. *To make the dressing:* In a medium bowl, mix the oil, lemon juice, lemon pepper, mustard and garlic. Remove ¼ cup of the dressing for the salad greens and set aside; you'll have about 1 scant tablespoon of dressing left in the bowl.

2. *To make the salad:* Add the lamb to the dressing remaining in the bowl. Toss thoroughly to coat each piece.

3. Place a large nonstick skillet over high heat until drops of water sprinkled into the skillet dance on the surface. Add half of the lamb and stir-fry for 2 to 3 minutes, or until the outside surfaces are no longer pink. Remove from the skillet with a slotted spoon and set aside. Repeat with the remaining lamb.

4. In a large bowl, mix the greens and Parmesan. Add the reserved dressing and mix well. Divide among 4 serving plates. Top with the lamb. Save the bread with the salads.

Makes 4 servings

⇥ In a Flash!

Ask your butcher to cut the lamb into ½" strips for you.

⇥ Spin Off

Leftover lamb makes fabulous sandwiches! In fact, I usually prepare more lamb than I plan to use in the salad just so that I have some left over for sandwiches the next day. My favorite is a pita pocket stuffed with cold lamb strips and diced tomatoes.

Hot Artichoke Dip

Pictured on page 132

Because of the amount of bread in this hearty dip, it is much better served with raw or blanched vegetables for dippers than with chips or crackers. It can also be served as a vegetable side dish or even as a vegetarian entrée.

Each 2-tablespoon serving contains approximately:

Calories: 77
Fat: 2 g.
Cholesterol: 2 mg.
Sodium: 135 mg.

- 4 slices whole-wheat bread, torn into pieces
- 2 cans (8½ ounces each) artichoke hearts packed in water, drained
- ⅓ cup fresh lemon juice
- 1 tablespoon extra-virgin olive oil
- 2 garlic cloves, halved
- ¾ teaspoon paprika
- ½ teaspoon dried oregano, crushed
- ½ teaspoon dried basil, crushed
- ¼ teaspoon dried thyme, crushed
- ¼ cup grated fresh Parmesan cheese

1. Preheat the oven to 350°. Coat a 9″ × 5″ loaf pan with nonstick vegetable cooking spray.

2. Place the bread in a blender container and process until the consistency of fine gravel. Pour into a small bowl and set aside.

3. To the blender, add the artichokes, lemon juice, oil, garlic, paprika, oregano, basil and thyme. Puree. Add the Parmesan and bread crumbs. Process just until mixed.

4. Spoon the mixture into the prepared pan. Bake for 15 minutes, or until lightly browned. Serve hot, warm or cold.

Makes 2 cups

⤳ In a Flash!
Use ¼ teaspoon garlic powder in place of the fresh garlic.

⤳ Spin Off
Spread leftover dip on toasted French bread for a great sandwich. Or thin the dip with stock or milk for use as a sauce.

Chunky Vegetarian Caponata

Caponata is the Italian version of the French ratatouille. I call this recipe vegetarian caponata because I have not used anchovies or anchovy paste. If you prefer to add a bit of anchovy, I recommend about 1 teaspoon of the paste. When a recipe calls for only a small amount of tomato paste, I always use the paste that comes in a tube rather than opening a can. Leftover paste keeps better and for a longer period of time in the tube. (Store in the refrigerator.)

Each ½-cup serving contains approximately:

Calories: 49
Fat: 2 g.
Cholesterol: 0 mg.
Sodium: 371 mg.

1	tablespoon extra-virgin olive oil
1	medium onion, thinly sliced
2	celery ribs, thinly sliced
2	small eggplants, unpeeled and diced
4	large plum tomatoes, peeled and diced
¼	cup capers
¼	cup sliced pimiento-stuffed olives
1	tablespoon chopped fresh basil
1	tablespoon tomato paste
1½	teaspoons freshly ground black pepper
½	teaspoon salt
1	lemon, sliced (optional)
	Parsley sprigs (optional)

Pictured on page 133

1. Warm the oil in a large nonstick skillet or Dutch oven over medium heat. Add the onions and celery; cook for about 5 minutes, or until lightly browned.

2. Add the eggplant, tomatoes, capers, olives, basil, tomato paste, pepper and salt. Cook for about 10 minutes, or until the eggplant is soft. Serve warm or cold garnished with the lemon slices (if using) and parsley sprigs (if using).

Makes 6 cups

↣ In a Flash!

Use 1 can (16 ounces) of drained plum tomatoes in place of the fresh tomatoes and reduce the salt to ¼ teaspoon. Replace the fresh basil with 1 teaspoon crushed dried basil.

↣ Spin Off

Leftovers keep well for several days in the refrigerator. Serve warm as a vegetable side dish or cold as an appetizer or salad. Caponata can also be used as a topping for pasta, polenta or pizza or as a filling for pita pockets.

Corn Casserole

This tasty dish actually takes a few more than 30 minutes start to finish when you include the baking time. But the timing is so close—and the recipe so easy—that I included it in this section. I sometimes sprinkle cheese on the top of this dish and serve it as an entrée.

Each serving contains approximately:

Calories: 325
Fat: 12 g.
Cholesterol: 31 mg.
Sodium: 305 mg.

1 can (16 ounces) salt-free cream-style corn
1 can (16 ounces) salt-free corn kernels
1 box (8½ ounces) Jiffy corn muffin mix
1 cup light sour cream
1 egg, lightly beaten

Pictured on page 134

1. Preheat the oven to 350°. Coat a 13″ × 9″ baking dish with non-stick vegetable cooking spray.

2. In a large bowl, mix the cream-style corn, corn kernels, muffin mix, sour cream and egg until well blended. Spoon into the baking dish. Bake for 30 minutes. Serve warm.

Makes 6 servings

↩ In a Flash!

This is already about as fast as I can make it!

↩ Spin Off

Crumble the leftovers and toast them in the oven to use as a topping on soups and salads.

Honeyed Rice

For a higher-fiber dish, use brown rice in place of the white. For a refreshing variation, stir in ½ cup fresh mint just before serving. I especially like the mint version with Baked Honey-Rosemary Lamb Shanks (page 260).

Each ½-cup serving contains approximately:

Calories: 137
Fat: 0 g.
Cholesterol: 0 mg.
Sodium: 102 mg.

1 **cup uncooked long-grain white rice**

2 **cups water**

2 **tablespoons honey**

1 **tablespoon reduced-sodium soy sauce**

1 **teaspoon dry sherry or apple juice**

1.   Combine the rice and water in a medium saucepan and bring to a boil over high heat. Reduce the heat to low, cover and cook for 15 minutes, or until the liquid is absorbed. Remove from the heat and fluff with a fork.

2.   Stir in the honey, soy sauce and sherry or apple juice. Mix well. Serve hot or cold.

Makes 3 cups

↔ In a Flash!

Use quick-cooking rice.

↔ Spin Off

Mix cold leftover rice with raisins and diced apples for a delicious rice salad.

Dirty Rice

To lighten this
Cajun specialty,
I left out the
traditional high-
cholesterol organ
meats and browned
the flour for the roux
in a very small
amount of oil rather
than chicken fat. For
extra fiber, I used
brown rice instead of
white. This dish
makes a wonderful
base for leftovers,
and it can be made
ahead and reheated
just before serving.

Each serving contains
approximately:

Calories: 187
Fat: 5 g.
Cholesterol: 0 mg.
Sodium: 370 mg.

1	tablespoon canola oil
2	tablespoons unbleached all-purpose flour
1	small onion, chopped
1	can (4 ounces) diced green chili peppers
2	garlic cloves, pressed or minced
1	bay leaf
½	cup defatted chicken stock
½	teaspoon dried oregano, crushed
½	teaspoon dried thyme, crushed
½	teaspoon salt
¼	teaspoon cayenne pepper
¼	teaspoon freshly ground black pepper
2	cups cooked brown rice
	Tabasco sauce (to taste)

1. Warm the oil in a large nonstick skillet over medium-high heat. Add the flour, stirring constantly. Reduce the heat to medium and continue stirring for about 3 minutes, or until the roux is a dark brown.

2. Add the onions, chili peppers, garlic and bay leaf. Cook, stirring frequently, for about 5 minutes, or until the onions are soft and translucent.

3. Stir in the stock, oregano, thyme, salt, cayenne and black pepper. Bring to a boil. Remove and discard the bay leaf.

4. Stir in the rice and Tabasco sauce. Heat through.

Makes 4 servings

↔ In a Flash!

Use 1 cup prechopped onions, ¼ teaspoon garlic powder and quick-cooking brown rice.

↔ Spin Off

Serve leftover rice cold as a salad or side dish.

Spicy Thai Rice

This piquant Asian rice dish is good served hot, cold or at room temperature. It can be used as a side dish or as a vegetarian entrée. The combination of the rice, which is a grain, and the tofu and peanut butter, which are both legumes, forms a complete protein.

Each ½-cup serving contains approximately:

Calories: 230
Fat: 9 g.
Cholesterol: 0 mg.
Sodium: 339 mg.

2	**cups water**
2	**teaspoons sugar**
½	**teaspoon salt**
1	**cup jasmine rice**
⅓	**cup unhomogenized peanut butter**
¼	**cup silken soft tofu**
2	**tablespoons rice vinegar**
1	**tablespoon reduced-sodium soy sauce**
2	**teaspoons fresh lime juice**
1	**teaspoon dark sesame oil**
1	**garlic clove, halved**
¼	**teaspoon crushed red-pepper flakes**
4	**scallions, chopped**
½	**cup chopped fresh cilantro**
	Cilantro sprigs (optional)

1. In a large saucepan, combine the water, sugar and salt. Bring to a boil over high heat. Stir in the rice. Reduce the heat to low, cover and simmer for 15 minutes, or until the rice is tender and the water has been absorbed. Remove from the heat, uncover and fluff with a fork.

2. In a blender, combine the peanut butter, tofu, vinegar, soy sauce, lime juice, oil, garlic and red-pepper flakes. Puree. Pour over the rice and mix well. Stir in the scallions and chopped cilantro. Serve garnished with the cilantro sprigs (if using).

Makes 3 cups

↝ In a Flash!
Use quick-cooking rice.

↝ Spin Off
Serve the leftovers cold as a salad. For a hearty entrée, add cooked poultry, meat or seafood, such as shrimp.

Savory Polenta
with Italian Salsa

Both the polenta and the salsa can be made up to a day ahead of time and stored in the refrigerator. You can serve the polenta warm, cold or at room temperature.

Each serving contains approximately:

Calories: 172
Fat: 6 g.
Cholesterol: 17 mg.
Sodium: 363 mg.

Polenta

1	**cup yellow cornmeal**
3	**cups defatted chicken stock**
2	**garlic cloves, pressed or minced**
4	**ounces goat cheese, crumbled**

Salsa

¼	**cup chopped sun-dried tomatoes**
4	**large plum tomatoes, peeled and finely diced**
¼	**cup finely chopped fresh parsley**
3	**tablespoons finely chopped fresh basil**
2	**tablespoons finely chopped pitted kalamata olives (optional)**
1	**tablespoon balsamic vinegar (or to taste)**
1	**garlic clove, pressed or minced**
¼	**teaspoon sugar**
¼	**teaspoon salt**
¼	**teaspoon freshly ground black pepper**

1. *To make the polenta:* Place the cornmeal in a large saucepan. Whisk in the stock until smooth. Add the garlic. Slowly bring to a boil over medium heat, stirring frequently. Reduce the heat to low, cover and cook, stirring occasionally, for 20 minutes. Remove from the heat and stir in the goat cheese.

2. Coat an 8″ round cake pan with nonstick vegetable cooking spray. Spoon the polenta into the pan. Let stand for a few minutes to cool slightly, then evenly press the top with wet hands. Let cool for at least 5 minutes, then turn onto a cutting board and cut into 6 pie-shaped wedges.

3. *To make the salsa:* While the polenta is cooking, place the sun-dried tomatoes in a large bowl and cover with boiling water. Let stand for 3 minutes. Drain and return to the bowl. Stir in the plum tomatoes, parsley, basil, olives (if using), vinegar, garlic, sugar, salt and pepper. Serve over the polenta.

Makes 6 servings

↔ In a Flash!

Use instant polenta, which cooks in just 5 minutes; follow package directions for the amount of liquid needed. Or use the precooked plain or garlic-flavored polenta and sprinkle the goat cheese over the top of each serving. Replace the fresh basil with 1½ teaspoons dried.

↔ Spin Off

Leftover polenta is great served cold for brown bag lunches and picnics. The salsa is good served over pasta, rice or baked potatoes. It is also a good condiment with fish, poultry and meat.

Mashed Potatoes with Horseradish

Pictured on page 151

Try adding diced cooked fish, poultry or meat to these tasty potatoes for a quick, easy and satisfying main dish.

Each serving contains approximately:

Calories: 170
Fat: 4 g.
Cholesterol: 10 mg.
Sodium: 263 mg.

6	medium boiling potatoes (2 pounds), peeled and cubed
2	tablespoons butter or margarine
½	teaspoon salt
½	teaspoon freshly ground black pepper
½	cup fat-free sour cream
3	tablespoons prepared horseradish

1. Place the potatoes in a large saucepan. Cover with cold water and bring to a boil over high heat. Cook for 8 to 10 minutes, or until tender. Drain thoroughly and place in a large bowl.

2. Add the butter or margarine, salt and pepper. Beat with an electric mixer on low speed or mash with a potato masher. Add the sour cream and horseradish; mix well.

Makes 6 servings

⇥ In a Flash!

Put the cooked potatoes and all other ingredients in a food processor and blend just until smooth. Don't overprocess or the potatoes could become gummy.

⇥ Spin Off

Make patties out of leftover potatoes and brown in a nonstick skillet. Or serve leftover potatoes cold as a salad with cooked poultry or meat.

Mexican Pizza

Kids love this "pizza," and it's such a snap to make that they can easily do it themselves. It can be served hot or cold, making it perfect for meals at home or for brown bag lunches. You can replace the Tabasco sauce with any bottled taco sauce you happen to have on hand or omit it completely for a more mild taste. I purposely call for unthawed frozen corn kernels because they retain their moisture better during baking and are therefore tastier. They also remain plump looking, creating a much more attractive dish.

Each serving contains approximately:

Calories: 295
Fat: 10 g.
Cholesterol: 20 mg.
Sodium: 994 mg.

4	whole-wheat tortillas
1	can (15 ounces) fat-free refried beans
½	teaspoon Tabasco sauce (or to taste)
1	cup salsa, well drained
1	cup frozen corn kernels, unthawed
½	cup chopped fresh cilantro
3	ounces reduced-fat Monterey Jack cheese, shredded or thinly sliced
3	ounces reduced-fat sharp Cheddar cheese, shredded or thinly sliced

1. Preheat the oven to 375°. Place the tortillas on a baking sheet and mist with nonstick vegetable cooking spray.

2. In a small bowl, mix the beans and Tabasco sauce. Spread evenly over the tortillas. Top with the salsa. Sprinkle with the corn and cilantro. Sprinkle with the Monterey Jack and Cheddar.

3. Bake for about 12 to 15 minutes, or until the cheese is melted and starting to brown. Remove from the oven and allow to cool for a few minutes before serving.

Makes 4 servings

↤ In a Flash!

Use already-shredded cheese. If you're really in a hurry, use only one type of cheese.

↤ Spin Off

Chop up leftovers and add to salads or soups.

Black Bean Chili

Pictured on page 152

You can serve this chili over rice or pasta as a vegetarian entrée. For meat eaters, add leftover chopped poultry or meat.

Each serving contains approximately:

Calories: 253
Fat: 3 g.
Cholesterol: 0 mg.
Sodium: 1,228 mg.

2   **medium onions, finely chopped**
2   **garlic cloves, pressed or minced**
1   **can (14½ ounces) ready-cut tomatoes, undrained**
1   **can (4 ounces) diced green chili peppers**
2   **teaspoons chili powder**
1   **teaspoon dried oregano, crushed**
1   **teaspoon ground cumin**
2   **cans (15 ounces each) black beans, rinsed and drained**

1. Place the onions and garlic in a large saucepan. Cover and cook over low heat for about 5 minutes, or until soft (stir occasionally and add a little water or stock, if necessary, to prevent scorching).

2. Stir in the tomatoes, peppers, chili powder, oregano and cumin. Bring to a boil over medium heat. Reduce the heat to low and simmer for 10 minutes. Add the beans, mix well and heat thoroughly.

Makes 4 servings

⇥ In a Flash!

Use about 1½ cups prechopped onions and ¼ teaspoon garlic powder.

⇥ Spin Off

Add vegetable or chicken stock to leftovers for black bean soup.

Mashed Potatoes with Horseradish (page 148)

Black Bean Chili (page 150)

Hot Crab Dip (page 159)

Pasta with Clam Sauce (page 160)

Scallops with Sage and Corn (page 161)

Fish Tacos (page 165)

Salmon and Red Onion Kabobs (page 167)

Grilled Swordfish on Herbed Couscous with Vegetable Minestrone (page 168)

Hot Crab Dip

This delicious dip
is good served with
raw vegetables,
crackers or chips.
I like it best warm
with rye toast.

Each ¼-cup serving
contains
approximately:

Calories: 60
Fat: 0 g.
Cholesterol: 33 mg.
Sodium: 278 mg.

2	cans (6 ounces each) white crab meat, rinsed and drained
1	package (8 ounces) fat-free cream cheese, softened
2	tablespoons fresh lemon juice
1	tablespoon skim milk
1	teaspoon horseradish (or to taste)
¼	teaspoon paprika

Pictured on page 153

1. Preheat the oven to 350°.

2. In a large bowl, mix the crab, cream cheese, lemon juice, milk, horseradish and paprika. Spoon into a small casserole dish and bake for 15 minutes, or until the mixture bubbles.

Makes about 2 cups

↦ In a Flash!

Serve the dip cold, rather than heating it in the oven.

↦ Spin Off

Serve leftover dip cold as a sandwich spread.

Pasta with Clam Sauce

This is one of my favorite pasta dishes. You can use any type of pasta you want. When fresh basil is available, I like to top each serving with a large sprig of it. Also, you may want to sprinkle a little fresh Parmesan cheese over the top.

Each serving contains approximately:

Calories: 342
Fat: 6 g.
Cholesterol: 31 mg.
Sodium: 1,047 mg.

8	ounces dry pasta
2	cans (6½ ounces each) chopped clams, undrained
1	tablespoon extra-virgin olive oil
3	garlic cloves, pressed or minced
2	tablespoons anchovy paste or minced anchovies
2	cans (14½ ounces each) ready-cut Italian-style tomatoes, undrained
¼	cup finely chopped fresh parsley
¼	teaspoon freshly ground black pepper
2	teaspoons fresh lemon juice
	Italian parsley sprigs (optional)

Pictured on page 154

1. Cook the pasta in a large pot of boiling water until tender but still firm to the bite. Drain thoroughly in a colander. Return to the pot and cover to keep warm.

2. Meanwhile, drain the clams, reserving the juice. Set aside the clam juice and the clams.

3. Warm the oil in a large saucepan over medium heat. Add the garlic and cook for 1 minute, or just until the garlic starts to sizzle. Stir in the anchovy paste, mixing well. Add the tomatoes, chopped parsley, pepper and the reserved clam juice. Mix well and slowly bring to a boil. Reduce the heat to low and simmer for 15 minutes.

4. Add the reserved clams and lemon juice; heat for 1 to 2 minutes. (Do not boil the sauce at this point or the clams will toughen.) Serve over the pasta and garnish with the parsley sprigs (if using).

Makes 4 servings

↣ In a Flash!

Use ½ teaspoon garlic powder.

↣ Spin Off

Combine leftover pasta and sauce and serve cold as a pasta salad.

Scallops with Sage and Corn

The first time I ever had scallops seasoned with sage was at the Blue Orchid Inn near Topton, Pennsylvania. I thought the combination was so delicious that I immediately went to work creating a recipe that took advantage of this rather unusual pairing of flavors. When fresh sage and fresh sweet summer corn are both readily available, it's the ideal time of the year for making this sensational scallop dish. When they are not readily available, however, you can use dried sage plus frozen corn.

Each serving contains approximately:

Calories: 197
Fat: 4 g.
Cholesterol: 38 mg.
Sodium: 343 mg.

1   **pound scallops**
1   **tablespoon fresh lemon juice**
¼   **teaspoon salt**
¼   **teaspoon freshly ground black pepper**
2   **teaspoons extra-virgin olive oil**
¼   **cup fresh sage, chopped**
1   **garlic clove, pressed or minced**
2   **cups fresh corn kernels**
1   **large red bell pepper, seeded and diced**
    Sage sprigs (optional)

Pictured on page 155

1. Wash the scallops in cold water and pat dry. Place them on a plate and sprinkle with the lemon juice, salt and black pepper.

2. Combine the oil, chopped sage and garlic in a large nonstick skillet and cook over medium heat for about 1 minute, or until the garlic starts to sizzle. Add the scallops and cook, stirring frequently, for about 2 minutes, or until the scallops turn from translucent to opaque. Remove the scallops from the pan and set aside.

3. Using the same skillet, cook the corn and red peppers, stirring frequently, for about 3 minutes, or until tender. Stir in the scallops and remove from the heat. Serve garnished with the sage sprigs (if using).

Makes 4 servings

↠ In a Flash!

Substitute 1 tablespoon dried sage for the fresh and use frozen corn kernels. This will save you the time of washing and chopping the fresh sage and cutting the fresh corn kernels off of the cob. You can also buy about 1 cup of red peppers at the salad bar of your supermarket.

↠ Spin Off

Refrigerate leftovers to serve over greens. Or toss them with cooked pasta or rice as a sage-scented scallop salad.

Fancy Fish Roll-Ups

This easy recipe is also amazingly delicious. I like to serve the rolled fish fillets over rice or pasta and spoon the sauce over the top. Sole is an excellent choice for this dish.

Each serving contains approximately:

Calories: 129
Fat: 2 g.
Cholesterol: 52 mg.
Sodium: 351 mg.

4 thin fish fillets (about 4 ounces each)
1 can (10¾ ounces) reduced-sodium tomato soup
¼ teaspoon Worcestershire sauce
Lemon slices (optional)
Chopped fresh parsley (optional)

1. Preheat the oven to 350°.

2. Rinse the fish with cold water and pat dry. Roll up the fillets lengthwise and arrange them, seam side down, in a 11″ × 7″ baking dish.

3. In a small bowl, mix the soup and Worcestershire sauce. Pour over the fish. Bake for 20 to 30 minutes, or until the fish flakes when tested with a fork. Serve garnished with the lemon slices (if using) and the parsley (if using).

Makes 4 servings

↔ In a Flash!

You can also cook the fish in a skillet, covered, over low heat for about 10 to 12 minutes.

↔ Spin Off

Leftover fish can be chopped, mixed with the sauce and served over pasta, rice or beans. It can also be added to soups.

Curried Fish

You can serve the curried fish over the rice rather than mixing them together, if you prefer. Also, you can replace the fish with chopped cooked chicken or turkey.

Each serving contains approximately:

Calories: 404
Fat: 9 g.
Cholesterol: 75 mg.
Sodium: 565 mg.

1½	tablespoons butter or corn-oil margarine
1	large onion, coarsely chopped
1	can (12 ounces) evaporated skim milk
½	cup defatted chicken stock
2½	tablespoons unbleached all-purpose flour
2	teaspoons curry powder
¼	teaspoon ground ginger
½	teaspoon salt
	Dash of freshly ground black pepper
4	cups cubed cooked fish
1	teaspoon fresh lemon juice
2	cups cooked white or brown rice

1. Melt the butter or margarine in a large nonstick skillet over medium heat. Add the onions and cook for about 5 minutes, or until tender. Remove from the heat and set aside.

2. Combine the milk and stock in a medium saucepan and bring to the boiling point over medium-high heat. Remove from the heat and set aside.

3. In a cup, mix the flour, curry powder, ginger, salt and pepper. Sprinkle over the onions and stir to make a paste. Cook for about 3 minutes; do not brown. Add the hot milk mixture to the skillet all at once, stirring with a wire whisk. Simmer, stirring occasionally, for about 10 minutes, or until thickened.

4. Add the fish and lemon juice to the skillet and mix well. Add the rice and fold in thoroughly. Heat through.

Makes 4 servings

⇥ In a Flash!
Use 2 cups prechopped onions and a 12-ounce can of water-packed white albacore tuna, drained and flaked.

⇥ Spin Off
Thin the leftovers with milk or chicken stock and serve as a curried fish and rice soup.

Pacific Rim Fish
with Fresh Plum Sauce

Rich and complex flavors combine to create an exciting and satisfying dish that can be prepared in about 30 minutes. The fish is excellent served over rice or pasta. For an even lighter presentation, serve it over wilted spinach leaves. This dish works well with other thick white-fleshed fish fillets, such as halibut.

Each serving contains approximately:

Calories: 227
Fat: 4 g.
Cholesterol: 36 mg.
Sodium: 340 mg.

- **8   plums, quartered**
- **2   tablespoons Chinese rice wine, dry sherry or apple juice**
- **2   tablespoons water**
- **2   teaspoons chopped fresh ginger**
- **½   teaspoon freshly ground black pepper**
- **½   teaspoon Chinese 5-spice blend**
- **4   sea bass fillets (4 ounces each)**
- **1   tablespoon fresh lemon juice**
- **½   teaspoon salt**
- **4   scallions, cut into 1" pieces**
- **½   cup chopped fresh cilantro**

1. Place about one-quarter of the plum pieces in a blender or food processor. Add the rice wine, sherry or apple juice and the water, ginger, pepper and Chinese 5-spice blend. Puree.

2. Remove any bones from the sea bass. Sprinkle the fish on both sides with the lemon juice and salt.

3. Coat a large nonstick skillet with nonstick vegetable cooking spray. Place over medium heat until drops of water sprinkled into the skillet dance on the surface. Add the sea bass and cook for 1 minute per side. Remove from the heat and pour the pureed plum mixture over the fish.

4. Add the scallions and the remaining plums. Return to the heat until the mixture starts to simmer. Reduce the heat to low, cover and simmer for 5 minutes. Serve sprinkled with the cilantro.

Makes 4 servings

⤞ In a Flash!

Have your fishmonger remove the bones from the fish. Use 1 teaspoon ground ginger in place of the fresh ginger.

⤞ Spin Off

Leftover fish is wonderful served cold by itself. Or chop it and add to salads.

Fish Tacos

These Mexican "sandwiches" are messy to eat but so delicious they're well worth the effort.

Each serving contains approximately:

Calories: 177
Fat: 5 g.
Cholesterol: 13 mg.
Sodium: 434 mg.

Pictured on page 156

1   **box (8½ ounces) frozen sole fillets with bread crumb coating**
¾   **cup salsa**
⅓   **cup fat-free mayonnaise**
6   **corn tortillas, warmed**
½   **small green cabbage, shredded**
½   **cup chopped fresh cilantro**
3   **limes, quartered**

1. Bake the fish fillets according to the package directions.

2. In a small bowl, mix the salsa and mayonnaise.

3. Cut each fillet in half lengthwise and place in the center of a tortilla. Top with the cabbage and cilantro. Spoon on the salsa mixture. Fold each taco in half. Serve with lime quarters to squeeze on the tacos.

Makes 6 servings

↬ In a Flash!

Use 1½ cups of packaged already-shredded coleslaw mix for the cabbage.

↬ Spin Off

Use leftover fish and sauce in salads.

Fillet of Sole
in Gingered Lemon Sauce

This recipe is good for other fish besides sole, but I find the texture of the sole is especially lovely with the ginger-lemon flavor.

Each serving contains approximately:

Calories: 98
Fat: 1 g.
Cholesterol: 70 mg.
Sodium: 237 mg.

¼   **cup fresh lemon juice**
1½   **teaspoons cornstarch**
1   **teaspoon grated fresh ginger**
1   **teaspoon grated lemon rind, yellow part only**
¼   **teaspoon ground cinnamon**
¼   **teaspoon salt**
4   **small sole fillets (about 4 ounces each)**
1   **lemon, peeled and thinly sliced (optional)**

1. Preheat oven to 350°.

2. Combine the lemon juice and cornstarch in a small saucepan and stir until the cornstarch is dissolved. Stir in the ginger, lemon rind, cinnamon and salt. Cook over low heat, stirring constantly, until slightly thickened.

3. Place the sole in an 11″ × 7″ baking dish. Pour the sauce evenly over the top. Cover tightly and bake for about 10 to 12 minutes, or until the fish turns opaque and is easily flaked with a fork. Transfer the fish to serving plates, top with the sauce and garnish with the lemon slices (if using).

Makes 4 servings

↔ In a Flash!

Use ¼ teaspoon pure lemon extract in place of the grated lemon rind.

↔ Spin Off

Mix together the leftover sole and sauce; serve over pasta shells.

Salmon and Red Onion Kabobs

You can use any kind of onions in this recipe, but the red onions make the prettiest presentation.

Each serving contains approximately:

Calories: 380
Fat: 11 g.
Cholesterol: 62 mg.
Sodium: 107 mg.

1 **large red onion, cut into 8 wedges**
2 **garlic cloves, pressed or minced**
2 **teaspoons extra-virgin olive oil**
1 **can (20 ounces) pineapple chunks packed in juice**
2 **teaspoons balsamic vinegar**
1 **teaspoon reduced-sodium soy sauce**
1 **salmon fillet (about 1 pound), cut into 2″ cubes**
2 **cups hot cooked white or brown rice**

Pictured on page 157

1. Soak 8 wooden skewers in cold water until needed. Preheat the oven to 400°.

2. Place the onions in a 13″ × 9″ baking dish. Sprinkle with the garlic and drizzle with the oil. Bake for 15 minutes, stirring after 10 minutes to roast evenly. Remove from the oven and set aside. Turn the oven temperature to broil.

3. Drain the pineapple, reserving the juice in a small bowl. Mix the vinegar and soy sauce with the juice.

4. Using the wooden skewers, alternate the onions with the pineapple chunks and salmon. Place the skewers back in the same baking dish. Pour the juice mixture over them.

5. Place under the broiler for about 3 minutes, or until the salmon turns from translucent to opaque.

6. Divide the rice among serving plates. Top with the kabobs and spoon the cooking liquid in the baking dish over the top.

Makes 4 servings

⟷ In a Flash!

Rather than making kabobs, just put the pineapple chunks and salmon on top of the baked onions; drizzle with the juice mixture and broil. Spoon the mixture over the rice. Use quick-cooking rice.

⟷ Spin Off

Serve leftovers cold with fresh fruit or vegetables.

Grilled Swordfish on Herbed Couscous with Vegetable Minestrone

Pictured on page 158

Bill Bracken, the executive chef of The Peninsula Beverly Hills, a glamorous hotel in southern California famous for its many world-famous celebrity guests, told me this was his own favorite dish. I ordered it and found it to be one of the most interesting and delicious fish entrées I have ever tasted. I immediately asked him if I could have the recipe to share with my readers. The good news is that this spectacular-tasting, impressive-looking dish is also easy to make!

Each serving contains approximately:

Calories: 416
Fat: 11 g.
Cholesterol: 57 mg.
Sodium: 423 mg.

Minestrone

- 1 tablespoon olive oil
- 1 garlic clove, pressed or minced
- 2 cups finely diced vegetables (such as yellow squash, zucchini, onions and red bell peppers)
- 1 can (11½ ounces) V-8 juice
- ¼ cup defatted chicken stock
- 1½ tablespoons chopped fresh basil
- 1 teaspoon chopped fresh thyme
- 1 teaspoon chopped fresh rosemary
- ¼ teaspoon freshly ground black pepper

Couscous

- 1½ cups defatted chicken stock
- 1 teaspoon olive oil
- 1 bay leaf
- 1 teaspoon chopped fresh thyme
- ½ teaspoon chopped fresh rosemary
- ¼ teaspoon freshly ground black pepper
- 1 cup dry couscous

Swordfish

- 4 swordfish steaks (6 ounces each)
- ½ teaspoon olive oil
  Dash of salt
  Dash of freshly ground black pepper
  Chopped fresh basil, thyme or rosemary (optional)
  Thyme or rosemary sprigs (optional)

1. *To make the minestrone:* Warm the oil in a large saucepan over medium heat. Add the garlic and cook for about 1 minute, or just until the garlic starts to sizzle. Add the mixed vegetables and cook, stirring frequently, for about 4 minutes, or just until tender. Add the juice, stock, basil, thyme, rosemary and pepper; bring to a boil. Reduce the heat to low and simmer for 3 minutes.

2. *To make the couscous:* Combine the stock, oil, bay leaf, thyme, rosemary and pepper in a medium saucepan and bring to a boil over high heat. Stir in the couscous and bring to a boil again. Reduce the heat to low, cover the pan and cook for 2 minutes, or until all the liquid has been absorbed. Remove from the heat. Remove and discard the bay leaf. Fluff with a fork. Cover and allow to stand for 5 minutes.

3. *To make the swordfish:* Wash the swordfish with cold water and pat dry. Rub with the oil, salt and pepper. Sprinkle with the chopped basil, thyme or rosemary (if using). Cook on a charcoal grill or under a broiler for about 3 to 4 minutes per side, or just until the fish turns from translucent to opaque; do not overcook or the fish will become tough.

4. Divide the couscous among serving plates. Top with the swordfish. Spoon the minestrone around each serving. Garnish with the thyme or rosemary sprigs (if using).

Makes 4 servings

↔ In a Flash!

Use canned water-packed white albacore tuna instead of the swordfish. Replace the fresh herbs with dried ones; use one-half to one-third the fresh amount.

↔ Spin Off

Dice leftover fish and mix it with leftover sauce and couscous. Thin with V-8 juice and chicken stock to serve as a soup.

Salmon with Fresh Ginger
Sauce on Angel Hair Pasta

Pictured on page 175

Dried fruits of all types offer a truly quick approach to gourmet cooking. In fact, they are an almost magical ingredient in fat-free sauces. When reconstituted in water, stock, wine or juice and then pureed, they give the sauce a rich and creamy texture. In this recipe, apples are reconstituted in chicken stock, then they're combined with Chinese spices and fresh ginger, which add a depth of flavor. I like to serve the sauce on a colored pasta, such as spinach or red pepper.

Each serving contains approximately:

Calories: 456
Fat: 12 g.
Cholesterol: 62 mg.
Sodium: 378 mg.

4	ounces dried apples
1	can (14½ ounces) defatted chicken stock
½	cup water
1½	tablespoons chopped fresh ginger
1	teaspoon rice vinegar
½	teaspoon Chinese 5-spice blend
¼	teaspoon salt
1	salmon fillet (about 1 pound), cut into 4 equal pieces
½	teaspoon garlic salt
½	teaspoon freshly ground black pepper
12	ounces fresh angel hair
1	tablespoon dark sesame oil
½	cup chopped fresh cilantro

1. Combine the apples, stock and water in a medium saucepan and bring to a boil over high heat. Reduce the heat to medium and boil for 5 minutes. Let cool for 5 minutes. Transfer to a blender or food processor. Add the ginger, vinegar, Chinese 5-spice blend and salt. Puree.

2. Meanwhile, sprinkle both sides of the salmon pieces evenly with the garlic salt and pepper. Coat a large nonstick skillet with nonstick vegetable cooking spray and place it over medium heat until drops of water sprinkled into the skillet dance on the surface. Arrange the salmon in the skillet and brown it lightly on both sides, about 30 seconds per side.

3. Pour the apple puree over the salmon. Cover and simmer over low heat for about 4 minutes, or until the salmon is the desired doneness; do not overcook.

4. While the salmon is cooking, cook the angel hair in a large pot of boiling water for about 2 minutes, or until tender but still firm to the bite. Drain thoroughly and return the noodles to the pot. Add the oil and toss to mix well.

5. To serve, divide the angel hair among serving plates. Top with the salmon. Stir the sauce in the skillet and spoon over the salmon. Sprinkle with the cilantro.

Makes 4 servings

↦ In a Flash!

Use 2 cups unsweetened applesauce in place of the dried apples. Mix with the other sauce ingredients and pour over the sautéed salmon. Heat through.

↦ Spin Off

Serve leftover salmon and sauce cold over greens as a salad.

Herbed Oven-Fried Chicken

This is a wonderful recipe for entertaining because you can bread the chicken in the morning, or even the night before, and then bake it just before serving. I like to serve it with a tossed green salad.

Each serving contains approximately:

Calories: 245
Fat: 9 g.
Cholesterol: 67 mg.
Sodium: 482 mg.

2	**tablespoons canola oil**
4	**boneless, skinless chicken breast halves (about 4 ounces each)**
¼	**cup buttermilk**
½	**cup whole-wheat bread crumbs**
1½	**teaspoons dried thyme, crushed**
½	**teaspoon salt**
½	**teaspoon freshly ground black pepper**

1. Preheat the oven to 400°. Place the oil in a 13″ × 9″ baking pan and place in the oven for 1 minute to heat. Remove and tilt the pan to coat the bottom with the oil.

2. Place the chicken in a single layer on a large plate and pour the buttermilk over it. Turn the pieces over until well coated with buttermilk.

3. Combine the bread crumbs, thyme, salt and pepper in a plastic bag. Add the chicken to the bag, one piece at a time. Close the bag and shake to coat the chicken. Transfer to the baking pan.

4. Bake for 5 minutes. Turn the pieces and bake for 5 minutes, or until the crumbs are browned and the chicken is cooked (no more than a total of 15 minutes).

Makes 4 servings

↔ In a Flash!

Use an herbed dressing or stuffing mix for the coating.

↔ Spin Off

Top leftover chicken with sliced tomatoes and cheese and broil until the cheese melts. Serve over fresh garden greens or on toast for open-faced sandwiches.

Chicken-Fried Steak
with Country Gravy

This recipe delivers the same "down home" taste associated with higher-fat recipes for this popular Southern dish. You can also use chicken tenders instead of steak in this recipe if you prefer.

Each serving contains approximately:

Calories: 340
Fat: 10 g.
Cholesterol: 62 mg.
Sodium: 458 mg.

2	teaspoons cornstarch
1	can (12 ounces) evaporated skim milk
¼	teaspoon poultry seasoning
¼	teaspoon salt
½	teaspoon freshly ground black pepper
2	egg whites
1	tablespoon water
18	fat-free saltine crackers, crushed
1	pound lean flank steak, trimmed of all visible fat and cut into 1" strips
1	tablespoon canola oil

1. Place the cornstarch in a medium bowl. Add a few tablespoons of the milk and stir to dissolve the cornstarch. Stir in the remaining milk and the poultry seasoning, salt and pepper. Set aside.

2. Combine the egg whites and water in a shallow bowl and whisk until frothy. Place the cracker crumbs on a large plate.

3. Dip each strip of steak into the egg whites, shaking off any excess liquid, then dip it into the crumbs to coat.

4. Place a large nonstick skillet over medium heat until drops of water sprinkled into the skillet dance on the surface. Add the oil, tilting the pan to coat the surface. Add the steak and cook for about 10 minutes, or until well browned on all sides. Remove the pan from the heat; transfer the steak to a plate.

5. Add the milk mixture to the skillet and cook over medium heat, stirring constantly, for 2 to 3 minutes, or until thickened. Spoon over the steak to serve.

Makes 4 servings

↔ In a Flash!

Add the poultry seasoning to a can of condensed reduced-fat cream of mushroom soup and heat it in the skillet instead of making the gravy.

↔ Spin Off

Chop up any leftover steak, mix it with leftover gravy and serve it as a topping for baked potatoes.

Chicken Florentine

This recipe also works well with fish. You can make it ahead of time and reheat it just before serving.

Each serving contains approximately:

Calories: 244
Fat: 7 g.
Cholesterol: 83 mg.
Sodium: 548 mg.

4 **boneless, skinless chicken breast halves (about 4 ounces each)**

1 **can (10¾ ounces) condensed reduced-fat cream of chicken soup, undiluted**

2 **ounces part-skim mozzarella cheese, shredded**

⅛ **teaspoon ground nutmeg**

⅛ **teaspoon freshly ground black pepper**

1 **box (10 ounces) frozen chopped spinach, thawed**

2 **tablespoons grated fresh Parmesan cheese**

1. Preheat the oven to 350°.

2. Place a large nonstick skillet over medium heat until drops of water sprinkled into the skillet dance on the surface. Add the chicken and brown well on both sides.

3. Meanwhile, combine the soup, mozzarella, nutmeg, and pepper in a medium saucepan. Stir over medium-low heat until the mozzarella is completely melted.

4. Line the bottom of a 13″ × 9″ baking dish with the spinach. Top with the chicken in a single layer. Pour the cheese sauce evenly over the top. Sprinkle with the Parmesan. Bake for 10 minutes, then place under the broiler until the top is lightly browned.

Makes 4 servings

⤙ In a Flash!

Use cooked chicken. Buy the mozzarella already shredded; use ½ cup.

⤙ Spin Off

Chop any leftover chicken and mix it with the spinach and sauce. Serve over pasta.

Salmon with Fresh Ginger Sauce on Angel Hair Pasta
(page 170)

Lemon-Tarragon Chicken on Cannellini Beans
(page 183)

Mediterranean Skillet Steaks (page 185)

Lamb Chops with Herbed Apricot Sauce (page 186)

**Asian Pork Chops (page 188) and Salad of Young
Greens with Fennel Dressing (page 196)**

Ham and Cheese Calzone (page 189)

**Marinated Mushrooms (page 192) and
Pickled Carrots (page 193)**

Maple-Glazed Pork Tenderloin (page 262)

Lemon-Tarragon Chicken on Cannellini Beans

This delicious dish is just as good served cold as it is hot and makes a wonderful entrée for summer luncheons.

Each serving contains approximately:

Calories: 331
Fat: 7 g.
Cholesterol: 66 mg.
Sodium: 1,013 mg.

2   **cans (15 ounces each) cannellini beans, rinsed and drained**

2   **teaspoons pure lemon extract, divided**

2   **teaspoons dried tarragon, crushed, divided**

1   **teaspoon freshly ground black pepper, divided**

4   **boneless, skinless chicken breast halves (about 4 ounces each)**

¼   **teaspoon salt**

1   **tablespoon extra-virgin olive oil**

Tarragon or parsley sprigs (optional)

Pictured on page 176

1. Preheat the oven to 400°.

2. Place the beans in an 11″ × 7″ baking dish. Add 1 teaspoon of the lemon extract, 1 teaspoon of the tarragon and ½ teaspoon of the pepper and mix well. Spread the beans evenly over the bottom of the dish. Arrange the chicken on top of the beans. Sprinkle with the salt and the remaining 1 teaspoon tarragon and ½ teaspoon pepper.

3. In a cup, mix the oil with the remaining 1 teaspoon lemon extract. Drizzle over the chicken.

4. Cover the dish with a lid or aluminum foil and bake for about 20 minutes, or until the chicken is tender. Serve garnished with the tarragon or parsley sprigs (if using).

Makes 4 servings

⤙ In a Flash!

Use sliced cooked chicken or turkey and just heat the dish to serving temperature.

⤙ Spin Off

Chop up the leftover chicken, mix it with the beans and serve it over greens for a salad.

Chicken Stir-Fry Fettuccine

This spicy chicken pasta is sure to become a family favorite. You can also prepare this dish with turkey or meat of any type.

Each serving contains approximately:

Calories: 435
Fat: 13 g.
Cholesterol: 125 mg.
Sodium: 824 mg.

2 tablespoons extra-virgin olive oil
3 garlic cloves, pressed or minced
¾ teaspoon freshly ground black pepper
1 pound chicken tenders
½ teaspoon salt
8 ounces fresh mushrooms, thinly sliced
1 can (4 ounces) diced green chili peppers
1 package (9 ounces) fresh fettuccine
¼ cup grated fresh Parmesan cheese

1. In a medium bowl, mix the oil, garlic and pepper. Add the chicken and toss to coat.

2. Place a large nonstick skillet over medium-high heat until drops of water sprinkled into the skillet dance on the surface. Add the chicken and stir-fry for about 2 minutes, or until the chicken is no longer pink. Remove from the skillet with a slotted spoon and sprinkle with the salt.

3. Add the mushrooms to the same skillet. Stir-fry for 3 minutes, or until tender. Stir in the chili peppers and cooked chicken.

4. Meanwhile, cook the fettuccine in a large pot of boiling water for 2 minutes, or until tender but still firm to the bite. Drain thoroughly in a colander. Return to the pot and add the chicken mixture. Toss well. Serve sprinkled with the Parmesan.

Makes 4 servings

↔ In a Flash!
Buy presliced fresh mushrooms or canned sliced mushrooms; use 2 cups.

↔ Spin Off
Serve leftovers cold as a pasta salad.

Mediterranean Skillet Steaks

If you're hungry for a steak but don't want to fire up the barbecue or heat up the oven, this recipe offers a perfect solution. The directions given are for a medium-rare steak. If you prefer a rare steak, start checking it after about 3 minutes per side; for a steak that's more well done, cook it longer.

Each serving contains approximately:

Calories: 248
Fat: 15 g.
Cholesterol: 73 mg.
Sodium: 415 mg.

Pictured on page 177

2	lean beef rib eye steaks, 1″ thick (8 ounces each)
1½	teaspoons dried oregano, crushed
1	teaspoon dried basil, crushed
½	teaspoon salt
¼	teaspoon freshly ground black pepper
1	tablespoon extra-virgin olive oil
3	garlic cloves, pressed or minced
2	tablespoons crumbled feta cheese
1	tablespoon fresh lemon juice
1	tablespoon chopped pitted kalamata olives

1. Sprinkle both sides of the steaks with the oregano, basil, salt and pepper; rub the seasonings into the meat.

2. Combine the oil and garlic in a large nonstick skillet. Cook over medium heat for about 1 minute, or until the garlic starts to sizzle. Add the steaks to the skillet and cook for about 5 minutes on each side for medium-rare.

3. Remove from the heat and sprinkle with the feta, lemon juice and olives. Cut each steak in half before serving.

Makes 4 servings

↦ In a Flash!

Use 1 teaspoon garlic powder in place of the fresh garlic.

↦ Spin Off

Use leftover meat to make Mediterranean steak sandwiches. Cut the meat into thin strips and stuff it into whole-wheat pita pockets.

Lamb Chops with Herbed Apricot Sauce

Dried apricots give this fat-free sauce a rich and creamy texture, and the combination of herbs adds a complex taste that goes well with the lamb.

Each serving contains approximately:

Calories: 359
Fat: 8 g.
Cholesterol: 75 mg.
Sodium: 525 mg.

Pictured on page 178

4	boneless skewered sirloin lamb chops (4 ounces each), trimmed of all visible fat
½	teaspoon garlic salt
½	teaspoon freshly ground black pepper
8	ounces dried apricot halves
1	can (14½ ounces) defatted chicken stock
½	teaspoon balsamic vinegar
½	teaspoon dried oregano, crushed
½	teaspoon dried thyme, crushed
¼	teaspoon dried rosemary, crushed
¼	teaspoon salt
⅛	teaspoon ground nutmeg

1. Sprinkle both sides of the lamb chops evenly with the garlic salt and pepper.

2. Place a large nonstick skillet over medium heat until drops of water sprinkled into the skillet dance on the surface. Arrange the lamb in the skillet and brown well on both sides.

3. Meanwhile, combine the apricots and stock in a medium saucepan and bring to a boil over high heat. Reduce the heat to medium and boil for 5 minutes.

4. Transfer half of the apricots and all of the liquid to a blender or food processor. Add the vinegar, oregano, thyme, rosemary, salt and nutmeg. Puree. Pour over the browned lamb chops. Sprinkle with the remaining cooked apricots. Reduce the heat to low, cover and simmer for 10 minutes.

5. To serve, remove the lamb from the skillet and remove the skewers. Stir the sauce well and spoon over the lamb.

Makes 4 servings

⤵ In a Flash!
Use 1½ teaspoons dried Italian herb seasoning in place of the oregano, thyme and rosemary.

⤵ Spin Off
Dice up leftover lamb, mix it with leftover sauce and serve over pasta or rice.

Greek Lamb Pasta

You can use ground chicken, turkey or beef in this recipe in place of the lamb if you prefer. Also, you can substitute any other type of pasta you happen to have on hand.

Each serving contains approximately:

Calories: 574
Fat: 11 g.
Cholesterol: 81 mg.
Sodium: 594 mg.

12	**ounces dry spirals**
1	**pound lean ground lamb**
1	**medium onion, finely chopped**
2	**garlic cloves, pressed or minced**
1	**can (28 ounces) crushed tomatoes, undrained**
1	**teaspoon dried oregano, crushed**
¼	**teaspoon ground cinnamon**
¼	**teaspoon freshly ground black pepper**
4	**tablespoons crumbled feta cheese**

1. Cook the spirals in a large pot of boiling water for 10 minutes, or until tender but still firm to the bite. Drain thoroughly in a colander. Return to the pot and keep warm.

2. While the spirals are cooking, combine the lamb, onions and garlic in a large nonstick skillet. Cook over medium-high heat, stirring frequently, for 5 minutes, or until the lamb is crumbly and the onions are translucent. Drain off any visible fat.

3. Add the tomatoes, oregano, cinnamon and pepper to the lamb. Bring to a boil. Reduce the heat to low and simmer for 10 minutes. Serve over the spirals. Sprinkle with the feta.

Makes 4 servings

↔ In a Flash!

Use couscous in place of the pasta and replace the fresh garlic with garlic powder.

↔ Spin Off

Use leftover sauce as a filling for pita sandwiches.

Asian Pork Chops

These pork chops are good served over either rice or pasta. I also like them on greens as a warm salad.

Each serving contains approximately:

Calories: 290
Fat: 15 g.
Cholesterol: 81 mg.
Sodium: 89 mg.

Pictured on
page 179

4	center-cut boneless pork chops (¾″ thick and about 4 ounces each), trimmed of all visible fat
½	teaspoon salt
¼	teaspoon freshly ground black pepper
3	tablespoons cider vinegar
2	tablespoons sugar
⅔	cup defatted chicken stock
⅔	cup dry sherry or apple juice
1	large Golden Delicious apple, peeled, cored and thinly sliced
2	tablespoons chopped fresh ginger
12	scallions, sliced diagonally into 1″ pieces
2	teaspoons cornstarch
2	tablespoons water

1. Place a large nonstick skillet over medium heat until drops of water sprinkled into the skillet dance on the surface. Add the pork and cook for 5 minutes per side. Sprinkle with the salt and pepper. Transfer the pork to a plate and set aside.

2. Add the vinegar and sugar to the skillet, stirring to dissolve the sugar. Pour in the stock and sherry or apple juice; bring to a boil.

3. Add the apples and ginger. Cook for 2 minutes. Add the scallions and cook for 2 minutes.

4. In a cup, dissolve the cornstarch in the water. Add to the skillet and cook, stirring, until thickened. Reduce the heat to low and return the pork and any juices from the plate to the skillet. Simmer gently for about 1 minute, or until the pork is heated through.

5. Serve the pork topped with the apples and scallions; spoon on the sauce.

Makes 4 servings

⇥ In a Flash!

Use 2 teaspoons of powdered ginger in place of the fresh ginger.

⇥ Spin Off

Chop up leftover pork chops, mix with the sauce and combine with some coleslaw mix for a delicious Asian salad.

Ham and Cheese Calzone

A calzone is a Neapolitan-inspired stuffed pizza that resembles a large turnover. I make a large one here, but you can also prepare smaller ones. It is equally good hot or at room temperature. In this recipe, I mix fat-free ricotta cheese and low-fat mozzarella to reduce the amount of fat. For a vegetarian calzone, omit the ham and add dried tomato bits. Using a ready-to-bake packaged pizza crust makes this recipe as easy to prepare as it is easy to eat!

Each serving contains approximately:

Calories: 277
Fat: 8 g.
Cholesterol: 21 mg.
Sodium: 696 mg.

⅓　**cup fat-free ricotta cheese**
½　**teaspoon dried oregano, crushed**
½　**teaspoon freshly ground black pepper**
¾　**cup shredded part-skim mozzarella cheese**
¼　**cup shredded fresh Parmesan cheese**
¼　**cup finely chopped ham**
1　**tube (10 ounces) ready-to-bake pizza dough**

Pictured on page 180

1. Preheat the oven to 425°. Coat a pizza pan or baking sheet with nonstick vegetable cooking spray.

2. In a medium bowl, mix the ricotta cheese, oregano and pepper. Stir in the mozzarella, Parmesan and ham; mix well.

3. Unroll the pizza dough onto the prepared pan. Using your hands, press it into a 10″ circle, starting in the center. Spoon the cheese mixture onto half of the circle, leaving a 1″ border. Fold the other half of the crust over the top, making a half-moon shape. Press the edges together tightly, pinching the dough to seal it shut.

4. Bake for 8 minutes. Turn the calzone over and bake for about 7 minutes, or until well browned. Remove from the oven and allow to cool slightly before cutting into 4 pie-shaped wedges.

Makes 4 servings

⇥ In a Flash!

Buy already-shredded cheeses. Use 2 tablespoons of bacon bits instead of chopping the ham.

⇥ Spin Off

Refrigerate leftover pieces of calzone in self-sealing plastic bags. You can either reheat them in a microwave or serve them cold as cheese sandwiches. Serve with a salad.

Hands-On Time:
Less Than 30 Minutes

In this section of the book, I have included all of the savory recipes that take longer than 30 minutes start to finish. However, none of them require more than 30 minutes of actual preparation time, and most take much less than that.

When you don't have time to cook, what could be more helpful than a dinner entrée that takes only 10 minutes of your time in the morning and is ready and waiting to be served when you come home? Or how about a holiday turkey that you can roast and have ready to serve in just a little over an hour?

This chapter also includes those recipes that take but a few minutes to assemble but benefit enormously from chilling or marinating.

Hands-on Time: Less Than 30 Minutes

Marinated Mushrooms

Serve these mushrooms on toothpicks for hors d'oeuvres or use them as garnishes for salads and sand-wiches.

Each ½-cup serving contains approximately:

Calories: 34
Fat: 1 g.
Cholesterol: 0 mg.
Sodium: 447 mg.

1 **pound fresh mushrooms**
⅔ **cup tarragon vinegar**
⅓ **cup water**
1 **tablespoon sugar**
2 **teaspoons extra-virgin olive oil**
1½ **teaspoons salt**
1 **garlic clove, pressed or minced**
⅛ **teaspoon Tabasco sauce**
Finely diced red bell peppers (optional)

Pictured on page 181

1. Wipe the mushrooms clean with a damp paper towel and trim off the stem ends.

2. In a large bowl, mix the vinegar, water, sugar, oil, salt, garlic and Tabasco sauce. Add the mushrooms and toss to coat thoroughly. Cover and refrigerate for several hours or overnight. Sprinkle with the red peppers (if using) before serving.

Makes 4 cups

⇢ In a Flash!
Buy prewashed, ready-to-use mushrooms.

⇢ Spin Off
Use the leftover marinade as a salad dressing.

Pickled Carrots

These spicy carrots are a traditional Mexican condiment called zanahorias en escabeche. *They are often found on the table, along with the salsa, in Mexican restaurants. They keep well for up to 2 weeks if stored tightly covered in the refrigerator.*

Each ¼-cup serving contains approximately:

Calories: 22
Fat: 0 g.
Cholesterol: 0 mg.
Sodium: 57 mg.

5	medium carrots, cut into ½" rounds
1	cup water
1	cup white wine vinegar
1	small onion, sliced
1	small jalapeño pepper, seeded and sliced (wear plastic gloves when handling)
2	garlic cloves, quartered
½	teaspoon dried oregano, crushed
¼	teaspoon salt

Pictured on page 181

1. In a large glass bowl, mix the carrots, water, vinegar, onions, peppers, garlic, oregano and salt. Cover and allow to marinate at room temperature for 2 days.

2. Refrigerate for 1 day before serving.

Makes about 3 cups

↦ In a Flash!

Use a 1-pound bag of peeled baby carrots.

↦ Spin Off

Serve as a condiment or as an ingredient in soups, salads, tacos and casseroles.

Hot and Spicy Apple and Cabbage Salad

This is a delightfully different salad that can be made with fresh ingredients any time of the year. If you don't have Chinese chili paste, you can substitute a spicy hot salsa. Also, when Asian pears are available, I often use one in place of the apple.

Each 1-cup serving contains approximately:

Calories: 41
Fat: 0 g.
Cholesterol: 0 mg.
Sodium: 11 mg.

Pictured on page 263

- **½ small cabbage, cut into 2″ pieces**
- **Salt**
- **¼ cup Chinese rice wine, dry sherry or apple cider**
- **1 garlic clove, pressed or minced**
- **2 teaspoons sugar**
- **1 teaspoon Chinese red-chili paste**
- **1 large crisp apple, peeled and thinly sliced**

1. Place the cabbage in a colander and sprinkle with the salt. Toss to mix well. Allow to stand for at least 1 hour. Rinse thoroughly and drain well. Place in a large bowl.

2. Place the rice wine, sherry or apple cider in a small bowl. Stir in the garlic, sugar and chili paste to mix well. Pour over the cabbage. Add the apples and mix well.

Makes 6 cups

↠ In a Flash!

Use 12 ounces of preshredded cabbage from the produce section of your supermarket. You can shorten the time allowed for the salted cabbage to stand before rinsing it. However, the longer it stands, the milder the cabbage.

↠ Spin Off

Just before serving, add sliced fresh fruit to leftover cabbage for a refreshing and unusual mixed-fruit salad.

Curried Waldorf Salad

Pictured on page 199

This popular combination of ingredients is a crowd pleaser any time of the year. It packs well for picnics and tailgate parties and is wonderful on holiday menus as well. I sometimes substitute fennel bulb for half of the celery because it adds a pleasant licorice taste to the salad.

Each ½-cup serving contains approximately:

Calories: 117
Fat: 5 g.
Cholesterol: 0 mg.
Sodium: 212 mg.

1	cup fat-free mayonnaise
1	tablespoon fresh lemon juice
1	teaspoon sugar
¾	teaspoon curry powder
¼	teaspoon ground cinnamon
⅛	teaspoon ground ginger
2	pounds Red Delicious apples, peeled, cored and diced
3	cups diced celery
2	scallions, cut into ½" pieces
½	cup raisins
1	cup chopped toasted almonds

1. In a large bowl, combine the mayonnaise, lemon juice, sugar, curry powder, cinnamon and ginger; mix well. Add the apples, celery, scallions and raisins. Cover and refrigerate for several hours.

2. Just before serving, stir in the almonds.

Makes 8 cups

⇥ In a Flash!

Buy cut celery and scallions at the salad-bar section of the market.

⇥ Spin Off

Add cooked poultry or meat to any leftover salad for a delicious main-course salad. If you are serving this salad for Thanksgiving, make more than you plan to serve so you can add turkey to the leftovers. It's fabulous!

Salad of Young Greens with Fennel Dressing

Pictured on page 179

This is a recipe I developed several years ago for a magazine on entertaining. I like it with so many different types of menus that I still serve it often. Even though the salad takes only minutes to prepare, I included it in this chapter because the dressing has to be refrigerated for at least 2 hours to thicken.

Each serving contains approximately:

Calories: 45
Fat: 1 g.
Cholesterol: 0 mg.
Sodium: 218 mg.

Dressing

2	tablespoons cold water
½	teaspoon unflavored gelatin
¼	cup boiling water
½	teaspoon sugar
½	teaspoon salt
¼	cup raspberry vinegar
1	tablespoon fresh lemon juice
¼	teaspoon dry mustard
¼	teaspoon anise extract or ground fennel seeds
⅛	teaspoon freshly ground black pepper
1½	teaspoons walnut oil

Salad

1	small fennel bulb
1	head Bibb lettuce, torn into bite-size pieces
1	head radicchio, torn into bite-size pieces
1	bunch arugula, torn into bite-size pieces
1	cup mâche or mixed greens
2	tablespoons pine nuts, toasted

1. *To make the dressing:* Place the cold water in a medium bowl. Sprinkle with the gelatin and allow to soften for 5 minutes. Add the boiling water and stir until the gelatin is completely dissolved. Add the sugar and salt; stir until completely dissolved. Stir in the vinegar, lemon juice, mustard, anise extract or fennel seeds and pepper; mix thoroughly. Slowly whisk in the oil.

2. Pour into a bottle with a tight-fitting lid. Refrigerate for at least 2 hours. Shake well before using.

3. *To make the salad:* Trim the fennel, reserving some of the feathery fronds for a garnish. Dice the fennel and place in a large bowl. Add the lettuce, radicchio, arugula and mâche or greens. Toss to mix. Add the dressing and toss until all of the leaves glisten. Serve sprinkled with the pine nuts and garnished with the fennel fronds.

Makes 6 servings

⤶ In a Flash!

Use a bag of ready-to-serve mixed spring greens in place of all of the salad greens in the recipe.

⤶ Spin Off

Use the dressing as a sauce on fish and poultry.

Potato and Stilton Salad

You can substitute any type of blue cheese for the Stilton called for in this recipe. This salad is also good made with sharp Cheddar cheese and can be served warm or chilled.

Each serving contains approximately:

Calories: 300
Fat: 4 g.
Cholesterol: 11 mg.
Sodium: 404 mg.

1	pound small new potatoes, scrubbed and quartered
1	tablespoon red wine vinegar
½	cup fat-free sour cream
½	teaspoon Worcestershire sauce
¼	teaspoon salt
¼	teaspoon freshly ground black pepper
1	stalk celery, finely chopped
2	scallions, finely chopped
2	ounces Stilton cheese, crumbled

Pictured on page 200

1. Place the potatoes in a large saucepan. Cover with cold water and bring to a boil over high heat. Reduce the heat to medium and cook for 20 minutes, or until tender. Drain thoroughly and place in a large bowl. Sprinkle with the vinegar. Let cool for 5 minutes.

2. In another large bowl, combine the sour cream, Worcestershire sauce, salt and pepper; mix well. Stir in the celery, scallions and Stilton. Toss to mix. Add the potatoes and mix well.

Makes 4 servings

⇥ In a Flash!

Use frozen blanched potatoes; cook according to the package directions. Buy the celery and scallions already chopped at the salad bar in your market. Buy the cheese already crumbled; use ½ cup.

⇥ Spin Off

Stir-fry leftover salad in a small amount of olive oil and serve as a potato side dish. Or add stock to the salad and serve it as a soup.

Curried Waldorf Salad (page 195)

Potato and Stilton Salad (page 198)

Sweet Potato Dip (page 208)

Roasted Root Vegetables (page 210)

Cinnamon Waffles (page 214)

Sweet Cinnamon Quick Bread (page 215)

Vegetable Pizza (page 218)

Pear and Gorgonzola Pizza with Walnuts (page 217)

Chinese Chicken and Pineapple Salad

Here's another salad that uses gelatin to thicken the dressing and give it the slightly creamy texture usually associated with higher-fat dressings. When possible, make this type of dressing the day before you plan to use it. Do not substitute fresh pineapple for the canned pineapple in this salad. Bromelin, an enzyme in fresh pineapple, will cause the chicken to become mushy. Also, never use fresh or fresh frozen pineapple in recipes containing gelatin because this same enzyme prevents jelling.

Each serving contains approximately:

Calories: 339
Fat: 9 g.
Cholesterol: 103 mg.
Sodium: 208 mg.

Dressing

2	tablespoons cold water
½	teaspoon unflavored gelatin
¼	cup boiling water
¼	cup rice vinegar
1	tablespoon dark brown sugar
2	teaspoons reduced-sodium soy sauce
½	teaspoon Chinese 5-spice blend
1	garlic clove, pressed or minced
2	teaspoons dark sesame oil

Salad

1	package (8 ounces) coleslaw mix
3	cups diced cooked chicken breast
1	can (20 ounces) pineapple chunks packed in juice, drained
¼	cup chopped toasted almonds

1. ***To make the dressing:*** Place the cold water in a medium bowl. Sprinkle with the gelatin and allow to soften for 5 minutes. Add the boiling water and stir until the gelatin is completely dissolved. Stir in the vinegar, brown sugar, soy sauce, Chinese 5-spice blend and garlic. Slowly whisk in the oil.

2. Pour into a bottle with a tight-fitting lid. Refrigerate for at least 2 hours. Shake well before using.

3. ***To make the salad:*** Place the coleslaw mix in a large bowl. Add the dressing and toss until all of the leaves glisten. Add the chicken and pineapple; toss thoroughly. Serve topped with the almonds.

Makes 4 servings

⇥ In a Flash!

Buy 12 ounces cooked and chopped chicken. Use ⅛ teaspoon garlic powder in the dressing in place of the fresh garlic.

⇥ Spin Off

Leftover salad keeps well if stored tightly covered in the refrigerator. You can also use this dressing as a sauce for fish and poultry.

Sweet Potato Dip

There are about 40 different varieties of sweet potatoes raised in this country, and they fall roughly into two categories. The ones that convert most of their starches to sugar during cooking and become sweet and soft are called the moist-fleshed varieties. Those that convert less starch and are less sweet are the dry-fleshed types. Although the sweeter varieties are often referred to as yams, they are not true yams, which are starchy tropical vegetables rarely found in our markets.

Each ¼-cup serving contains approximately:

Calories: 96
Fat: 2 g.
Cholesterol: 0 mg.
Sodium: 84 mg.

2	**medium sweet potatoes**
1	**tablespoon dried marjoram, crushed**
½	**teaspoon ground nutmeg**
¼	**teaspoon salt**
⅛	**teaspoon freshly ground black pepper**
⅛	**teaspoon crushed red-pepper flakes**
1	**tablespoon extra-virgin olive oil**

Pictured on page 201

1. Preheat the oven to 400°. Wash and dry the sweet potatoes and poke holes in them with the tines of a fork. Place them on a baking sheet and bake for 1 hour, or until soft. Set aside until cool enough to handle. Remove and discard the skins.

2. Place the sweet potatoes in a food processor. Add the marjoram, nutmeg, salt, black pepper and red-pepper flakes. Blend until satin smooth. With the processor running, slowly add the oil through the feed tube.

Makes 1¾ cups

↦ In a Flash!
Use 4 jars (4 ounces each) pureed baby food sweet potatoes. Stir in the other ingredients.

↦ Spin Off
Thin leftover dip with a little skim milk for a wonderful sauce for pasta or rice. Or thin it further for a soup.

Italian Spaghetti Sauce

This sensational recipe for spaghetti sauce was sent to me by a reader several years ago. The first time I made it, I cut it in half and was sorry I did. Everyone in my family liked it so much they wanted me to make it again a few days later. It isn't any more trouble to make 18 cups of this sauce than it is to make 9 cups, and it freezes beautifully!

Each ½-cup serving contains approximately:

Calories: 149
Fat: 9 g.
Cholesterol: 28 mg.
Sodium: 368 mg.

¼ **cup extra-virgin olive oil**

4 **medium onions, sliced**

4 **garlic cloves, pressed or minced**

3 **pounds extra-lean ground round**

1 **can (46 ounces) tomato juice**

1 **can (29 ounces) tomato puree**

1 **can (12 ounces) tomato paste**

8 **whole dried chili peppers**

2 **teaspoons sugar**

2 **teaspoons salt**

¼ **teaspoon freshly ground black pepper**

24 **pimiento-stuffed olives, chopped (optional)**

1. In a Dutch oven or large pot, warm the oil over medium heat. Add the onions and garlic; cook for 10 minutes, or until softened. Crumble the beef into the pot. Cook, stirring frequently, for 10 minutes, or until the beef is browned.

2. Add the tomato juice, tomato puree, tomato paste, chili peppers, sugar, salt and black pepper. Cover and simmer, stirring occasionally, for 2 hours. Remove and discard the chili peppers. Add the olives (if using) just before serving.

Makes about 18 cups

↔ **In a Flash!**

Cutting the recipe in half reduces the cooking time by half.

↔ **Spin Off**

Freeze some of the sauce in ice cube trays until solid. Remove the cubes from the tray and store in self-sealing plastic bags. When you need a small amount of sauce for another dish, just thaw a few cubes in a microwave for a couple of minutes.

Roasted Root Vegetables

Roasting onions, carrots and other root vegetables is not only an easy way to prepare them but also a wonderful way to intensify their flavors. If you like, you can add other vegetables such as celery, fennel or brussels sprouts.

Each serving contains approximately:

Calories: 133
Fat: 5 g.
Cholesterol: 0 mg.
Sodium: 245 mg.

2 tablespoons extra-virgin olive oil
2 large garlic cloves, pressed or minced
1 tablespoon dried thyme, crushed
½ teaspoon salt
½ teaspoon freshly ground black pepper
1 pound small red-skinned potatoes, scrubbed and halved
1 large onion, quartered
8 ounces carrots, peeled and cut into 1" rounds
8 ounces turnips, peeled and cut into bite-size cubes

Pictured on page 202

1. Preheat the oven to 425°. Combine the oil and garlic in a large roasting pan and place in the oven for 2 minutes, or until the garlic starts to sizzle. Remove the pan from the oven and stir in the thyme, salt and pepper.

2. Add the potatoes, onions, carrots and turnips; toss until well coated. Cover with a lid or aluminum foil and bake for 30 minutes.

3. Increase the oven temperature to 450° and bake, uncovered, for 30 minutes, or until the vegetables are lightly browned and can be easily pierced with a fork.

Makes 6 servings

⇥ In a Flash!
Buy the vegetables already cut in the salad-bar section of the market.

⇥ Spin Off
Roasted vegetables are great served cold as a side dish or in salads.

Rice Pilaf

This is my favorite pilaf recipe. You can customize it by adding your own favorite herbs and spices. You can also turn it into an entrée by adding leftover cooked fish, poultry, meat or beans.

Each ½-cup serving contains approximately:

Calories: 148
Fat: 3 g.
Cholesterol: 0 mg.
Sodium: 155 mg.

1	**tablespoon canola oil**
1	**cup uncooked long-grain white rice**
½	**medium onion, thinly sliced**
2	**cups defatted chicken stock**
2	**tablespoons reduced-sodium soy sauce**
1	**teaspoon dried thyme, crushed**

1. Warm the oil in a large saucepan over medium heat. Add the rice and onions. Cook, stirring frequently, for 5 minutes, or until browned.

2. Add the stock, soy sauce and thyme. Bring to a boil. Reduce the heat to low, cover and cook for 20 minutes, or until all of the liquid has been absorbed.

Makes 4 cups

↬ In a Flash!

Use 1 cup sliced onions from the supermarket salad bar. Freeze pilaf in the size portions you most frequently use and just reheat to serve.

↬ Spin Off

Leftover pilaf is good served cold as a rice salad. Use it alone or mixed with other ingredients.

Crock-Pot Black Beans

I like to serve these beans over rice or pasta and garnish them with concentric circles of chopped green peppers, onions and pimientos. You'll need to think ahead a little when making this dish because the dried beans need to soak overnight in cold water.

Each serving contains approximately:

Calories: 286
Fat: 2 g.
Cholesterol: 0 mg.
Sodium: 810 mg.

1   **green bell pepper, seeded and chopped**
1   **medium onion, chopped**
1   **pound dried black beans, soaked overnight and drained**
3   **tablespoons rice vinegar**
2   **tablespoons ground cumin**
1   **tablespoon sugar**
3   **bay leaves**
2   **teaspoons salt**

1.   In a large nonstick skillet, combine the peppers and onions. Cover and cook over low heat for about 10 minutes, or until the onions are translucent; if needed, add a little water to prevent scorching.

2.   Place the beans in a 6-quart Crock-Pot or other slow cooker. Add water until 2″ above beans. Add the onion mixture, vinegar, cumin, sugar, bay leaves and salt. Cook on high for 8 hours, or until the beans are tender. Remove and discard the bay leaves.

Makes 6 servings

↠ In a Flash!

Keep presoaked and drained beans in self-sealing plastic bags in your freezer to use when you want them in a hurry.

↠ Spin Off

Leftover beans are great in salads, soups, burritos and tostadas. Or mash them for dips.

Jelled Breakfast Coffee Delight

Now you can "eat" your breakfast coffee and juice rather than drinking them!

Each serving contains approximately:

Calories: 98
Fat: 0 g.
Cholesterol: 0 mg.
Sodium: 8 mg.

¼ **cup cool water**
1 **envelope unflavored gelatin**
1 **cup boiling water**
1 **can (6 ounces) prune juice**
2 **teaspoons instant coffee granules**
2 **teaspoons sugar (or to taste)**
   Milk or yogurt (optional)

1. Place the cool water in a medium heatproof bowl. Sprinkle with the gelatin and let soften for 5 minutes. Add the boiling water and stir until the gelatin is completely dissolved.

2. Stir in the prune juice, coffee and sugar. Refrigerate until firm before serving.

3. Serve topped with the milk or yogurt (if using).

Makes 2 servings

↔ In a Flash!
This is as fast as it gets!

↔ Spin Off
Put leftovers in a blender with skim milk or yogurt for a creamy shake.

Cinnamon Waffles

Most waffle recipes call for beaten egg whites to be folded into the batter as the last step. These easy cinnamon waffles skip that time-consuming step. In fact, they can be made in minutes, and they freeze well.

Each waffle contains approximately:

Calories: 204
Fat: 7 g.
Cholesterol: 29 mg.
Sodium: 553 mg.

Pictured on page 203

1   cup whole-wheat flour
1   cup unbleached all-purpose flour
⅓   cup instant nonfat dry milk
1   tablespoon ground cinnamon
1   tablespoon baking powder
½   teaspoon baking soda
½   teaspoon salt
2   egg whites
1   egg
3   tablespoons canola oil
2   teaspoons vanilla
2   cups buttermilk

1.   In a large bowl, combine the whole-wheat flour, unbleached flour, dry milk, cinnamon, baking powder, baking soda and salt; mix well.

2.   In a medium bowl, mix the egg whites, egg, oil and vanilla. Pour over the dry ingredients. Add the buttermilk and mix well.

3.   Spray a nonstick waffle iron with nonstick vegetable cooking spray and preheat according to the manufacturer's directions. Pour ½ cup of the batter into the center of the hot waffle iron and cook until the batter stops steaming, about 6 minutes. (Cooking time will vary greatly depending on the type of waffle iron you are using.) Repeat to make 7 more waffles, coating the waffle iron lightly with spray between waffles.

Makes 8 waffles

↦ In a Flash!

Use only unbleached flour; use ½ cup liquid egg substitute in place of the egg and egg whites.

↦ Spin Off

Freeze leftover waffles and reheat them in a toaster.

Sweet Cinnamon Quick Bread

At first glance, this may not look like a recipe for people who don't have time to cook. However, it can literally be mixed in minutes, and it is so delicious you'll want to make it often.

Each slice contains approximately:

Calories: 147
Fat: 4 g.
Cholesterol: 14 mg.
Sodium: 311 mg.

Batter

Pictured on page 204

2	cups unbleached all-purpose flour
¾	cup sugar
4	teaspoons baking powder
2	teaspoons ground cinnamon
¾	teaspoon salt
1	cup buttermilk
¼	cup canola oil
2	egg whites
1	egg
2	teaspoons vanilla

Streusel

2	tablespoons sugar
1	teaspoon ground cinnamon
2	teaspoons corn-oil margarine, softened

1. Preheat the oven to 350°. Coat a 9″ × 5″ loaf pan with nonstick vegetable cooking spray.

2. *To make the batter:* In a large bowl, mix the flour, sugar, baking powder, cinnamon and salt. Add the buttermilk, oil, egg whites, egg and vanilla. Beat with an electric mixer on medium speed for 3 minutes. Pour the batter into the prepared pan.

3. *To make the streusel:* In a small bowl, mix the sugar, cinnamon and margarine until crumbly. Sprinkle over the batter and swirl slightly with a knife to marble it through the batter.

4. Bake for about 55 minutes, or until a skewer inserted in the center comes out clean. Cool for 10 minutes in the pan on a wire rack, then remove from the pan to finish cooling.

Makes 1 loaf; 16 slices

⇢ In a Flash!

Make 2 loaves at a time. Slice and freeze individual slices in plastic bags for toast in the morning.

⇢ Spin Off

Use for fabulous French toast!

Whole-Wheat Stuffing

This is a great holiday stuffing or dressing. It is also good served in place of rice or potatoes with fish, poultry or meat any time of the year. You'll need about 5 or 6 slices of bread. Omit the added salt if your stock contains salt.

Each ½-cup serving contains approximately:

Calories: 75
Fat: 2 g.
Cholesterol: 0 mg.
Sodium: 212 mg.

3	cups crumbled whole-wheat toast
1	teaspoon ground sage
¼	teaspoon freshly ground black pepper
¼	teaspoon salt (optional)
1	tablespoon corn-oil margarine
1	medium onion, finely chopped
1	cup chopped celery
½	cup chopped fresh parsley
1½	cups defatted chicken stock

1. Preheat the oven to 350°. Coat a 9″ × 5″ loaf pan with nonstick vegetable cooking spray.

2. In a large bowl, combine the toast, sage, pepper and salt (if using); mix well.

3. Melt the margarine in a large nonstick skillet over medium-low heat. Add the onions, celery and parsley. Cover and cook for 10 minutes, or until the onions are soft and translucent. Add to the bowl with the toast. Stir in the stock and mix well. Spoon the mixture into the prepared pan. Bake for 45 minutes.

Makes 4 cups

⇥ In a Flash!

Use 1½ cups prechopped onions, and buy chopped celery in the salad-bar section of your market.

⇥ Spin Off

Add leftovers to soups, stews and casseroles.

Pear and Gorgonzola Pizza with Walnuts

Pictured on page 206

I created this unusual pizza for Trattoria Acqua, an elegant Italian restaurant in La Jolla, California, with a spectacular ocean view. When the owners, Victoria and Michael McGreath, asked me if I would design a pizza for their new menu, I wanted it to be both delicious and totally different from the other pizzas they served. In the restaurant, the McGreaths make a whole-wheat pizza crust, but it is easier—and certainly much faster—if you buy already-prepared pizza dough.

Each slice contains approximately:

Calories: 226
Fat: 7 g.
Cholesterol: 12 mg.
Sodium: 366 mg.

6	ounces dried pears
⅔	cup water
⅔	cup dry white wine
¼	teaspoon freshly ground black pepper
¼	teaspoon balsamic vinegar
1	tube (10 ounces) ready-to-bake pizza dough
1	teaspoon walnut oil
1	Bartlett pear, peeled, cored and thinly sliced
3	ounces Gorgonzola cheese, crumbled
¼	cup reduced-fat ricotta cheese
2	tablespoons chopped walnuts

1. Combine the dried pears, water, wine and pepper in a medium saucepan and bring to a boil over high heat. Reduce the heat to low, cover and simmer for 25 minutes. Remove from the heat and allow to cool for 5 minutes. Transfer to a blender or food processor. Add the vinegar and blend until coarsely chopped.

2. Preheat the oven to 450°. Coat a 12″ pizza pan with nonstick vegetable cooking spray.

3. Place the pizza dough on a floured board and roll into a 12″ circle. Place on the prepared pan. Brush with the oil. Spread the cooked pears evenly over the top, leaving a ½″ border around the edge. Arrange the pear slices on top of the sauce.

4. In a small bowl, combine the Gorgonzola and ricotta; mash together with a fork. Sprinkle over the top of the sliced pears. Sprinkle with the walnuts.

5. Bake on the lowest oven shelf for about 12 to 15 minutes, or until the crust is crisp and the cheese is bubbly. Remove from the oven and transfer to a cutting board for slicing.

Makes 8 slices

↪ In a Flash!

Eliminate the sliced fresh pear. Buy the Gorgonzola or another blue cheese already crumbled; use ⅓ cup.

↪ Spin Off

Allow leftover pizza to come to room temperature and store it in self-sealing plastic sandwich bags for great brown bag lunches.

Hands-On Time: Less Than 30 Minutes

Vegetable Pizza

You can use this same recipe to make small individual pizzas. They are ideal for party "participation cooking." Just put out bowls of lightly cooked cut vegetables, sauce and cheese. Then give the guests some dough and a pizza pan, and let them create their own personalized pizzas.

Each serving contains approximately:

Calories: 392
Fat: 12 g.
Cholesterol: 33 mg.
Sodium: 758 mg.

Pictured on page 205

1 tablespoon yellow cornmeal
1 medium onion, thinly sliced
4 ounces fresh mushrooms, thinly sliced
1 cup thinly sliced red bell peppers
1 cup thinly sliced zucchini
1 tube (10 ounces) ready-to-bake pizza dough
1 cup fat-free pasta sauce
8 ounces part-skim mozzarella cheese, shredded

1. Preheat the oven to 425°. Coat a 12″ pizza pan with nonstick vegetable cooking spray and sprinkle it evenly with the cornmeal.

2. Place the onions in a large nonstick skillet. Cover and cook over low heat for about 10 minutes, or until soft. Add the mushrooms, peppers and zucchini. Cover and cook for 5 minutes. Remove from the heat and set aside until cool enough to handle.

3. Place the pizza dough on a floured board and roll into a 12″ circle. Place on the prepared pan. Spread evenly with the pasta sauce, leaving a ½″ border. Top with the vegetables.

4. Bake on the lowest oven shelf for 10 minutes. Remove from the oven and sprinkle with the mozzarella. Bake for 10 minutes, or until the mozzarella is melted and starting to brown.

Makes 4 servings

↦ In a Flash!

Use already-sliced vegetables from the salad bar section of the market; you'll want about 1½ cups of onions and 1 cup of mushrooms. Buy preshredded mozzarella.

↦ Spin Off

Cold leftover pizza makes good brown bag lunches.

Baked Quesadillas

Baking these Mexican grilled-cheese sandwiches is much faster than cooking them individually on a grill or in a skillet. They can be served as appetizers or as the main course in a vegetarian meal.

Each serving contains approximately:

Calories: 443
Fat: 16 g.
Cholesterol: 26 mg.
Sodium: 805 mg.

1   **can (10¾ ounces) condensed reduced-fat cream of mushroom soup, undiluted**
2   **cups fat-free sour cream**
1   **can (7 ounces) diced green chili peppers**
1   **teaspoon chili powder**
½   **teaspoon ground cumin**
12   **whole-wheat flour tortillas**
6   **ounces reduced-fat sharp Cheddar cheese, shredded**
    Chopped scallions
    Chopped fresh cilantro
2   **cups salsa**

1. Preheat the oven to 350°. Coat two 10″ pie plates or quiche dishes with nonstick vegetable cooking spray.

2. In a medium bowl, combine the soup, sour cream, peppers, chili powder and cumin; mix well.

3. Place 1 tortilla in the bottom of each prepared dish. Spoon ⅓ cup of the mushroom sauce over each tortilla; sprinkle with about 2 tablespoons of the Cheddar. Repeat the layering 4 more times to use all the sauce, Cheddar and all but the last 2 tortillas; top each with 1 tortilla.

4. Mist the top tortillas with the nonstick spray and bake for about 25 minutes, or until the tops are browned and the cheese has melted.

5. Cut the quesadillas into wedges and top with the scallions and cilantro. Serve the salsa on the side.

Makes 6 servings

⇢ In a Flash!

Buy the scallions and cilantro chopped in the salad-bar section of the market.

⇢ Spin Off

Leftover quesadillas make great snacks and are wonderful in brown bag lunches.

Chili Relleno Casserole

For a real Southwestern treat that can be assembled in minutes, this recipe takes first place. Serve it with hot corn tortillas and lots of salsa!

Each serving contains approximately:

Calories: 479
Fat: 12 g.
Cholesterol: 185 mg.
Sodium: 195 mg.

2   **cans (4 ounces each) whole green chili peppers**
4   **ounces reduced-fat sharp Cheddar cheese, shredded**
3   **eggs**
2   **cups skim milk**
½   **cup unbleached all-purpose flour**
¼   **teaspoon salt**

1. Preheat the oven to 350°.

2. Coat a 11″ × 7″ baking dish with nonstick vegetable cooking spray. Line the bottom with the peppers in a single layer. Sprinkle evenly with the Cheddar.

3. Place the eggs in a medium bowl. Whisk in the milk, flour and salt until smooth. Pour into the baking dish. Bake for 45 minutes, or until set and lightly browned.

Makes 4 servings

↦ In a Flash!

Buy the cheese already shredded.

↦ Spin Off

Leftovers are good served cold on greens for a salad; top with salsa. Leftovers also travel well for brown bag lunches and picnics.

Zucchini Bake

This is a great recipe to have during the summer, when zucchini is so abundant we are all looking for new and different ways to use it. You can serve this as a vegetarian entrée or as a side dish with fish, poultry or meat.

Each serving contains approximately:

Calories: 203
Fat: 9 g.
Cholesterol: 7 mg.
Sodium: 437 mg.

Pictured on page 223

1	**pound zucchini, shredded**
1	**cup reduced-fat biscuit mix**
¾	**cup liquid egg substitute**
½	**cup grated fresh Parmesan cheese**
1	**small onion, shredded**
⅓	**cup buttermilk**
2	**tablespoons canola oil**

1. Preheat the oven to 350°. Coat a 9″ pie plate or an 11″ × 7″ baking dish with nonstick vegetable cooking spray.

2. In a large bowl, combine the zucchini, biscuit mix, egg substitute, Parmesan, onions, buttermilk and oil. Mix well. Pour into the prepared dish.

3. Bake for about 1 hour, or until lightly browned. Remove from the oven and allow to stand for 5 minutes before cutting.

Makes 4 servings

↦ In a Flash!

Make this the day before you plan to serve it and then reheat it in a microwave.

↦ Spin Off

Include leftovers cold in brown bag lunches.

Mushroom Soufflé

This soufflé is good for breakfast, brunch, lunch or dinner. Serve it with fresh fruit or vegetables. Large eggs are the best choice for this recipe.

Each serving contains approximately:

Calories: 188
Fat: 6 g.
Cholesterol: 48 mg.
Sodium: 582 mg.

8	slices whole-wheat bread, crusts removed
1½	cups skim milk
2	tablespoons corn-oil margarine
½	medium onion, chopped
1½	pounds fresh mushrooms, chopped
2	tablespoons finely chopped fresh parsley
1	egg yolk
¾	teaspoon salt
4	egg whites
2	tablespoons plain dried bread crumbs

1. Preheat the oven to 350°. Coat a 3-quart casserole or soufflé dish with nonstick vegetable cooking spray.

2. Combine the bread and milk in a large bowl. Let stand for 15 minutes and then mash the bread thoroughly with a fork.

3. Meanwhile, melt the margarine in a large nonstick skillet over medium heat. Add the onions and cook for 5 minutes. Add the mushrooms and cook for about 5 to 7 minutes, or until soft.

4. Transfer the mushroom mixture to the bowl with the bread. Add the parsley, egg yolk and salt. Mix well.

5. In a medium bowl, whisk the egg whites for a few minutes until soft peaks form. Fold into the mushroom mixture until no streaks of white show.

6. Spoon the mixture into the prepared dish. Sprinkle the top with the bread crumbs. Bake for about 1 hour, or until a knife inserted in the center comes out clean. Serve immediately.

Makes 6 servings

↪ In a Flash!

Use ¾ cup prechopped onions and 8 cups of packaged presliced mushrooms (chop the mushrooms briefly in a food processor).

↪ Spin Off

Cold soufflé is great in brown bag lunches.

Zucchini Bake (page 221)

Rapidly Roasted Turkey (page 235)

Brown Bag Chicken (page 237) (page 237)

225

Cheesy Chicken with Tomatoes and Sunflower Seeds
(page 243)

Chicken Stew Provençale (page 244)

Roasted Italian Chicken on Rotini (page 247)

Turkey Loaf (page 249)

Chuck Wagon Stew (page 257)

Overnight Cheddar
Cheese Strata

This dish is perfect for Sunday brunch. You can assemble it on Saturday and refrigerate it until Sunday morning. Then you can put it into a cold oven, set the timer to turn on the oven an hour before you want to eat, go to church and have brunch as soon as you return. If you don't have beau monde seasoning, substitute a little celery salt.

Each serving contains approximately:

Calories: 365
Fat: 10 g.
Cholesterol: 29 mg.
Sodium: 597 mg.

4	slices whole-wheat bread, cut into ¼″ squares
4	ounces reduced-fat sharp Cheddar cheese, shredded
1	can (12 ounces) evaporated skim milk
1	cup liquid egg substitute
2	tablespoons chopped chives or scallion tops
¼	teaspoon salt
¼	teaspoon beau monde seasoning
¼	teaspoon dry mustard
¼	teaspoon Worcestershire sauce
⅛	teaspoon freshly ground black pepper
4	medium oranges, peeled and sliced

1. Evenly distribute half of the bread in an 11″ × 7″ baking dish. Sprinkle with half of the Cheddar. Repeat to use the remaining bread and Cheddar.

2. In a medium bowl, mix the milk, egg substitute, chives or scallion tops, salt, beau monde seasoning, mustard, Worcestershire sauce and pepper. Pour over the bread and Cheddar.

3. Cover and refrigerate overnight.

4. Remove the strata from the refrigerator 2 hours before baking. Place the baking dish in a larger pan. Add cold water to come about halfway up the sides of the strata dish. Turn the oven on to 300° and bake for 1 hour, or until puffy and lightly browned.

Serve garnished with the oranges.

Makes 4 servings

↪ In a Flash!

Buy oranges already sliced in the salad-bar section of the market. Buy shredded Cheddar; you'll need 1 cup.

↪ Spin Off

Serve leftover soufflé cold with a salad or in a brown bag lunch.

Vegetarian Lasagna

You can add cooked chopped poultry or meat to this lasagna, if you wish. In fact, it is a great way to use up small amounts of leftovers.

Each serving contains approximately:

Calories: 245
Fat: 4 g.
Cholesterol: 43 mg.
Sodium: 474 mg.

1 **jar (26 ounces) fat-free meatless spaghetti sauce**
1 **pound fresh mushrooms, sliced**
1 **medium onion, chopped**
3 **small zucchini, sliced**
1 **carton (15 ounces) fat-free ricotta cheese**
½ **cup chopped fresh parsley**
1 **egg**
½ **teaspoon salt**
¼ **teaspoon freshly ground black pepper**
1 **cup shredded part-skim mozzarella cheese, divided**
4 **tablespoons shredded fresh Parmesan cheese, divided**
6 **no-boil lasagna noodles**

1. Preheat the oven to 350°. Coat a 13″ × 9″ baking dish with non-stick vegetable cooking spray.

2. In a large saucepan, combine the spaghetti sauce, mushrooms, onions and zucchini. Bring to a boil over medium-high heat. Reduce the heat to low, cover and cook for 10 minutes.

3. In a large bowl, combine the ricotta, parsley, egg, salt and pepper; mix well. Stir in ¾ cup of the mozzarella and 2 tablespoons of the Parmesan.

4. Place a third of the sauce mixture in the bottom of the prepared dish. Top with half of the ricotta mixture and 3 of the uncooked noodles (spaced about ½″ apart). Repeat the layering.

5. Top with the remaining sauce. Sprinkle with the remaining ¼ cup mozzarella and the remaining 2 tablespoons Parmesan.

6. Cover with a lid or aluminum foil and bake for 40 minutes. Uncover and bake for 20 minutes, or until lightly browned.

Makes 8 servings

⇥ In a Flash!

Buy already-sliced zucchini and fresh mushrooms in the salad-bar section of your market. Use 1½ cups prechopped onions. Buy preshredded mozzarella and fresh Parmesan.

⇥ Spin Off

Freeze leftovers in individual portions in self-sealing plastic bags. Reheat in the microwave. (Or place still-frozen portions in a brown bag lunch— they will thaw by noon and are truly tasty cold.)

Pasta Shells
with Dilled Crab Filling

This is a delightfully different taste combination. For a less-expensive dish, you can substitute water-packed white albacore tuna for the crab.

Each serving contains approximately:

Calories: 277
Fat: 5 g.
Cholesterol: 33 mg.
Sodium: 949 mg.

8	dry jumbo pasta shells
1	tablespoon corn-oil margarine
1	garlic clove, pressed or minced
½	medium onion, finely chopped
2	cups reduced-fat cottage cheese
1	can (6 ounces) white crab, rinsed and drained
1	tablespoon chopped fresh dill
1	teaspoon grated lemon rind, yellow part only
¼	teaspoon salt
¼	teaspoon freshly ground black pepper
1	jar (14–16 ounces) fat-free pasta sauce

1. Preheat the oven to 350°.

2. Cook the shells in a large pot of boiling water for about 12 minutes, or until tender but still firm to the bite. Drain thoroughly in a colander.

3. Meanwhile, melt the margarine in a large nonstick skillet. Add the garlic and cook over medium heat for 1 minute, or until the garlic sizzles. Add the onions and cook, stirring frequently, for about 10 minutes, or until soft and translucent. Remove from the heat and stir in the cottage cheese, crab, dill, lemon rind, salt and pepper.

4. Spoon the mixture into the cooked shells.

5. Spread the pasta sauce evenly over the bottom of an 11″ × 7″ or 8″ × 8″ baking dish. Arrange the shells on top of the sauce. Cover with a lid or aluminum foil and bake for 20 minutes.

Makes 4 servings

↪ In a Flash!

Use ½ teaspoon pure lemon extract to replace the grated lemon rind. Use 1 teaspoon dried dill weed in place of fresh dill. Serve the crab filling over cooked pasta rather than filling shells.

↪ Spin Off

Mash up any leftover filled pasta shells with the sauce and spread on toasted rye bread for tasty open-face sandwiches.

Italian Fish Dish

This is one of my favorite fish dishes—it also works well with chicken breasts. When using chicken, cook it for 2 minutes per side and check to make certain it has turned from translucent to opaque before serving.

Each serving contains approximately:

Calories: 386
Fat: 12 g.
Cholesterol: 56 mg.
Sodium: 963 mg.

1	**tablespoon olive oil**
2	**garlic cloves, pressed or minced**
2	**cups finely shredded carrots**
1	**medium onion, finely chopped**
¼	**cup finely chopped fresh parsley**
1	**can (28 ounces) ready-cut tomatoes, undrained**
1	**can (6 ounces) tomato paste**
1	**teaspoon dried oregano, crushed**
½	**teaspoon freshly ground black pepper**
¼	**teaspoon salt**
4	**halibut fillets (4 ounces each)**
1	**cup shredded part-skim mozzarella cheese**
¼	**cup grated fresh Parmesan cheese**

1. Place a large nonstick skillet over medium heat and add the oil; warm for 1 minute. Add the garlic and cook for 1 minute, or until the garlic sizzles. Add the carrots and onions; cook, stirring frequently, for 3 minutes.

2. Add the parsley and cook, stirring occasionally, for about 8 minutes, or until the vegetables are tender. Add the tomatoes, tomato paste, oregano, pepper and salt. Simmer for 30 minutes.

3. Coat a medium or large nonstick skillet with nonstick vegetable spray and place over medium heat until drops of water sprinkled into the skillet dance on the surface. Add the halibut and cook for 1 minute per side.

4. Use a spatula to place the halibut on top of the tomato sauce. Sprinkle with the mozzarella and Parmesan. Cover, reduce the heat to low and cook for about 4 minutes, or until the cheese is melted.

Makes 4 servings

↪ In a Flash!

Buy an 8-ounce bag of shredded carrots; buy preshredded mozzarella and grated fresh Parmesan.

↪ Spin Off

Chop leftover fish, mix it with leftover sauce and serve over pasta or rice.

Rapidly Roasted Turkey

This rapid method of roasting the holiday bird is much faster than traditional recipes and still produces a great-tasting turkey. If you want to use the pan drippings to make gravy, pour them into a bowl and place in the freezer while the bird is resting before carving. The fat will congeal on the top and can be easily removed for fat-free gravy.

1   turkey (about 12 pounds)
1   tablespoon lemon pepper

Pictured on page 224

1.   Place the oven rack on the second to the lowest position in the oven. Preheat the oven to 500°.

2.   Remove the package of giblets from inside the turkey. (Set aside to add to gravy or dressing, or freeze for future use.) Rinse the turkey inside and out with cold water and pat dry with paper towels. Place the bird, breast side up, in a large roasting pan. (The bird should not touch the sides of the pan.) Cut off and discard the wing tips. Rub the outside of the turkey with the lemon pepper.

3.   Place in the oven legs first. Roast for about 20 minutes; run a metal spatula under the turkey, moving it around a bit, to prevent its sticking to the bottom of the pan. Continue to roast for 1 hour, or until the leg joint can easily be moved and the juices run clear when the thigh is pierced with a sharp knife.

4.   Remove the turkey from the oven and allow to stand for 20 minutes before carving.

Makes about 12 servings

⇥ In a Flash!
The deli section of most supermarkets will roast your turkey or chicken for you.

⇥ Spin Off
You name it! Sandwiches, salads, soups . . .

Each 3-ounce serving of white meat without skin contains approximately:

Calories: 134
Fat: 3 g.
Cholesterol: 59 mg.
Sodium: 67 mg.

Each 3-ounce serving of dark meat without skin contains approximately:

Calories: 159
Fat: 6 g.
Cholesterol: 72 mg.
Sodium: 67 mg.

Hands-On Time: Less Than 30 Minutes

Herbed Lemon Chicken

1   **tablespoon unbleached all-purpose flour**
3   **tablespoons fresh lemon juice**
2   **teaspoons dried tarragon, crushed**
1   **teaspoon dried thyme, crushed**
1   **teaspoon seasoned salt**
1   **teaspoon grated lemon rind, yellow part only**
4   **skinless, bone-in chicken breast halves**
1   **large onion, sliced and separated into rings**

1. Preheat the oven to 350°. Put the flour in a large ($14'' \times 20''$) oven-cooking bag and shake to coat the inside of the bag. (Leave the flour in the bag to prevent bursting.)

2. Add the lemon juice, tarragon, thyme, salt and lemon rind to the bag; knead the bag to blend the ingredients. Place the chicken in the bag and turn to coat it with the lemon mixture.

3. Place the bag in a $13'' \times 9''$ baking dish. Arrange the chicken in an even layer and top with the onion rings. Close the bag with the tie provided. Cut six ½″ slits in the top of the bag. Make sure the bag does not overhang the baking dish.

4. Bake for about 30 to 35 minutes, or until the juices run clear when the chicken is pierced with a sharp knife. Allow to stand in the bag for 5 minutes. Carefully cut the bag open with scissors.

Makes 4 servings

⇢ In a Flash!

Use prechopped onions in place of the whole onion cut into rings.

⇢ Spin Off

This flavorful chicken is good cold in sandwiches and salads. You can also chop up any leftover chicken and reheat it to serve over pasta or rice.

Brown Bag Chicken

This is a recipe I created for another of my books, Cook It Light: One-Dish Meals. *This incredibly easy meal takes only about 10 minutes to assemble and literally uses every ingredient you brought home from the market to make it—including the shopping bag! You can vary the vegetables and herbs in this recipe to suit your own tastes. You can even stuff the chicken with your favorite dressing, if you prefer.*

Each serving contains approximately:

Calories: 417
Fat: 16 g.
Cholesterol: 100 mg.
Sodium: 499 mg.

1	**frying chicken (3–4 pounds)**
½	**teaspoon seasoned salt**
½	**teaspoon freshly ground black pepper**
¼	**teaspoon garlic powder**
	Several sprigs of fresh thyme
1	**medium onion, quartered**
4	**small red-skinned potatoes, scrubbed and halved**
4	**small carrots, peeled**
1	**box (10 ounces) frozen peas**

Pictured on page 225

1. Preheat the oven to 400°.

2. Rinse the chicken inside and out with cold water and pat dry with paper towels. Rub the chicken with the salt, pepper and garlic powder. Stuff the chicken with the thyme and onions.

3. Place the chicken, breast side up, in a 13″ × 9″ baking dish. Scatter the potatoes and carrots around the chicken; sprinkle the frozen peas over the top of the vegetables.

4. Place the dish inside a large brown paper grocery bag. Fold over the ends of the bag and staple shut.

5. Carefully place the bag-covered baking dish in the center of the oven *(make sure the bag is low enough that it doesn't touch the upper heating element and that it's high enough not to touch the lower heating element)*. Bake for 1½ hours.

6. Remove from the oven and carefully cut the bag open with scissors. Allow the chicken to stand for 10 minutes before cutting into serving pieces. Serve with the vegetables.

Makes 4 servings

⇥ In a Flash!

Buy packaged ready-to-cook potatoes and already-cut carrots from the salad-bar section of the market. Use 1 teaspoon dried thyme in place of the fresh sprigs.

⇥ Spin Off

Cold leftover chicken is wonderful served with the Curried Waldorf Salad on page 195.

Chinese Chicken in a Bag

This one recipe is reason enough to buy a box of oven-cooking bags. The chicken is so flavorful and tender—and so easy to prepare—that I often make it just to have the leftovers for salad. You can either remove the skin from the chicken prior to serving it or serve it Chinese-style with the skin left on and let your guests take it off themselves.

Each serving contains approximately:

Calories: 288
Fat: 8 g.
Cholesterol: 101 mg.
Sodium: 945 mg.

  1 **frying chicken (3–4 pounds)**
  1 **teaspoon ground ginger**
  ½ **teaspoon Chinese 5-spice powder**
1½ **teaspoons salt, divided**
  3 **scallions, cut into 3″ pieces**
  1 **tablespoon unbleached all-purpose flour**
  3 **tablespoons hoisin sauce**
  3 **tablespoons honey**
  2 **tablespoons dry sherry or apple juice**
  ½ **teaspoon freshly ground black pepper**

1. Rinse the chicken inside and out with cold water and pat dry with paper towels.

2. In a cup, mix the ginger, Chinese 5-spice powder and ½ teaspoon of the salt. Rub the mixture all over the cavity of the chicken and then put the scallions inside the chicken.

3. Put the flour in a large (14″ × 20″) oven-cooking bag and shake to coat the inside of the bag. (Leave the flour in the bag to prevent bursting.)

4. In a small bowl, mix the hoisin sauce, honey, sherry or apple juice, pepper and the remaining 1 teaspoon salt. Rub all over the chicken. Place the chicken in the oven bag; pour any remaining sauce into the bag. Close the bag with the tie provided.

5. Place the bag in a 13″ × 9″ baking dish. If possible, refrigerate for at least 4 hours before baking to allow the chicken to marinate. Cut six ½″ slits in the top of the bag.

6. Preheat the oven to 350°. Place the baking dish in the oven; make sure the bag does not overhang the dish. Bake for 1 hour, or until the leg joint can easily be moved and the juices run clear when the thigh is pierced with a sharp knife.

7. Remove the chicken from the oven and allow to stand for 10 minutes. Carefully cut the bag open with scissors. Remove the chicken from the bag and pour the cooking liquid into a bowl. Place the bowl in the freezer for a few minutes so the fat can congeal on the top for easy removal. Cut the chicken into serving pieces and serve with the defatted liquid poured over it.

Makes 4 servings

↔ In a Flash!

Omit the marination step. Just rub the seasonings on the chicken, inside and out, fill the cavity with the scallions and bake. This way, you can have it ready to eat in just a little over an hour.

↔ Spin Off

Remove the skin and bones from the leftover chicken and cut it into bite-size pieces. Also save any leftover cooking liquid. You can use the chicken in salad or soup. Or you can mix the chicken with the liquid and serve it over pasta, rice or a baked potato. The defatted cooking liquid can also be mixed with a little rice vinegar for a delicious salad dressing.

Baked Italian Chicken

I'm calling this Italian chicken because I'm using Italian seasoning. If you prefer, you can turn this same recipe Cajun or South-western just by changing the seasoning. You can also add a little Dijon mustard and dried thyme to the mayonnaise for French chicken.

Each serving contains approximately:

Calories: 379
Fat: 21 g.
Cholesterol: 102 mg.
Sodium: 399 mg.

½ **cup reduced-fat mayonnaise**

2 **teaspoons dried Italian herb seasoning**

1 **frying chicken (3–4 pounds), cut into serving pieces and skin removed**

3 **slices whole-wheat bread**

1. Preheat the oven to 425°.

2. In a cup, mix the mayonnaise and Italian seasoning. Rub on all sides of the chicken.

3. Put the bread in a blender or food processor and grind into crumbs. Place the crumbs in a plastic bag. Add the chicken, one piece at a time, and shake to coat well. Arrange the chicken on a rack in a broiler pan.

4. Bake for about 40 minutes, or until the chicken is golden brown and the juices run clear when the chicken is pierced with a sharp knife.

Makes 4 servings

↩ In a Flash!

Keep herbed fresh bread crumbs in the freezer. Then all you have to do is coat the chicken with mayonnaise and shake it in the already-seasoned crumbs.

↩ Spin Off

This chicken is great cold for picnics and brown bag lunches.

Chicken Breast in Fragrant Sauce

This is an authentic Chinese recipe with a very delicate flavor. Soaking the chicken in cold water prior to cooking gives it an almost velvet-like texture. In fact, in some Chinese restaurants, this is called Velvet Chicken.

Each serving contains approximately:

Calories: 248
Fat: 7 g.
Cholesterol: 72 mg.
Sodium: 384 mg.

1	pound chicken tenders
5	tablespoons cornstarch, divided
1	tablespoon canola oil
1	teaspoon grated fresh ginger
¼	cup water
1	cup defatted chicken stock
½	teaspoon salt
½	cup Chinese rice wine, dry sherry or apple juice
1	can (8 ounces) sliced water chestnuts, drained

1. Place the chicken in a large bowl. Add very cold water and set aside for 1½ hours. Drain thoroughly and pat dry with paper towels.

2. Put 4 tablespoons of the cornstarch in a plastic bag. Add the chicken, one piece at a time, and shake to coat well; shake off any excess cornstarch.

3. Place a wok or large nonstick skillet over medium heat until drops of water sprinkled into the pan dance on the surface. Add the oil, tilting the pan to coat the surface. Add the ginger and cook for 1 minute, or until the ginger sizzles.

4. Add the chicken and cook, stirring frequently, for 2 to 3 minutes, or until it turns from translucent to opaque. Remove the chicken from the pan and set aside.

5. In a small bowl, dissolve the remaining 1 tablespoon cornstarch in the water. Stir in the stock, salt and the rice wine, sherry or apple juice. Add to the pan the chicken was cooked in. Bring to a boil over medium heat and stir constantly until just slightly thickened. Stir in the chicken and water chestnuts.

Makes 4 servings

↪ In a Flash!

You can reduce the amount of time you soak the chicken in cold water. However, the soaking gives the chicken a velvety texture, so soak it for as long as you can.

↪ Spin Off

Serve leftovers cold in a salad or reheat and serve over pasta or rice.

Honey-Mustard Chicken

This is a wonderful entrée for entertaining because you can assemble it in the morning, store it in the refrigerator and bake it just in time for your dinner.

Each serving contains approximately:

Calories: 329
Fat: 6 g.
Cholesterol: 72 mg.
Sodium: 925 mg.

1½	cups herb-seasoned dry stuffing
½	cup hot water
¼	cup raisins
1	tablespoon corn-oil margarine, melted
4	boneless, skinless chicken breast halves (about 4 ounces each)
⅓	cup fat-free mayonnaise
3	tablespoons honey
1	tablespoon Dijon mustard

1. Preheat the oven to 400°. Coat a 13" × 9" baking dish with non-stick vegetable cooking spray.

2. In a medium bowl, mix the stuffing, water, raisins and margarine. Allow to stand for 2 minutes. Spoon 4 mounds of the mixture into the prepared pan and top each mound with a chicken breast.

3. In a small bowl, combine the mayonnaise, honey and mustard. Mix well and spoon over the chicken.

4. Cover the dish with a lid or aluminum foil. Bake for 25 minutes. Uncover and bake for about 5 minutes. To serve, spoon the sauce in the pan over the chicken and stuffing mixture.

Makes 4 servings

↤ In a Flash!

In place of the stuffing mixture, use leftover pasta, rice or beans under the chicken.

↤ Spin Off

Cut any leftover chicken into very small pieces. Mix with defatted chicken stock and any remaining stuffing for a truly delicious and satisfying soup.

Cheesy Chicken with Tomatoes and Sunflower Seeds

This easy chicken dish has a wonderful variety of tastes and textures. I like to serve it for dinner parties with rice pilaf.

Each serving contains approximately:

Calories: 266
Fat: 10 g.
Cholesterol: 92 mg.
Sodium: 627 mg.

Pictured on page 226

- 1 **tablespoon raw sunflower seeds**
- 4 **boneless, skinless chicken breast halves (about 4 ounces each)**
- 1 **tablespoon fresh lemon juice**
- ½ **teaspoon freshly ground black pepper**
- ¼ **teaspoon salt**
- 1 **can (14½ ounces) ready-cut tomatoes, drained**
- 4 **ounces reduced-fat Monterey Jack cheese, shredded**

1. Preheat the oven to 350°. Put the sunflower seeds in a pan and bake for about 10 minutes, or until golden brown; watch carefully, as the seeds burn easily.

2. Place the chicken in an 11″ × 7″ baking dish. Sprinkle with the lemon juice, pepper and salt. Cover with a lid or aluminum foil. Bake for 20 to 30 minutes, or until the chicken turns from translucent to opaque. Remove from the oven and pour off any excess liquid.

3. Spoon the tomatoes evenly over the chicken. Sprinkle the sunflower seeds and Monterey Jack evenly over the top. Place the dish under the broiler for about 1 minute, or just until the cheese is completely melted; do not brown.

Makes 4 servings

↔ In a Flash!

Use toasted sunflower seeds. Buy the Monterey Jack already shredded; use 1 cup.

↔ Spin Off

Leftovers are good cold chopped up in salads or reheated and mixed with pasta or rice.

Chicken Stew Provençale

This stew is one of my favorite dishes. I love the licorice-like flavor that is achieved with both the fresh fennel and the anise extract. If you can't find fresh fennel, use celery and add ½ teaspoon of ground fennel seeds or anise seeds to the stew. If you don't have anise extract, add more of the ground fennel or anise.

Each serving contains approximately:

Calories: 347
Fat: 10 g.
Cholesterol: 79 mg.
Sodium: 512 mg.

Pictured on page 227

1 **large fennel bulb**
1 **large onion, coarsely chopped**
2 **large tomatoes, peeled and chopped**
3 **garlic cloves, pressed or minced**
2 **bay leaves**
2 **teaspoons dried thyme, crushed**
½ **teaspoon salt**
½ **teaspoon freshly ground black pepper**
⅛ **teaspoon cayenne pepper (or taste)**
2 **cups defatted chicken stock**
4 **chicken legs, skin removed**
8 **small new potatoes, scrubbed and halved**
½ **teaspoon pure anise extract**

1. Trim the fennel; coarsely chop the bulb and the fronds. Place in a large pot or a Dutch oven. Add the onions, tomatoes, garlic, bay leaves, thyme, salt, black pepper and cayenne. Cover and slowly bring to a boil over medium-low heat. Reduce the heat to low and cook, covered, for 30 minutes.

2. Add the stock, chicken and potatoes to the pot. Cook for 30 minutes, or until the chicken and potatoes are tender and easily pierced with a sharp knife. Add the anise extract and mix well. Remove and discard the bay leaves.

Makes 4 servings

↔ In a Flash!

Use 2 cups prechopped onions, a 1-pound package of prescrubbed new potatoes, a 14½-ounce can of ready-cut tomatoes and a 14½-ounce can of defatted stock plus ¼ cup water.

↔ Spin Off

Cut any leftover chicken off the bone, dice it and mix with the remainder of the stew; use as a topping for rice or pasta. Or mix the chopped chicken with the leftover stew, add a little more chicken stock and have a wonderful chicken soup.

Brunswick Stew

Not only is this tasty stew a snap to make, but there are no dirty pans to wash because you cook it in a bag that gets thrown away!

Each serving contains approximately:

Calories: 349
Fat: 5 g.
Cholesterol: 72 mg.
Sodium: 640 mg.

¼   cup unbleached all-purpose flour
1   can (15¼ ounces) lima beans, drained
1   can (14½ ounces) stewed tomatoes, undrained
1   can (11 ounces) salt-free corn kernels, drained
1   medium onion, finely chopped
4   boneless, skinless chicken breast halves (about 4 ounces each), cut into thin strips
1   garlic clove, pressed or minced
½   teaspoon lemon pepper
1   can (14½ ounces) defatted chicken stock

1.   Preheat the oven to 350°. Put the flour in a large (14″ × 20″) oven-cooking bag and shake to coat the inside of the bag. (Leave the flour in the bag to prevent bursting.) Place the bag in a 13″ × 9″ baking dish.

2.   Add the lima beans, tomatoes, corn, onions, chicken, garlic and lemon pepper. Knead the bag to mix the ingredients. Add the stock and close the bag with the tie provided. Press the ingredients into an even layer. Cut six ½″ slits in the top of the bag. Make sure the bag does not overhang the baking dish.

3.   Bake for 45 to 50 minutes, or until the chicken turns from translucent to opaque.

Makes 4 servings

↦ In a Flash!

Use 1½ cups prechopped onions. Replace the garlic with ⅛ teaspoon garlic powder.

↦ Spin Off

Add more stock to leftovers and serve as a soup.

Tarragon Chicken
and Pasta Bake

To turn this into a vegetarian entrée, just substitute cream of celery or cream of mushroom soup for the cream of chicken called for and use 2 cups of chopped cooked broccoli in place of the chicken.

Each serving contains approximately:

Calories: 449
Fat: 10 g.
Cholesterol: 77 mg.
Sodium: 504 mg.

8 **ounces dry ziti pasta**

1 **can (10¾ ounces) condensed reduced-fat cream of chicken soup, undiluted**

1 **cup low-fat milk**

2 **teaspoons dried tarragon, crushed**

½ **teaspoon freshly ground black pepper**

2 **cups cubed cooked chicken**

¼ **cup grated fresh Parmesan cheese**
      Paprika (optional)

1. Preheat the oven to 350°.

2. Cook the ziti in a large pot of boiling water for about 10 minutes, or until tender but still firm to the bite. Drain thoroughly in a colander.

3. In a large bowl, mix the soup, milk, tarragon and pepper. Stir in the chicken and ziti. Transfer to a 13″ × 9″ baking dish. Sprinkle with the Parmesan and paprika (if using). Bake for about 30 minutes, or until heated through.

Makes 4 servings

↦ In a Flash!
Buy already-grated fresh Parmesan. Use leftover cooked pasta.

↦ Spin Off
Serve leftovers cold as a pasta salad.

Roasted Italian Chicken on Rotini

You can make this dish without using an oven bag by just baking it in a covered casserole. I prefer using the bag because the chicken cooks faster and cleanup is so much easier.

Each serving contains approximately:

Calories: 420
Fat: 4 g.
Cholesterol: 72 mg.
Sodium: 268 mg.

2	tablespoons unbleached all-purpose flour
1	teaspoon dried rosemary, crushed
1	jar (16 ounces) low-fat pasta sauce
4	skinless, bone-in chicken breast halves
1	medium green bell pepper, seeded and coarsely chopped
8	ounces dry multicolored rotini

Pictured on page 228

1. Preheat the oven to 350°. Put the flour and rosemary in a large (14″ × 20″) oven-cooking bag and shake to coat the inside of the bag. (Leave the flour in the bag to prevent bursting.)

2. Add the pasta sauce to the bag and knead to blend in the flour and rosemary. Add the chicken and peppers. Turn the bag to coat the chicken with the sauce. Place the bag in a 13″ × 9″ baking dish and arrange the chicken in an even layer. Close the bag with the tie provided.

3. Cut six ½″ slits in the top of the bag. Make sure the bag does not overhang the baking dish. Place in the oven and bake for about 45 minutes, or until the chicken is tender and the juices run clear when the chicken is pierced with a sharp knife.

4. While the chicken is baking, cook the rotini in a large pot of boiling water for about 10 minutes, or until tender but still firm to the bite. Drain thoroughly in a colander. Divide among serving plates. Top with the chicken and sauce.

Makes 4 servings

↔ In a Flash!

For a faster dish with a little more zing, replace the bell pepper called for with a 7-ounce can of diced green chili peppers. Use leftover cooked pasta; reheat in the microwave.

↔ Spin Off

Dice any leftover chicken and mix it with the leftover sauce and pasta for a cold pasta salad.

Turkey in a Bag

Cooking in an oven bag not only eliminates the time-consuming basting process but also keeps the oven clean! You can use either a fresh turkey here or a thawed frozen one.

Each 3-ounce serving of white meat without skin contains approximately:

Calories: 134
Fat: 3 g.
Cholesterol: 59 mg.
Sodium: 67 mg.

Each 3-ounce serving of dark meat without skin contains approximately:

Calories: 159
Fat: 6 g.
Cholesterol: 72 mg.
Sodium: 67 mg.

2   **tablespoons unbleached all-purpose flour**
1   **turkey (about 12 pounds)**
1   **medium onion, quartered**
2   **celery ribs, sliced**
2   **lemons, scored**

1.   Preheat the oven to 350°. Put the flour in a turkey-size (19″ × 23½″) oven-cooking bag and shake to coat the inside of the bag. (Leave the flour in the bag to prevent bursting.)

2.   Remove the package of giblets from inside the turkey. (Set aside to add to gravy or dressing, or freeze for future use.) Rinse the turkey inside and out with cold water and pat dry with paper towels.

3.   Put the onions, celery and lemons inside the turkey. Place the turkey in the bag and put in a large roasting pan at least 2″ deep. Close the bag with the tie provided. Cut six ½″ slits in the top of the bag. (You may insert a meat thermometer through a slit in the bag into the thigh, making sure it does not touch the bone.) Make sure the bag does not overhang the baking dish.

4.   Bake for 2½ to 3½ hours, or until the meat thermometer registers 180° and the juices run clear when the thigh is pierced with a sharp knife. Allow to stand for 20 minutes before slicing.

Makes about 12 servings

⇥ In a Flash!
The deli section of most supermarkets will roast your turkey for you.

⇥ Spin Off
You name it! Sandwiches, salads, soups and more.

Turkey Loaf

Pictured on page 229

This unusual low-fat dish gets its moisture from the undiluted apple juice that is both in it and glazing it.

Each serving contains approximately:

Calories: 212
Fat: 6 g.
Cholesterol: 68 mg.
Sodium: 141 mg.

2	**pounds lean ground turkey breast**
½	**cup fresh bread crumbs**
½	**cup chopped onions**
¼	**cup chopped fresh parsley**
¼	**cup chopped celery**
¼	**cup toasted walnuts**
1	**tablespoon corn-oil margarine, softened**
¾	**teaspoon lemon pepper**
½	**teaspoon salt**
1	**garlic clove, pressed or minced**
4	**tablespoons frozen unsweetened apple juice concentrate, thawed, divided**

1. Preheat the oven to 350°. Coat a 13″ × 9″ baking dish with non-stick vegetable cooking spray.

2. In a large bowl, combine the turkey, bread crumbs, onions, parsley, celery, walnuts, margarine, lemon pepper, salt, garlic and 3 tablespoons of the apple juice concentrate. Mix well.

3. Shape the mixture into a loaf and place in the prepared pan. Brush the loaf with the remaining 1 tablespoon apple juice concentrate. Bake for about 1½ hours, or until nicely browned and cooked through.

Makes 8 servings

↔ In a Flash!

Use ⅛ teaspoon garlic powder.

↔ Spin Off

Leftover turkey loaf makes great sandwiches as well as a tasty filling for omelets. For a low-fat sandwich, try spreading the bread with cranberry sauce instead of mayonnaise.

Easy Turkey Enchiladas

This is a wonderful recipe for using up cooked turkey after the holidays. However, you can buy cooked turkey breast in any supermarket and make this delicious Southwestern-style dish any time of the year. You can also use chicken or meat instead of the turkey. For vegetarian enchiladas, use tempeh and cream of mushroom soup.

Each serving contains approximately:

Calories: 412
Fat: 14 g.
Cholesterol: 62 mg.
Sodium: 1,106 mg.

1   **cup diced cooked turkey**

1   **package (10 ounces) frozen chopped spinach, thawed and drained**

1½   **cups shredded reduced-fat Monterey Jack cheese, divided**

1   **cup chopped scallions, including the tops, divided**

8   **corn tortillas**

1   **can (10¾ ounces) condensed reduced-fat cream of chicken soup, undiluted**

1   **can (4 ounces) diced green chili peppers**

¼   **cup skim milk**

1   **cup salsa**

¼   **cup fat-free sour cream**

1. Preheat the oven to 350°. Coat a 13″ × 9″ baking dish with non-stick vegetable cooking spray.

2. In a medium bowl, combine the turkey, spinach, 1 cup of the Monterey Jack and ½ cup of the scallions.

3. Soften the tortillas according to the package directions. Spoon about ⅓ cup of the turkey mixture onto each tortilla, roll the tortilla around the filling and place, seam side down, in the prepared baking dish.

4. In a medium bowl, combine the soup, peppers and milk; mix well. Pour the mixture over the enchiladas. Sprinkle with the remaining ½ cup Monterey Jack. Bake for 45 minutes, or until lightly browned.

5. Serve topped with the salsa, sour cream and the remaining ½ cup scallions.

Makes 4 servings

↔ In a Flash!

Layer the tortillas and other ingredients in a casserole instead of rolling the tortillas around the filling.

↔ Spin Off

Chop leftover enchiladas and serve over lettuce for a Southwestern salad.

Rapid Roast

This rapid-roasting method works equally well for a 6-pound leg of lamb. The technique, timing and yield are identical. The only real difference is that the lamb is a little leaner. Thirty minutes gives a rare roast. If you like prime rib more well done, cook it for 33 to 36 minutes before turning the oven off. The general rule is: 5 minutes per pound for rare and 5½ to 6 minutes per pound for more-well-done meat.

Each 3-ounce serving contains approximately:

Calories: 185
Fat: 8 g.
Cholesterol: 81 mg.
Sodium: 75 mg.

1 **prime rib of beef (6 pounds)**
2 **garlic cloves, pressed or minced**
1 **tablespoon lemon pepper**

1. Preheat the oven to 500°. Rub the roast with the garlic and lemon pepper. Place in a roasting pan and bake for 30 minutes, then turn the heat off. Do not open the oven door for exactly 2 hours.

2. Remove the roast from the oven and allow to stand for 15 minutes for easier carving.

Makes about 16 servings

↔ In a Flash!

Use garlic powder to rub the roast.

↔ Spin Off

Leftover roast is great for salads, sandwiches, soups and casseroles.

Chilean Corn and Meat Pie

On a recent trip to Chile, I discovered one of their favorite dishes, Pastel de Choclo, *a fresh corn and meat pie. It is tasty enough to become habit forming and so easy and inexpensive that it's perfect for entertaining. I even brought home the bowls traditionally used for cooking and serving this dish. They are 5" wide, 2" deep and made of terra-cotta that has to be "cured" before use by filling the bowls with milk and baking them at 250° for 2 hours. However, you certainly don't need these special bowls. Use individual ramekins or a large casserole.*

Meat Mixture

- 1 **boneless, skinless chicken breast half (about 4 ounces)**
- 8 **ounces extra-lean ground round**
- ½ **cup raisins**
- 2 **tablespoons chopped pitted kalamata olives**
- ¼ **teaspoon salt**
- ¼ **teaspoon freshly ground black pepper**

Corn Topping

- ½ **tablespoon canola oil**
- ⅛ **teaspoon paprika**
- 1 **medium onion, finely chopped**
- 1 **bag (16 ounces) frozen corn kernels, thawed**
- ½ **cup skim milk**
- ¾ **teaspoon ground cumin**
- ¼ **teaspoon salt**
- ¼ **teaspoon freshly ground black pepper**
- 2 **teaspoons sugar**

1. Preheat the oven to 400°.

2. *To make the meat mixture:* Coat a large nonstick skillet with nonstick vegetable cooking spray. Place over medium heat until drops of water sprinkled into the skillet dance on the surface. Add the chicken and cook for 2 minutes on each side. Remove from the skillet, cut into quarters and set aside.

3. Crumble the beef into the skillet. Cook, stirring, for 4 to 5 minutes, or until the beef is browned. Remove from the heat and stir in the raisins, olives, salt and pepper. Divide among 4 small ovenproof bowls or an 8″ × 8″ baking dish. Top with the chicken.

Each serving contains approximately:

Calories: 333
Fat: 7 g.
Cholesterol: 52 mg.
Sodium: 415 mg.

4. *To make the corn topping:* Combine the oil and paprika in the same skillet and place over medium heat for about 1 minute. Add the onions; cook, stirring frequently, for about 5 minutes, or until soft and translucent.

5. In a food processor, combine the corn, milk, cumin, salt and pepper; puree. Add to the skillet and mix well. Cook for 5 minutes. Spoon over the meat and chicken. Sprinkle evenly with the sugar.

6. Bake for 35 to 40 minutes, or until bubbly and browned.

Makes 4 servings

⤙ In a Flash!

Eliminate the chicken from the recipe and save a step.

⤙ Spin Off

Leftover pie is delicious served cold.

Beef Spaghetti Pie Olé

This is a slightly modified version of the recipe that won the first prize for Sherry Druary in the Alabama state Beef Cook Off. I met Sherry at the National Beef Cook Off in Little Rock in 1995. She's an interior decorator, married to a Presbyterian minister and the mother of two young daughters. She is also committed to keeping daily dinners as a time for the family to be together, despite her busy schedule. For this reason, she frequently makes use of healthy convenience foods.

Each serving contains approximately:

Calories: 514
Fat: 16 g.
Cholesterol: 146 mg.
Sodium: 847 mg.

Shell

1	package (7 ounces) dry spaghetti
1/3	cup shredded reduced-fat Monterey Jack or Cheddar cheese
1	egg
1/4	teaspoon salt
1/4	teaspoon garlic powder

Filling

1	pound extra-lean ground round
1	teaspoon garlic powder
1/2	teaspoon ground cumin
1/4	teaspoon salt
1	can (10 ounces) diced tomatoes with green chilies, undrained
3/4	cup fat-free sour cream
1	cup shredded reduced-fat Monterey Jack or Cheddar cheese

1. Preheat the oven to 350°.

2. *To make the shell:* Cook the spaghetti in a large pot of boiling water for about 8 minutes, or until tender but still firm to the bite. Drain thoroughly in a colander.

3. In a large bowl, whisk together the cheese, egg, salt and garlic powder. Add the spaghetti and toss to coat. Transfer to a 9″ pie plate. Press evenly in the bottom and up the sides to form a shell.

4. *To make the filling:* Place a large nonstick skillet over medium heat until drops of water sprinkled into the skillet dance on the surface. Crumble the beef into the pan and cook, stirring often, for about 4 to 5 minutes, or until lightly browned. Pour off any drippings. Season the beef with the garlic powder, cumin and salt.

5. Stir in the tomatoes and bring to a boil. Cook, stirring occasionally, for about 3 to 5 minutes, or until most of the liquid has evaporated.

6. Reserve 2 tablespoons of the beef mixture for a garnish. Stir the sour cream into the remaining beef mixture and spoon it into the prepared shell. Sprinkle the cheese over the beef, leaving a 2″ border around the edge. Spoon the reserved beef mixture onto the center of the cheese. Bake for 15 minutes, or until heated through. Serve the pie cut into wedges.

Makes 4 servings

↪ In a Flash!

Serve the cooked beef mixture over cooked pasta and top with the cheese instead of assembling a pie and baking it.

↪ Spin Off

Freeze leftovers and reheat for a future meal.

Meat Loaf
with Mashed Potato Frosting

Everyone loves meat loaf with mashed potatoes. Here's a dramatic and fun way to present this popular combination.

Each serving contains approximately:

Calories: 337
Fat: 9 g.
Cholesterol: 104 mg.
Sodium: 1,037 mg.

1½   pounds extra-lean ground round
1   jar (12 ounces) fat-free beef gravy, divided
1   cup soft whole-wheat bread crumbs
¼   cup finely chopped onions
1   egg, lightly beaten
½   teaspoon freshly ground black pepper
2½   cups hot mashed potatoes
1   teaspoon extra-virgin olive oil
     Paprika (optional)

1. Preheat the oven to 350°.

2. In a large bowl, mix the beef with ¼ cup of the gravy. Add the bread crumbs, onions, egg and pepper; mix well.

3. Shape into a loaf and place in an 11″ × 7″ baking dish. Bake for 1 hour. Carefully drain off the fat.

4. Spread the mashed potatoes over the top and sides of the meat loaf. Drizzle with the oil and sprinkle with the paprika (if using).

5. Bake for 20 minutes. Remove from the oven and allow to stand for 5 minutes before slicing. Place the remaining gravy in a small saucepan and warm over medium heat. Serve over the meat loaf slices.

Makes 6 servings

↝ In a Flash!
Use instant mashed potatoes.

↝ Spin Off
Use cold meat loaf for sandwiches.

Chuck Wagon Stew

This stew is so good and freezes so well that I always make more than I need for one meal.

Each serving contains approximately:

Calories: 285
Fat: 8 g.
Cholesterol: 66 mg.
Sodium: 917 mg.

2	tablespoons unbleached all-purpose flour
1	tablespoon paprika
2	teaspoons salt
1	teaspoon plus 3 tablespoons chili powder, divided
2	pounds lean beef, trimmed of all visible fat and cut into 1″ cubes
1	tablespoon canola oil
2	medium onions, sliced
1	garlic clove, pressed or minced
1	can (28 ounces) whole tomatoes, broken up into pieces and undrained
1	tablespoon ground cinnamon
1	teaspoon ground cloves
½	teaspoon crushed red-pepper flakes
2	small potatoes, diced
3	carrots, diced

Pictured on page 230

1. In a large bowl, mix the flour, paprika, salt and 1 teaspoon of the chili powder. Add the beef and mix until well coated.

2. Warm the oil in a large pot or Dutch oven over medium-high heat. Add the beef and cook, stirring frequently, until well browned. Add the onions and garlic. Cook for about 5 minutes, or until the onions are soft and translucent.

3. Add the tomatoes, cinnamon, cloves, red-pepper flakes and the remaining 3 tablespoons chili powder. Cover and simmer for 2 hours. Add the potatoes and carrots. Cook for about 45 minutes, or until the vegetables are tender.

Makes 8 servings

↔ In a Flash!

Buy already-cubed beef. Use prechopped onions and frozen chopped potatoes and carrots.

↔ Spin Off

Store leftovers in single-portion sizes in freezer bags for fast future meals.

Middle Eastern Lamb Stew in a Crock-Pot

Stew

4	garlic cloves, quartered
1	pound lean lamb, cubed
1	can (28 ounces) whole tomatoes, broken up into pieces and undrained
1	medium onion, thinly sliced
1	medium green bell pepper, seeded and cut into thin 2"-long strips
½	cup dry red wine
2	bay leaves
1	tablespoon lemon pepper
1	tablespoon Worcestershire sauce
1	teaspoon sugar
1	teaspoon dried oregano, crushed
½	teaspoon ground coriander
½	teaspoon ground allspice
½	teaspoon paprika
¼	teaspoon salt

Couscous

2	cups defatted chicken or beef stock
2	teaspoons extra-virgin olive oil
½	teaspoon freshly ground black pepper
¼	teaspoon salt
1	cup dry whole-wheat couscous

1. ***To make the stew:*** Coat a large skillet with nonstick vegetable cooking spray. Add the garlic and cook over medium-high heat for about 1 minute, or just until the garlic starts to sizzle. Add the lamb and cook, stirring frequently, for about 2 to 3 minutes, or until browned.

2. Transfer to a 6-quart Crock-Pot or other slow cooker. Add the tomatoes, onions, green peppers, wine, bay leaves, lemon pepper, Worcestershire sauce, sugar, oregano, coriander, allspice, paprika and salt. Mix well and cook on high for 8 hours. Remove and discard the bay leaves.

3. *To make the couscous:* Bring the stock, oil, pepper and salt to a boil in a medium saucepan over high heat. Stir in the couscous and bring to a boil again. Reduce the heat to low, cover the pan and cook for 2 minutes, or until all water has been absorbed. Remove from the heat. Fluff with a fork. Cover and allow to stand for 5 minutes.

4. Serve the stew over the couscous.

Makes 4 servings

↔ In a Flash!

For the stew, use ½ teaspoon garlic powder, prechopped onions and ready-cut canned tomatoes. For the couscous, use 1 can (14½ ounces) stock and ¼ cup water.

↔ Spin Off

Mix leftover stew with the couscous (or with cooked rice, pasta or beans) for a terrific casserole dish.

Baked Honey-Rosemary Lamb Shanks

The hands-on preparation time for these lamb shanks is so short and the rich "down home" flavor so satisfying that once you've made this recipe it's sure to become a family favorite. I like to serve the lamb shanks over pasta or rice or with Fiesta Corn Surprise (page 75). If you prefer not to use wine, replace it with ¼ cup water and 1 teaspoon white vinegar.

Each serving contains approximately:

Calories: 275
Fat: 8 g.
Cholesterol: 75 mg.
Sodium: 722 mg.

4   **medium lamb shanks, trimmed of all visible fat**
1   **can (8 ounces) tomato sauce**
1   **medium onion, chopped**
¼   **cup honey**
¼   **cup dry white wine**
1   **tablespoon dried rosemary, crushed**
1   **teaspoon freshly ground black pepper**
½   **teaspoon salt**
3   **garlic cloves, pressed or minced**

1. Preheat the oven to 325°.

2. Coat a large, ovenproof skillet with nonstick vegetable cooking spray. Place over medium-high heat until drops of water sprinkled into the skillet dance on the surface. Add the lamb and cook, turning, until browned on all sides.

3. In a medium bowl, mix the tomato sauce, onions, honey, wine, rosemary, pepper, salt and garlic. Pour over the lamb. Cover and bake for 2½ hours, or until the lamb is fork tender.

Makes 4 servings

↔ In a Flash!

Omit browning the lamb; use 1½ cups prechopped onions and ½ teaspoon garlic powder. Place all the ingredients in a casserole, cover and bake as directed.

↔ Spin Off

This recipe makes much more sauce than you will need. That's wonderful, because the leftover sauce can be used to cook broccoli florets, which are sensational served over pasta or rice for another meal.

Leg of Lamb
with Rosemary Gravy

I developed this recipe for Diabetes Forecast *magazine a few years ago for an article on alternative Christmas dinner menus. It has become my favorite way to cook a leg of lamb. The seasonings add wonderful flavor to the meat, and the oven-bag method keeps it very moist. If you prefer not to use the sherry in this recipe, you can substitute apple juice and add 1 tablespoon wine vinegar and ½ teaspoon sherry extract.*

Each 3-ounce serving contains approximately:

Calories: 220
Fat: 14 g.
Cholesterol: 79 mg.
Sodium: 356 mg.

1   tablespoon unbleached all-purpose flour
1   leg of lamb (7–8 pounds), trimmed of all visible fat
1   tablespoon extra-virgin olive oil
¼   cup Dijon mustard
4   garlic cloves, pressed or minced
1   tablespoon dried rosemary, crushed
1   teaspoon salt
½   teaspoon freshly ground black pepper
¼   cup dry sherry

1. Preheat the oven to 325°. Put the flour in a turkey-size (19″ × 23½″) oven-cooking bag and shake to coat the inside of the bag. (Leave the flour in the bag to prevent bursting.)

2. Rub the lamb with the oil. In a small bowl, mix the mustard, garlic, rosemary, salt and pepper. Rub the mixture all over the lamb. Place the lamb in the bag and pour in the sherry.

3. Close the bag with the tie provided. Cut six ½″ slits in the top of the bag. Place the bag in a roasting pan at least 2″ deep; make sure the bag does not overhang the pan. Insert a meat thermometer through a slit in the bag into the thickest part of the lamb, not touching the bone.

4. Bake for 1½ hours, or until the thermometer reads 140° for rare or 150° for medium. Remove the lamb from the oven and allow to remain in the bag for 15 minutes. Cut the top of the bag open with scissors. Remove the lamb and place it on a cutting board for slicing.

5. Pour the pan juices into a bowl and place in the freezer for a short time for the fat to congeal on the top. Spoon off the fat and reheat the juices in a small saucepan. Serve over the lamb.

Makes about 18 servings

↔ In a Flash!

Drag a damp paper towel through the pan juices to remove most of the fat or pour the juices into one of the gravy-separator pitchers designed to remove fat from the liquid.

↔ Spin Off

Use leftovers to make cold lamb salads and sandwiches.

Maple-Glazed Pork Tenderloin

The maple flavor goes well with the pork, and the combination of all the other flavors makes this a truly outstanding dish.

Each serving contains approximately:

Calories: 371
Fat: 6 g.
Cholesterol: 106 mg.
Sodium: 694 mg.

Pictured on page 182

1¼ **pounds pork tenderloin, trimmed of all visible fat**

¾ **cup pure maple syrup**

2 **tablespoons chili sauce**

2 **tablespoons reduced-sodium soy sauce**

1 **tablespoon unsweetened frozen orange juice concentrate, thawed**

1 **tablespoon Dijon mustard**

1 **tablespoon Worcestershire sauce**

1 **tablespoon curry powder**

1 **garlic clove, pressed or minced**

1 **teaspoon toasted sesame seeds**

1. Preheat the oven to 350°.

2. Place the pork in an 11″ × 7″ baking dish. In a medium bowl, mix the maple syrup, chili sauce, soy sauce, orange juice concentrate, mustard, Worcestershire sauce, curry powder and garlic. Pour over the pork.

3. Bake for about 30 to 40 minutes, or until a meat thermometer inserted into the tenderloin reads 150°.

4. Remove from the oven and allow to stand for 10 minutes before slicing into ¼″ slices; spoon the sauce on top and sprinkle with the sesame seeds.

Makes 4 servings

↠ In a Flash!

Use ¼ teaspoon garlic powder in place of the fresh garlic.

↠ Spin Off

Chop leftover pork, mix it with leftover sauce and serve it hot or cold over Asian noodles.

Hot and Spicy Apple and Cabbage Salad (page 194)

Honeyed Oranges (page 279)

Baked Delicious Apples (page 282)

Warm Pear Slices in Honey-Pepper Sauce (page 283)

Pumpkin Whip (page 287)

Lemon Bread Pudding (page 290)

Lemon-Ginger Ice Milk (page 294)

Tropical Sorbet (page 295)

Perfect Pork Chops

The beauty of this recipe is that the timing doesn't have to be exact to ensure "perfect pork chops." Leaving them in the oven longer than required for proper doneness won't overcook them. So if your dinner is running a little late, there is no cause for panic.

Each serving contains approximately:

Calories: 275
Fat: 15 g.
Cholesterol: 81 mg.
Sodium: 777 mg.

4	center-cut boneless pork chops (¾" thick and about 4 ounces each), trimmed of all visible fat
½	teaspoon garlic salt
½	teaspoon freshly ground black pepper
1½	cups finely chopped fresh parsley
½	cup Dijon mustard
3	tablespoons plain dried bread crumbs
½	teaspoon dried thyme, crushed

1. Preheat the oven to 500°.

2. Lightly sprinkle both sides of the pork chops with the garlic salt and pepper, and place them in an 11" × 7" baking dish.

3. In a medium bowl, combine the parsley, mustard, bread crumbs and thyme; mix well. Spoon the mixture on top of the pork chops, packing it down with your hands.

4. Bake for 4 minutes. Turn the oven off and do not open the door for at least 35 minutes.

Makes 4 servings

↔ In a Flash!

Ready the pork chops for the oven in the morning—or even a day ahead. Store, tightly covered, in the refrigerator until you're ready to cook them.

↔ Spin Off

Chop leftover pork chops, mix with the topping and add to mixed greens. Dress with an herbed vinaigrette for a delicious and unusual salad.

Polynesian Pork

*This is a great recipe
for entertaining
because you can
put it on to cook in
the morning, and
it's ready when your
guests arrive.*

Each serving contains
approximately:

Calories: 435
Fat: 10 g.
Cholesterol: 68 mg.
Sodium: 375 mg.

1	**pound lean pork, cubed**
1	**can (20 ounces) pineapple chunks packed in juice, undrained**
1	**medium onion, thinly sliced**
1	**green bell pepper, seeded and cut into strips**
¼	**cup fresh lime or lemon juice**
2	**tablespoons chopped fresh ginger**
1	**teaspoon ground cinnamon**
1	**teaspoon ground nutmeg**
½	**teaspoon salt**
¼	**teaspoon freshly ground black pepper**
2	**cups hot cooked white or brown rice**

1. Place a large nonstick skillet over medium-high heat until drops of water sprinkled into the skillet dance on the surface. Add the pork and cook, stirring frequently, until browned. Transfer to a 6-quart Crock-Pot or other slow cooker.

2. Add the pineapple, onions, green peppers, lime or lemon juice, cinnamon, nutmeg, salt and pepper. Mix well. Cook on low for about 8 hours, or until tender. Serve spooned over the rice.

Makes 4 servings

↤ In a Flash!
Omit the step of browning the pork.

↤ Spin Off
Mix leftover pork with the rice and serve cold as a salad.

Ham and Cheese Roll-Ups

These tasty rolled-up sandwiches are wonderful for brown bag lunches, picnics and tailgate parties. You can add variety to this recipe by using other kinds of deli meats and cheeses.

Each serving contains approximately:

Calories: 379
Fat: 11 g.
Cholesterol: 66 mg.
Sodium: 909 mg.

6	ounces fat-free cream cheese, softened
¼	cup finely chopped chives or scallion tops
1	tablespoon Dijon mustard (or to taste)
4	large flour tortillas
1	cup shredded reduced-fat Swiss cheese
8	leaves green leaf lettuce
8	ounces thinly sliced turkey ham

1. In a medium bowl, combine the cream cheese, chives or scallion tops and mustard; mix well. Divide among the tortillas and spread evenly.

2. Sprinkle with the Swiss. Top each tortilla with a lettuce leaf and slice of ham, leaving a ½″ border around the edges. Roll the tortillas tightly and wrap in plastic wrap. Refrigerate for at least 30 minutes before serving.

3. To serve, cut each roll diagonally in half.

Makes 4 servings

↣ In a Flash!
Put the roll-ups in the freezer for 10 minutes to chill.

↣ Spin Off
Serve leftover sandwiches warm for a real breakfast treat.

Fast Desserts for a Fabulous Finish

Many low-fat desserts are just as delicious and satisfying as their high-fat counterparts. However, when a favorite dessert simply cannot be lightened without appreciably changing its taste and texture, I firmly believe that a very small portion of something truly wonderful is a whole lot better than a plateful of some "make do" dish.

That said, I assure you that this dessert chapter contains good examples of tasty, low-fat desserts that can be made with a minimum of fuss. Some require time in the oven, refrigerator or freezer to finish them off, but your hands-on time is brief.

Try adding your own touches and favorite flavors to some of these recipes. I'm certain that your family and friends will be more than happy to act as a "taste panel" for your project!

Fast Desserts for a Fabulous Finish

Creamy Caramel Dip

I particularly like this caramel dip served with thinly sliced wedges of cold crisp apple. It is also good as a topping on yogurt, ice milk and cake.

Each ¼-cup serving contains approximately:

Calories: 104
Fat: 0 g.
Cholesterol: 3 mg.
Sodium: 218 mg.

1 **package (8 ounces) fat-free cream cheese, softened**
¾ **cup packed dark brown sugar**
1 **cup fat-free sour cream**
1 **package (3.4 ounces) fat-free instant vanilla pudding mix**
1 **cup skim milk**
2 **teaspoons vanilla extract**
2 **teaspoons fresh lemon juice**

1. Combine the cream cheese and brown sugar in a large bowl and mix until smooth. Stir in the sour cream and pudding mix.

2. Stir in the milk, vanilla and lemon juice; mix well. Cover and chill for at least 1 hour.

Makes 3½ cups

↔ In a Flash!

It is faster to mix the cream cheese with an electric mixer on low speed than to do it by hand with a whisk or a spoon.

↔ Spin Off

Use as a breakfast spread on waffles, pancakes and toast.

Meringue

Meringue is a wonderfully festive-looking, fast, fat-free topping for pies and tarts of all types. To use the meringue, spread it evenly over the top of a pie or on tarts. Bake in a pre-heated 350° oven for about 10 minutes, or until the meringue is golden brown.

Each serving contains approximately:

Calories: 22
Fat: 0 g.
Cholesterol: 0 mg.
Sodium: 20 mg.

2	**egg whites**
¼	**teaspoon cream of tartar**
3	**tablespoons sugar**

1. Place the egg whites in a medium bowl and beat with a whisk or electric mixer until frothy. Add the cream of tartar and beat until the mixture forms firm peaks when the whisk or beaters are lifted. Add the sugar, 1 tablespoon at a time, beating after each addition. Do not overbeat; the mixture should be stiff but not dry. Use as indicated on the left or below.

Makes 8 servings

↔ In a Flash!

Use packaged egg whites such as Just Whites in place of the raw egg whites and whip according to the package directions.

↔ Spin Off

Meringue is also a delightful and very light topping for fresh or canned fruit. Just put the fruit in an ovenproof dish, cover with the meringue and bake at 350° for about 10 minutes, or until golden brown.

Caramelized Milk

This is the least labor-intensive sauce I have ever made in my life.

1 can (14 ounces) sweetened condensed skim milk

1. Pour the milk into the top of a double boiler. Place over simmering water, cover and cook over medium-low heat for 1½ hours, or until thickened and light caramel in color (check the water level occasionally to make sure it doesn't boil away).

2. Remove from the heat and stir until smooth. Serve warm or cold (cool to room temperature, cover and store in the refrigerator).

Makes 1 cup

↝ In a Flash!
It can't be made any faster!

↝ Spin Off
Thin the caramelized milk with skim milk and serve in place of syrup on pancakes and waffles. Or pour over yogurt or ice milk.

Each 2-tablespoon serving contains approximately:

Calories: 138
Fat: 0 g.
Cholesterol: 0 mg.
Sodium: 50 mg.

Secret Sauce

This is a fake copy of crème anglaise, an outrageously rich custard sauce made with egg yolks.

1 cup vanilla ice milk, melted
1½ teaspoons orange-flavored liqueur, such as Grand Marnier

1. In a small bowl, mix the ice milk and liqueur.

Makes 1 cup

↝ In a Flash!
This is already a "no work" sauce.

↝ Spin Off
Store leftover sauce, covered, in the refrigerator to use on any fresh, frozen or canned fruit.

Each 2-tablespoon serving contains approximately:

Calories: 27
Fat: 1 g.
Cholesterol: 2 mg.
Sodium: 13 mg.

Honeyed Oranges

This is a Native American recipe that is so easy to make and so surprisingly delicious I often serve it when I want a light dessert. It is particularly good following a South-western meal.

Each serving contains approximately:

Calories: 128
Fat: 0 g.
Cholesterol: 0 mg.
Sodium: 3 mg.

4   **large navel oranges**
2   **tablespoons honey**

Pictured on
page 264

1.   Cut the oranges in half crosswise. Carefully scoop the orange sections from the rind cups, being careful not to tear the rind. Set the rind cups aside.

2.   Dice the oranges and place them in a medium bowl. Add the honey and mix well. Spoon into the reserved rind cups. Cover and refrigerate for at least 2 hours.

Makes 4 servings

↤ In a Flash!

Make this dessert a day ahead of time. It will taste better and be ready whenever you want to serve it.

↤ Spin Off

Serve leftovers as a breakfast fruit.

Cider-Poached Bananas

This sugar-free dessert is amazingly delicious. It is best served immediately, because the bananas tend to harden if allowed to get cold.

Each serving contains approximately:

Calories: 193
Fat: 0 g.
Cholesterol: 1 mg.
Sodium: 29 mg.

2   **cups apple cider**
¼   **cup raisins**
1   **cinnamon stick**
1   **tablespoon vanilla extract**
4   **small firm bananas**
    Ground cinnamon
½   **cup fat-free vanilla yogurt**

1. In a large saucepan wide enough to hold the bananas, combine the cider, raisins, cinnamon stick and vanilla. Bring to a boil over high heat. Reduce the heat to medium-low and simmer for 5 minutes.

2. Add the bananas and simmer for about 8 minutes, or until tender. Remove the bananas with a slotted spoon and place on individual serving plates. Sprinkle with the cinnamon. Top with the yogurt and serve immediately.

Makes 4 servings

↔ In a Flash!
Slice the bananas so they cook faster.

↔ Spin Off
Puree leftover bananas with a little vanilla yogurt for a delicious pudding.

Poached Dried Apricots

This recipe can be used for other dried fruits, such as peaches, pears and apples. For dessert, I like to serve the apricots topped with vanilla ice milk and Caramelized Milk (page 278). For breakfast, I like the fruit with vanilla yogurt.

Each serving contains approximately:

Calories: 154
Fat: 0 g.
Cholesterol: 0 mg.
Sodium: 0 mg.

1   **cup dried apricot halves**
1   **teaspoon sugar**
1   **teaspoon vanilla extract**
2   **cinnamon sticks**

1.   Place the apricots in a medium saucepan and cover with cold water to a depth of 2″. Allow to soak for several hours or overnight.

2.   Add the sugar, vanilla and cinnamon sticks. Bring to a boil over high heat. Reduce the heat to low and simmer for 15 minutes. Remove from the heat and set aside to cool.

3.   To serve, remove the apricots from the poaching liquid with a slotted spoon.

Makes 4 servings

⇢ In a Flash!

Cover the apricots with boiling water and shorten the soaking time to 1 hour.

⇢ Spin Off

Use leftover poached apricots in fruit salads and as a topping for breakfast cereals.

Baked Delicious Apples

My favorite apple for baking is the Golden Delicious, because it is so sweet you don't need to add any sugar. Many food writers claim Delicious apples lose their flavor when cooked, but I don't agree. The Golden Delicious has a very subtle flavor to start with, and its sweetness more than compensates for its rather mild flavor when baked. These literally delicious baked apples are not only a light and healthy dessert but also a wonderful breakfast. Try topping them with a little vanilla yogurt.

Each serving contains approximately:

Calories: 125
Fat: 0 g.
Cholesterol: 0 mg.
Sodium: 0 mg.

4 large Golden Delicious apples
2 cups apple juice
2 teaspoons vanilla extract
1 tablespoon ground cinnamon

Pictured on page 265

1. Preheat the oven to 350°.

2. Wash and core the apples. Remove the peel from the top third of each apple. Place the apples in an 8″ × 8″ baking dish.

3. Combine the apple juice and vanilla in a medium bowl. Pour over the apples. Sprinkle with the cinnamon and cover with a lid or aluminum foil.

4. Bake for about 1 hour, or until the apples can easily be pierced with a fork. Serve hot or cold.

Makes 4 servings

↪ In a Flash!

Dice the apples instead of leaving them whole, so they bake faster.

↪ Spin Off

Make applesauce out of any leftover baked apples. Chop them and put them in a blender or food processor. Blend slightly for chunky applesauce or puree for a smooth texture.

Warm Pear Slices
in Honey-Pepper Sauce

I serve these pears as a topping on fish, poultry and meat entrées as well as for dessert. For a nice presentation, slice the pears lengthwise and serve the slices arranged into fan shapes.

Each serving contains approximately:

Calories: 210
Fat: 2 g.
Cholesterol: 3 mg.
Sodium: 113 mg.

3   tablespoons red wine vinegar
3   tablespoons honey
1   teaspoon freshly ground black pepper
⅛   teaspoon salt
3   large Bartlett pears, peeled, cored and sliced
1   cup low-fat vanilla yogurt
    Mint sprigs (optional)

Pictured on
page 266

1.   In a large saucepan, combine the vinegar, honey, pepper and salt. Mix well. Add the pears and bring to a boil over medium-high heat. Reduce the heat to low, cover and cook for about 7 minutes, or until the pears are tender.

2.   Using a slotted spoon, transfer the pears to a large plate. Bring the remaining liquid to a rapid boil over high heat. Boil for 1 minute and pour over the pears. Serve topped with the yogurt and garnished with the mint sprigs (if using).

Makes 4 servings

⇢ In a Flash!

Use canned sliced pears packed in water or juice and heat them in the sauce.

⇢ Spin Off

Use leftover pears in salads.

Peaches with Almond Sauce

This speedy Italian dessert tastes so delicious it is bound to become a family favorite. Besides, you can make it in 5 minutes!

Each serving contains approximately:

Calories: 100
Fat: 2 g.
Cholesterol: 5 mg.
Sodium: 26 mg.

1   cup vanilla ice milk, melted
1   teaspoon vanilla extract
½   teaspoon almond extract
1   bag (16 ounces) frozen unsweetened sliced peaches, thawed

1.   In a small bowl, mix the ice milk, vanilla and almond extract. Serve spooned over the peaches.

Makes 4 servings

↔ In a Flash!
Use 1 can (16 ounces) sliced peaches packed in water, drained, to save the thawing time.

↔ Spin Off
The sauce is good on any fresh, frozen or canned fruit.

Gingered Fruit Compote
with Cinnamon Sauce

This deceivingly rich-tasting dessert is perfect for winter menus, when really good fresh fruits are more difficult to find and very expensive.

Each serving contains approximately:

Calories: 114
Fat: 0 g.
Cholesterol: 0 mg.
Sodium: 29 mg.

1	**tablespoon finely chopped fresh ginger**
1½	**cups water**
1	**cup chopped dried apples**
¾	**cup chopped dried apricots**
¼	**cup currants**
1	**cup fat-free sour cream**
¼	**cup unsweetened frozen apple juice concentrate, thawed**
1½	**teaspoons vanilla extract**
½	**teaspoon ground cinnamon**

1. Put the ginger in a small saucepan and cover with 3″ of water. Bring to a boil over high heat and cook for 10 minutes. Drain and set aside.

2. In a medium saucepan, combine the water, apples and apricots. Bring to a boil over high heat. Reduce the heat to low, cover and simmer for 25 minutes, or until tender. Remove from the heat and mix in the currants and reserved ginger.

3. Cool to room temperature. Cover and refrigerate for at least 2 hours.

4. In a small bowl, mix the sour cream, apple juice concentrate, vanilla and cinnamon. Serve spooned over the fruit mixture.

Makes 8 servings

⟴ In a Flash!

Make both the compote and the sauce the day before you plan to serve them so you truly can serve dessert "in a flash"!

⟴ Spin Off

Serve leftover compote and sauce on hot oatmeal for a sensational breakfast treat.

Banana Cream Dream

*This is my favorite
new banana recipe.
It was sent to me by
a reader in St. Peter,
Minnesota, who
called it Banana
Cream Dessert. She
said it tasted just
like a banana cream
pie, was easier to
make and was so
good! After making
it, I agreed with her
enough to rename
this "dreamy"
dessert.*

Each serving contains
approximately:

Calories: 102
Fat: 3 g.
Cholesterol: 0 mg.
Sodium: 165 mg.

2   cups skim milk

**1   package (1.5 ounces) fat-free, sugar-free
    instant vanilla pudding mix**

1   cup fat-free sour cream

1   container (12 ounces) thawed light whipped topping, divided

3   small bananas, sliced

16   reduced-fat vanilla wafers, broken into thirds

1.   Pour the milk into a large bowl. Add the pudding mix and stir
with a whisk for 1 full minute, or until smooth and creamy. Add the
sour cream and three-quarters of the whipped topping. Mix well.

2.   Pour into a 13″ × 9″ glass baking dish and smooth the surface
with a rubber spatula. Push the banana slices into the surface of the
mixture, distributing them evenly. Then push the wafer pieces in all
over the surface.

3.   Spread the remaining one-quarter of the whipped topping over
the surface. Cover and refrigerate for at least 1 hour.

Makes 16 servings

⤭ In a Flash!

*Make this the morning of your party for an even tastier dessert that's
ready when you are.*

⤭ Spin Off

*Put any leftovers into a blender and puree for a delicious banana shake
or a wonderful topping for fresh fruit.*

Pumpkin Whip

Pictured on page 267

For a fancier presentation of this quick dessert, use a pastry bag to pipe it into bowls or sherbet glasses. For a still more elaborate dessert, have available low-fat whipped topping or Secret Sauce (page 278) to spoon over each serving.

Each serving contains approximately:

Calories: 84
Fat: 0 g.
Cholesterol: 6 mg.
Sodium: 33 mg.

1   **can (16 ounces) solid-pack pumpkin**
2   **cups fat-free ricotta cheese**
¼   **cup packed light brown sugar**
1   **tablespoon ground cinnamon**
1½ **tablespoons vanilla extract**
1   **teaspoon ground allspice**
¼   **teaspoon ground nutmeg**

1. In a food processor bowl, combine the pumpkin, ricotta, brown sugar, cinnamon, vanilla, allspice and nutmeg. Blend until satin smooth. Cover and refrigerate for at least 3 hours.

Makes 8 servings

↔ In a Flash!
Serve immediately at room temperature.

↔ Spin Off
Use as a spread on turkey sandwiches.

Pink Panna Cotta
with Red Raspberries

Panna cotta is a smooth-textured Italian pudding that is like a custard without the eggs. It is becoming increasingly popular in this country. The name actually means "cooked cream"; however, this low-fat version made with milk is a tasty alternative. Panna cotta is usually white, but the addition of berry syrup gives it a delightful pink color that perfectly complements the red berries. I use red Italian coffee syrup such as raspberry or strawberry.

Each serving contains approximately:

Calories: 182
Fat: 2 g.
Cholesterol: 6 mg.
Sodium: 88 mg.

¼	**cup cold water**
2	**envelopes unflavored gelatin**
3¾	**cups low-fat milk**
2	**tablespoons sugar**
2	**teaspoons vanilla extract**
¾	**teaspoon almond extract**
½	**cup red berry syrup, divided**
2	**cups fresh raspberries**
	Mint sprigs (optional)

1. Place the water in a cup and sprinkle with the gelatin. Allow to soften for 5 minutes.

2. In a medium saucepan, combine the milk and sugar. Cook over medium heat, stirring frequently, until the mixture just comes to the boiling point. Remove from the heat, add the softened gelatin and stir until it is completely dissolved.

3. Stir in the vanilla, almond extract and ¼ cup of the berry syrup. Pour into six 6-ounce molds or custard cups. Cover and refrigerate for at least 4 hours.

4. To serve, dip the molds briefly into hot water and then loosen the panna cotta with a knife, if necessary. Unmold each panna cotta on a serving plate. Surround with berries and drizzle with the remaining ¼ cup berry syrup. Garnish with the mint (if using).

Makes 6 servings

↣ In a Flash!

Make the panna cotta in a large mold, rather than 6 small ones, and cut it into pie-shaped pieces to serve.

↣ Spin Off

Leftover panna cotta is delicious with any fresh or canned fruit for breakfast. You can also put it in the blender for a tasty and satisfying beverage.

Pecan Pudding

This easy-to-make pudding is a lighter, lower-calorie version of the ever-popular Southern pecan pie.

Each serving contains approximately:

Calories: 267
Fat: 12 g.
Cholesterol: 3 mg.
Sodium: 151 mg.

½ **cup chopped pecans**
2 **tablespoons cold water**
1½ **teaspoons unflavored gelatin**
1 **can (12 ounces) evaporated skim milk**
⅓ **cup packed dark brown sugar**
1 **tablespoon corn-oil margarine**
1 **teaspoon vanilla extract**

1. Place the pecans in a large nonstick skillet over medium heat and stir until well toasted; watch carefully, as they burn easily. Divide among 4 small ramekins or custard cups.

2. Place the water in a cup and sprinkle with the gelatin. Allow to soften for 5 minutes.

3. In a medium saucepan, combine the milk, brown sugar and margarine. Bring slowly just to the boiling point over medium-low heat. Remove from the heat and add the softened gelatin and the vanilla. Stir until the gelatin is completely dissolved. Allow to cool slightly.

4. Pour into the ramekins or custard cups. Cover and refrigerate for at least 4 hours.

Makes 4 servings

↔ In a Flash!

Make this in a large dish and spoon it into smaller ones before serving. Serve with fresh berries.

↔ Spin Off

Put leftover pudding in a blender and puree to make a sauce for pancakes and waffles.

Lemon Bread Pudding

Pictured on
page 268

*To further intensify
the lemon flavor of
this light bread pud-
ding, combine lemon
juice and sugar to
taste and pour a
little over each
serving.*

Each serving contains
approximately:

Calories: 123
Fat: 1 g.
Cholesterol: 3 mg.
Sodium: 292 mg.

1 **can (12 ounces) evaporated skim milk**
⅓ **cup sugar**
1 **tablespoon grated lemon rind, yellow part only**
1 **teaspoon vanilla extract**
¼ **teaspoon ground cinnamon**
¼ **teaspoon salt**
3 **cups diced French bread trimmed of crust**

1. Preheat the oven to 325°. Coat a 9″ × 5″ loaf pan with nonstick vegetable cooking spray.

2. In a large bowl, combine the milk, sugar, lemon rind, vanilla, cinnamon and salt. Stir until the sugar has completely dissolved. Add the bread, mix well and allow to stand for 20 minutes, or until the bread has absorbed all the liquid.

3. Spoon the mixture into the prepared pan and press down firmly using your hands. Serve warm or cover with a lid or aluminum foil and bake for 40 to 45 minutes, or until a knife inserted in the center comes out clean. Cool on a rack. Cover and refrigerate for at least 3 hours.

Makes 8 servings

↪ In a Flash!
Use 1½ teaspoons pure lemon extract instead of grated lemon rind.

↪ Spin Off
Warm leftover pudding and serve it for breakfast with fresh fruit.

Sticky Coconut Rice with Mango Sauce

This is one of the most popular desserts in Thailand, and it is excellent served following any type of Asian meal. In Asia, the rice is made with coconut milk. But because coconut is such a highly saturated fat, I replaced it with canned milk and added coconut extract for the flavor. The sauce is so delicious, and tastes so complex, that no one will ever guess the only ingredient is pureed mango. Sticky rice can be found in the Asian section of most supermarkets, and it is available in all Asian markets.

Each serving contains approximately:

Calories: 270
Fat: 2 g.
Cholesterol: 8 mg.
Sodium: 167 mg.

1	cup sticky white rice
1	can (12 ounces) evaporated low-fat milk
1	cup water
¼	cup sugar
¼	teaspoon salt
1½	teaspoons coconut extract
2	large ripe mangoes, peeled, seeded and chopped

1. Place the rice in a large heavy saucepan or the top of a double boiler. Cover generously with cold water and allow to soak for at least 2 hours. Drain and return to the pan.

2. Stir in the milk, water, sugar and salt. Bring to a boil over medium heat. Reduce the heat to low, cover and cook for 15 minutes, stirring occasionally. Remove from the heat and stir in the coconut extract.

3. Allow to cool. Cover and refrigerate for at least 2 hours.

4. Place the mango in a blender or food processor and puree. Refrigerate for at least 2 hours.

5. Spoon the rice into serving dishes and top with the mango sauce.

Makes 6 servings

↔ In a Flash!

Use regular white rice, which does not have to be soaked, in place of the Asian sticky rice. Serve the mango diced instead of pureed.

↔ Spin Off

Combine leftover rice and mango puree for an unusual breakfast cereal, which can be served hot or cold. Or serve the rice with milk and sliced bananas. Use the sauce on other fruit or on fish or poultry.

Jelled Cappuccino

This speedy dessert is perfect following an Italian meal. It is also a satisfying snack or an unusual breakfast treat.

Each ½-cup serving contains approximately:

Calories: 152
Fat: 2 g.
Cholesterol: 3 mg.
Sodium: 187 mg.

2	tablespoons cold water
1	envelope unflavored gelatin
¼	cup boiling water
3	tablespoons instant cappuccino powder
2	tablespoons sugar (or to taste)
1	can (12 ounces) evaporated skim milk

1. Place the cold water in a medium bowl and sprinkle with the gelatin. Allow to soften for 5 minutes.

2. Add the boiling water and stir until the gelatin is dissolved. Add the cappuccino powder and sugar; stir until completely dissolved. Add the milk and mix well.

3. Cover and refrigerate for at least 3 hours.

Makes 2 cups

⤝ In a Flash!
I really can't think of a faster method!

⤝ Spin Off
Blend with cold skim milk and serve as a chilled caffe latte.

Frozen Strawberry Yogurt

You can add a tropical taste to this light and satisfying frozen dessert with a teaspoon of coconut extract. If you do not have an ice-cream freezer, pour the mixture into a metal bowl and freeze it for 5 to 6 hours, or until it's almost solid. Then break it into pieces and blend it in a food processor until smooth. Either way, you can serve the yogurt immediately or store it for up to 4 days. (Take the yogurt out of the freezer about 15 minutes before serving for it to soften.)

Each serving contains approximately:

Calories: 333
Fat: 2 g.
Cholesterol: 6 mg.
Sodium: 87 mg.

4 **cups fresh strawberries**
1 **banana, sliced**
½ **cup packed light brown sugar**
½ **cup frozen unsweetened orange juice concentrate, thawed**
1 **teaspoon vanilla extract**
2 **cups low-fat plain yogurt**

1. Place the strawberries, bananas, brown sugar, orange juice concentrate and vanilla in the bowl of a food processor. Puree. Add the yogurt and blend just until mixed.

2. Pour the mixture into an ice-cream freezer and freeze according to the manufacturer's directions.

Makes 4 servings

⟿ In a Flash!
Use 2 bags (16 ounces each) frozen strawberries, thawed.

⟿ Spin Off
Melt the frozen yogurt and serve over fruit as a sauce.

Lemon-Ginger Ice Milk

This fabulous fat-free frozen dessert will remind you of the richest, creamiest, highest-fat ice cream you ever tasted. The recipe was developed by my friend Shirley Corriher of Atlanta. She teaches both food science and cooking classes all over the country. Her knowledge is legendary, and her effervescent personality keeps her in constant demand by amateurs and professionals alike.

Each serving contains approximately:

Calories: 199
Fat: 0 g.
Cholesterol: 1 mg.
Sodium: 129 mg.

¾ cup packed light brown sugar
2 cartons (16 ounces each) fat-free sour cream
1 carton (8 ounces) fat-free lemon yogurt
2 tablespoons candied ginger, minced
2 tablespoons light corn syrup
2 teaspoons vanilla extract
2 teaspoons grated lemon rind, yellow part only
⅛ teaspoon salt

Pictured on page 269

1. Push the brown sugar through a large-mesh strainer to remove any lumps. Transfer to a blender or a food processor. Add the sour cream, yogurt, ginger, corn syrup, vanilla, lemon rind and salt. Process to blend well. Transfer to a large bowl and place in the freezer to chill for 10 minutes.

2. Transfer the mixture to an ice-cream maker and freeze according to the manufacturer's directions. (If you do not have an ice-cream maker, see page 293.)

Makes 8 servings

⇥ In a Flash!
Don't bother to freeze the mixture—just serve it as a cold custard.

⇥ Spin Off
Thaw leftover ice milk and serve it as a sauce over baked bananas or sliced oranges.

Tropical Sorbet

Pictured on
page 270

1　can (20 ounces) unsweetened crushed
　　pineapple packed in juice, drained and frozen
1　large banana, sliced and frozen
¼　cup orange juice
1　tablespoon sugar
½　teaspoon coconut extract

When making this refreshing dessert, put the drained pineapple into a large self-sealing plastic bag and press it out flat before freezing. Do the same thing with the banana slices. Break the fruit pieces apart before putting them into the blender or food processor—it is much easier to puree the mixture that way.

Each ½-cup serving contains approximately:

Calories: 72
Fat: 0 g.
Cholesterol: 0 mg.
Sodium: 1 mg.

1.　Place one-quarter of the frozen pineapple and one-quarter of the frozen bananas in a blender or food processor. Add the orange juice, sugar and coconut extract. Puree.

2.　Add the remaining pineapple and bananas a little at a time, blending until smooth after each addition, until the mixture is completely pureed and light and frothy in texture.

3.　Pour into a large bowl. Cover and freeze for 1 hour before serving.

Makes 4 cups

⇥ In a Flash!

Serve the pureed mixture as a cold dessert soup instead of freezing it for a sorbet. You can also freeze it in ice cube trays for ice pops.

⇥ Spin Off

Puree leftover sorbet and use it as a sauce on fruit or thin it with more orange juice and serve it as a drink.

Spa Strawberry Mousse

This creamy-textured mousse was created by the acclaimed pastry chef Joel Gaillot for the final banquet of an International Spa and Fitness Association Conference. Both the delicious taste and the dramatic presentation of his fat-free dessert won rave reviews for him. I was so thrilled by his spectacular dessert that I asked him for his recipe to share with all of my readers.

- **2 tablespoons cold water**
- **2 envelopes unflavored gelatin**
- **¼ cup boiling water**
- **1 package (16 ounces) unsweetened strawberries, thawed**
- **½ cup sugar**
- **2 cups fat-free plain yogurt**

1. Place the cold water in a small bowl and sprinkle with the gelatin. Allow to soften for 5 minutes. Add the boiling water and stir until the gelatin is dissolved.

2. Place the strawberries, sugar and gelatin mixture in a blender and puree. Add the yogurt and blend just until mixed. Divide among 4 serving dishes or goblets. Cover and refrigerate for at least 3 hours, or until firm.

Makes 4 servings

↔ In a Flash!
Eliminate the gelatin and serve the liquid mixture as a dessert soup.

↔ Spin Off
Leftover mousse can be frozen and served as a frozen dessert.

Each serving contains approximately:

Calories: 213
Fat: 0 g.
Cholesterol: 2 mg.
Sodium: 94 mg.

Piña Colada Mousse

You can spoon this mousse into a prepared graham cracker pie crust for a sensational tropical pie.

Each ½-cup serving contains approximately:

Calories: 110
Fat: 0 g.
Cholesterol: 0 mg.
Sodium: 15 mg.

1 **can (8 ounces) unsweetened crushed pineapple packed in juice, undrained**
1 **container (8 ounces) thawed light whipped topping**
1 **cup fat-free sour cream**
2 **tablespoons sugar**
1 **teaspoon vanilla extract**
1 **teaspoon coconut extract**

1. In a large bowl, combine the pineapple, whipped topping, sour cream, sugar, vanilla and coconut extract. Mix well.

2. Pour into a serving dish, cover and refrigerate for at least 4 hours.

Makes 4 cups

↔ In a Flash!

Just cover the bowl you made the mousse in and save washing another dish.

↔ Spin Off

Fold other fruit into leftover mousse for another dessert or puree the mousse and use it as a sauce on other fruit.

Blueberry Mousse
with Raspberry Sauce

Pictured on
page 319

Although this dessert requires a fair amount of refrigerator time, your hands-on involvement is quite limited. You can make this delicious dessert in individual molds or custard cups if you prefer. If you'd rather not use orange liqueur, replace it with thawed frozen orange juice concentrate.

Each serving contains approximately:

Calories: 100
Fat: 1 g.
Cholesterol: 1 mg.
Sodium: 38 mg.

Mousse

- 1 **can (12 ounces) evaporated skim milk**
- ¼ **cup cold water**
- 2 **envelopes unflavored gelatin**
- ¼ **cup boiling water**
- 1 **package (16 ounces) frozen unsweetened blueberries, thawed**
- 3 **tablespoons orange-flavored liqueur, such as Grand Marnier**
- 2 **tablespoons fresh lemon juice**
- ¼ **cup sugar**

Sauce

- 1 **package (12 ounces) frozen unsweetened raspberries, thawed**
- ¼ **cup sugar**
- 1 **tablespoon orange-flavored liqueur, such as Grand Marnier**
- 1 **teaspoon lemon juice**

1. *To make the mousse:* Several hours before you plan to make the mousse, put the can of milk in the refrigerator to chill. Place a large metal or glass bowl and the beaters from an electric mixer in the freezer. (Chilling these items ensures that the milk will whip properly.)

2. Place the cold water in a small bowl and sprinkle with the gelatin. Allow to soften for 5 minutes. Add the boiling water and stir until the gelatin is dissolved.

3. Place the blueberries in a blender. Add the liqueur, lemon juice and gelatin mixture. Puree. Transfer to a medium bowl and refrigerate until needed.

4. Remove the bowl and beaters from the freezer. Pour the chilled milk into the bowl and beat until soft peaks form when the beaters are lifted. Slowly add the sugar and continue beating until firm peaks form.

5. Pour the blueberry mixture over the whipped milk. Using a rubber spatula, carefully fold in the blueberry mixture until no streaks of white show. Pour into a mold, cover and refrigerate for at least 4 hours.

6. *To make the raspberry sauce:* While the mousse is chilling, combine the raspberries, sugar, liqueur and lemon juice in a blender container; puree. With a spatula, press through a fine strainer (to remove the seeds) into a medium bowl. Cover and refrigerate until ready to serve.

7. Unmold the mousse onto a serving platter. Spoon into individual bowls and top with the sauce.

Makes 12 servings

↔ In a Flash!

Pour the mousse into a serving dish rather than a mold to save the time of unmolding it. If you want to use a decorative mold for the mousse, use a hair dryer to lightly warm the outside of the mold for easy unmolding.

↔ Spin Off

Freeze leftover mousse for a delicious frozen dessert.

Milk Chocolate–Raspberry Mousse

Pictured on page 320

This opulent-tasting dessert can be made in minutes and is sure to get rave reviews from your guests.

Each serving contains approximately:

Calories: 135
Fat: 3 g.
Cholesterol: 0 mg.
Sodium: 250 mg.

2	cups skim milk
1	package (2.1 ounces) fat-free instant chocolate pudding mix
1	cup fat-free sour cream
1	container (8 ounces) thawed light whipped topping
3	cups fresh raspberries, divided
16	reduced-fat chocolate graham crackers, broken into pieces

1. Pour the milk into a large bowl. Add the pudding mix and stir with a whisk for 1 full minute, or until smooth and creamy. Add the sour cream and whipped topping; whisk until smooth. Fold in 2 cups of the raspberries.

2. Pour into a 13″ × 9″ baking dish and spread evenly with a rubber spatula. Press the graham cracker pieces into the mousse, distributing them evenly. Sprinkle the remaining raspberries over the top. Cover and refrigerate for at least 3 hours.

Makes 16 servings

⇥ In a Flash!

Use a 12-ounce bag of frozen raspberries in place of the fresh.

⇥ Spin Off

Stir leftover mousse together and spoon it over other berries, ice milk or cake.

Carefree Chiffon Cheesecake

I call this "carefree" cheesecake because you don't have to bake it, and it's so low in fat that you can eat it without guilt. I call it "chiffon" because is as light as a mousse or a cold soufflé.

Each serving contains approximately:

Calories: 262
Fat: 8 g.
Cholesterol: 5 mg.
Sodium: 320 mg.

1 **package (8 ounces) fat-free cream cheese, softened**

½ **cup sugar**

1 **cup fat-free sour cream**

2 **teaspoons vanilla extract**

½ **teaspoon grated lemon rind, yellow part only**

1 **container (8 ounces) thawed light whipped topping**

1 **prepared 9″ graham cracker pie crust**

1. Put the cream cheese in a large bowl. Using an electric mixer, beat until smooth. Add the sugar and beat until smooth. Beat in the sour cream, vanilla and lemon rind.

2. Fold in the whipped topping, mixing well. Spoon the mixture into the pie crust. Cover and refrigerate for at least 3 hours.

Makes 8 servings

⇢ In a Flash!

Use ½ teaspoon pure lemon extract in place of the grated lemon rind.

⇢ Spin Off

Fold applesauce and a touch of ground cinnamon into leftover cheesecake and crust for another delicious dessert.

Chocolate Mocha Cheesecake

This easy chocolate treat doesn't even have to be baked. It's sure to get cheers from your chocoholic friends.

Each serving contains approximately:

Calories: 270
Fat: 9 g.
Cholesterol: 5 mg.
Sodium: 271 mg.

Pictured on page 321

2   **teaspoons instant coffee powder**
1   **tablespoon boiling water**
1   **package (8 ounces) fat-free cream cheese, softened**
⅔   **cup sugar**
3   **tablespoons unsweetened cocoa powder, sifted**
2   **teaspoons vanilla extract**
1   **container (8 ounces) thawed light whipped topping**
1   **prepared 9″ chocolate pie crust**
    Confectioners' sugar (optional)

1. In a cup, dissolve the coffee powder in the water.

Put the cream cheese in a large bowl. Add the coffee, sugar, cocoa powder and vanilla. Using an electric mixer, beat until smooth. Fold in the whipped topping, mixing well.

2. Spoon the mixture into the pie crust. Cover and refrigerate for at least 3 hours. Dust with confectioners' sugar (if using) before serving.

Makes 8 servings

⇥ In a Flash!

Use chocolate syrup (to taste) in place of the cocoa powder. This will save the time necessary to sift the cocoa.

⇥ Spin Off

Mix leftover cheesecake and crust together and spoon it into sherbet glasses for a different presentation. Fold raspberries or diced angel food cake into leftover cheesecake for another delicious dessert.

Peachy Cream Pie

In place of the canned peaches called for in this "peach of a pie," you can use fresh peaches or sliced frozen peaches. If you do, however, add a little fruit juice to compensate for the liquid that would otherwise come from the can.

Each serving contains approximately:

Calories: 210
Fat: 9 g.
Cholesterol: 12 mg.
Sodium: 325 mg.

1 **can (8 ounces) sliced peaches packed in juice, undrained**
1 **box (3.4 ounces) fat-free instant vanilla pudding mix**
1 **cup reduced-fat sour cream**
½ **teaspoon vanilla extract**
¼ **teaspoon ground cinnamon**
1 **prepared 9″ graham cracker pie crust**

1. Pour the peaches (and juice) into a blender or food processor and process just until coarsely chopped. Transfer to a large bowl.

2. Add the pudding mix, sour cream, vanilla and cinnamon. Mix until well blended. Pour the mixture into the crust and chill for at least 3 hours.

Makes 8 servings

↠ In a Flash!
Eliminate the crust and serve the filling immediately as a soft pudding.

↠ Spin Off
Serve leftover pie for breakfast instead of a sweet roll.

Light Lemon Pie

Now that it's possible to buy nonfat sweetened condensed skim milk, we can all make a fabulous fat-free lemon pie filling in a jiffy. You don't even have to bake it because the reaction of the milk and lemon juice does the thickening. You can spread light whipped topping over the top. For an even more festive pie, cover it with a colorful assortment of diced fresh fruit.

Each serving contains approximately:

Calories: 247
Fat: 5 g.
Cholesterol: 0 mg.
Sodium: 185 mg.

1   **can (14 ounces) sweetened condensed skim milk**
⅓   **cup fresh lemon juice**
1   **tablespoon grated lemon rind, yellow part only**
¼   **teaspoon salt**
1   **prepared 9" graham cracker pie crust**

1. In a large bowl, combine the milk, lemon juice, lemon rind and salt. Stir until thickened.

2. Pour into the pie crust. Cover and refrigerate for at least 3 hours.

Makes 8 servings

↦ In a Flash!

Use 1½ teaspoons pure lemon extract in place of the grated lemon rind.

↦ Spin Off

Put leftover pie, crust and all, in a blender or food processor and puree. It is a great sauce for fresh fruit, frozen yogurt or ice milk.

This is a rich-tasting peasant dessert from France. It is also the easiest way imaginable to make a fruit pie! Clafouti, which originated in the Limousin region of France, is traditionally made with cherries. However, any fruit, such as nectarines, plums or pears, may be used. This recipe uses peaches because they happen to be my favorite. The reason I suggest placing the quiche dish or pie plate on a baking sheet in this recipe is that it is almost impossible to put the clafouti into the oven without spilling a little bit of the batter.

Each serving contains approximately:

Calories: 161
Fat: 1 g.
Cholesterol: 27 mg.
Sodium: 89 mg.

Fresh Peach Clafouti

1⅓ **cups skim milk**
¾ **cup unbleached all-purpose flour**
½ **cup packed light brown sugar**
3 **egg whites**
1 **egg**
2 **teaspoons vanilla extract**
1 **teaspoon ground cinnamon**
⅛ **teaspoon salt**
3 **cups sliced fresh peaches**
2 **tablespoons confectioners' sugar**
  Ground cinnamon (optional)

Pictured on page 322

1. Preheat the oven to 350°. Coat a 10″ quiche dish or pie plate with nonstick vegetable cooking spray.

2. Place the milk, flour, brown sugar, egg whites, egg, vanilla, 1 teaspoon cinnamon and salt in a blender. Blend on high speed for 1 minute, or until well mixed.

3. Pour a thin layer of the batter into the prepared baking dish and place it in the center of the oven for 8 minutes.

4. In a medium bowl, mix the peaches and confectioners' sugar.

5. Remove the baking dish from the oven and place it on a baking sheet. Spoon the peaches evenly into the dish. Pour the remaining batter evenly over the top. Carefully place the baking sheet in the oven.

6. Bake for about 1 hour, or until the clafouti is puffed up and browned. Remove from the oven and allow to cool for at least 30 minutes. Sprinkle the top lightly with additional cinnamon (if using).

Makes 8 servings

⇢ In a Flash!

Use 3 cups frozen unsweetened sliced peaches, thawed and completely drained.

⇢ Spin Off

Serve leftover clafouti as a breakfast treat.

Fat-Free Fudgy Brownies

Pictured on page 323

This is a dessert I originally developed for the National Milk Producers' Light Milk and Cookie Break program. This very chocolatey brownie is sure to be a hit with your whole family. And it is truly best served with a cold glass of milk!

Each brownie contains approximately:

Calories: 60
Fat: 0 g.
Cholesterol: 0 mg.
Sodium: 95 mg.

⅓ **cup unsweetened cocoa powder**
⅔ **cup unbleached all-purpose flour**
⅔ **cup sugar**
¾ **teaspoon baking soda**
½ **teaspoon baking powder**
⅛ **teaspoon salt**
1 **teaspoon instant coffee powder**
⅓ **cup boiling water**
⅓ **cup skim milk**
1 **jar (2½ ounces) baby-food pureed prunes**
2 **egg whites**
1½ **teaspoons vanilla extract**
   Confectioners' sugar (optional)

1. Preheat the oven to 350°. Coat an 8″ × 8″ baking pan with non-stick vegetable cooking spray.

2. Sift the cocoa powder into a large bowl. Add the flour, sugar, baking soda, baking powder and salt; mix well.

3. In a medium bowl, dissolve the coffee powder in the water. Add the milk, prunes, egg whites and vanilla. Mix well. Pour over the cocoa mixture and mix well.

4. Pour the batter into the prepared pan and bake for about 30 minutes, or until a knife inserted in the center comes out clean.

5. Place the pan on a wire rack and allow to cool for 10 minutes. Invert the brownies onto a cutting board and let cool completely before cutting. Dust with confectioners' sugar (if using) before serving.

Makes 16 brownies

↤ **In a Flash!**
Use ⅓ cup of already-made strong coffee.

↤ **Spin Off**
Freeze brownies individually for brown bag lunches. Put them in lunch bags while still frozen; by lunchtime, they will be thawed and delicious.

California Fruit Bake

The recipe was developed sort of by accident. I was working on a recipe for strawberry bars that turned out to be much too fragile and moist to be cut into bars. But they were entirely too delicious to change! So I made the recipe again, baked it in a pie plate rather than a baking dish, cut it into wedges and served it warm topped with fat-free vanilla yogurt. My guests loved it. It can be served as a dessert or as a coffeecake for breakfast. The moisture in this delicious dish comes not from fat but from the addition of pureed prunes.

Each serving contains approximately:

Calories: 141
Fat: 5 g.
Cholesterol: 27 mg.
Sodium: 134 mg.

1	**egg**
2	**egg whites**
½	**cup packed light brown sugar**
1	**jar (2½ ounces) baby-food pureed prunes**
1	**tablespoon corn-oil margarine, melted**
1	**teaspoon vanilla extract**
½	**cup unbleached all-purpose flour**
½	**teaspoon baking powder**
¼	**teaspoon salt**
1	**pint fresh strawberries, sliced**
¼	**cup chopped walnuts, toasted**

1. Preheat the oven to 350°. Coat a 9″ or 10″ pie plate with nonstick vegetable cooking spray.

2. Combine the egg and egg whites in a large bowl. Beat by hand or with an electric mixer until frothy. Beat in the brown sugar. Add the prunes, margarine and vanilla. Mix well.

3. In a medium bowl, combine the flour, baking powder and salt; mix well. Add to the prune mixture and mix until the dry ingredients are completely moistened. Stir in the strawberries and walnuts.

4. Pour the batter into the prepared pan. Bake for about 35 minutes, or until the center is set, the top is lightly browned and the edges are starting to crisp.

5. Cool on a wire rack for 10 minutes before cutting.

Makes 8 servings

↔ In a Flash!
I have already taken every conceivable shortcut in this recipe!

↔ Spin Off
Wrap leftovers for brown bag lunches or picnic baskets.

Apple and Cheddar Cheese Snackin' Cake

Not only is this cake delicious and easy to make but cleanup is a snap because the cake pan never actually touches the cake. This cake is wonderful for portable meals, like picnics and tailgate parties, because it bakes in its "wrapper."

Each serving contains approximately:

Calories: 107
Fat: 3 g.
Cholesterol: 8 mg.
Sodium: 160 mg.

Cake

- 1⅓ cups unbleached all-purpose flour
- 2 teaspoons baking powder
- ⅓ cup sugar
- 1 tablespoon corn-oil margarine, softened
- ½ cup shredded reduced-fat sharp Cheddar cheese
- 2 egg whites
- ⅓ cup skim milk
- 1 teaspoon vanilla extract
- 1 pound Golden Delicious apples, peeled, cored and sliced

Topping

- ¼ cup unbleached all-purpose flour
- 3 tablespoons sugar
- ½ cup shredded reduced-fat sharp Cheddar cheese

1. *To make the cake:* Preheat the oven to 350°. Line a 9″ × 9″ baking pan with aluminum foil (allowing about 6″ to hang over each end so the cake can be removed from the pan and wrapped after being baked and cooled). Coat the foil with nonstick vegetable cooking spray.

2. In a large bowl, mix the flour and baking powder.

3. In a medium bowl, combine the sugar and margarine; mix well. Stir in the Cheddar and egg whites; mix well. Add the milk and vanilla; mix well. Pour over the flour and mix just until all the flour is moistened; do not overmix.

4. Spread the batter in the prepared pan. Press the apples into the batter in 3 rows.

5. *To make the topping:* In a small bowl, mix the flour and sugar. Add the Cheddar and mix until the consistency of coarse gravel. Sprinkle evenly over the batter.

6. Bake for about 45 minutes, or until the top is golden brown. Place on a wire rack and allow to cool to room temperature. Lift the cake out of the pan. Serve immediately or wrap tightly with the overhanging foil and store in the refrigerator.

Makes 12 servings

⇝ In a Flash!

Use sliced dried apples in place of the fresh apples to save the time of peeling, coring and slicing.

⇝ Spin Off

Freeze individual servings in self-sealing plastic bags. Add to sack lunches and picnic baskets. To thaw for instant eating, microwave for about 45 seconds.

Raspberry Tiramisu

This is the lightest version of this popular Italian dessert that I have ever come upon—yet it has the rich and satisfying taste of the original dish. I created this for an article in Cooking Light *magazine that featured fruit and cheese desserts. I have been making tiramisu this way ever since. Even though tiramisu is not classically made with raspberries, they are a delightful addition. If you prefer not to use the cognac called for, replace it with 1½ tablespoons apple cider plus ½ teaspoon brandy extract.*

½	**cup cold espresso, divided**
6	**tablespoons sugar, divided**
1	**package (3 ounces) ladyfingers**
4	**ounces mascarpone cheese**
4	**ounces fat-free cream cheese, softened**
1½	**tablespoons cognac**
1¼	**cups fresh or thawed unsweetened frozen raspberries, divided**
1	**teaspoon unsweetened cocoa powder**

1. In a shallow bowl or 8″ × 8″ baking dish, combine ¼ cup of the espresso with 4 tablespoons of the sugar; stir until completely dissolved. Separate the top and bottom halves of the ladyfingers and place 12 of the halves in the bowl or baking dish, touching but not overlapping each other.

2. In a food processor, combine the mascarpone, cream cheese, cognac and the remaining 2 tablespoons sugar. Blend until satin smooth.

3. Spoon half of the cheese mixture over the ladyfingers. Top with 1 cup of the raspberries. Place the remaining ladyfingers on top of the raspberries. Carefully drizzle with the remaining ¼ cup espresso.

4. Top with the remaining cheese mixture. Place the cocoa in a small sieve and sift evenly over the top. Decorate with the remaining ¼ cup raspberries. Cover and refrigerate for at least 4 hours.

Makes 6 servings

↔ In a Flash!
Teach your children how to make it!

↔ Spin Off
Freeze leftover tiramisu and serve as a frozen dessert.

Each serving contains approximately:

Calories: 246
Fat: 9 g.
Cholesterol: 102 mg.
Sodium: 189 mg.

Raspberry–Cream Cheese Brûlée

Pictured on page 324

This is a recipe I developed for the Chilean Fruit Board. They used it in a brochure featuring ways to use all of the fresh Chilean fruits available during our winter months, when it is summer in Chile.

Each serving contains approximately:

Calories: 200
Fat: 8 g.
Cholesterol: 23 mg.
Sodium: 196 mg.

1　can (12 ounces) evaporated skim milk
2　tablespoons cornstarch
⅓　cup packed light brown sugar
4　egg whites, slightly beaten
2　teaspoons canola oil
1　teaspoon vanilla extract
1　package (8 ounces) reduced-fat cream cheese, cut into cubes
1　pint fresh raspberries
8　teaspoons sugar

1.　Combine the milk and cornstarch in the top of a double boiler and stir until the cornstarch is completely dissolved. Add the brown sugar, egg whites and oil; whisk to mix well.

2.　Place the top of the double boiler over simmering water and cook, stirring constantly, for about 4 minutes, or until the mixture comes to a simmer and thickens. Remove from the heat and stir in the vanilla.

3.　Add the cream cheese and continue stirring until the cheese melts and the mixture is smooth. Fold in the raspberries and spoon into 8 ramekins or custard cups. Cover and refrigerate for at least 2 hours.

4.　To serve, sprinkle 1 teaspoon of sugar evenly over the top of each brûlée. Arrange on a baking sheet and broil until the sugar melts, bubbles and starts to brown. Serve immediately.

Makes 8 servings

↦ **In a Flash!**
Eliminate the glazing step and serve this as a lovely raspberry custard.

↦ **Spin Off**
Spoon leftovers over other fruits, yogurt or cake.

Instant Cherry Trifle

If you like trifle but don't have the time to make the traditional custard, this is an ideal recipe for you. It uses light cherry pie filling, fat-free instant pudding mix and angel food cake. They can be quickly layered in a traditional trifle dish for a delicious and impressive-looking dessert. If you prefer not to use sherry, you can substitute sherry, rum or brandy extract to taste.

Each ½-cup serving contains approximately:

Calories: 111
Fat: 0 g.
Cholesterol: 1 mg.
Sodium: 161 mg.

2   **cups skim milk**
1   **package (3.4 ounces) fat-free instant vanilla pudding mix**
2   **tablespoons dry sherry**
10   **ounces angel food cake, cut into 1″ cubes**
1   **container (21 ounces) light cherry pie filling**

1. Pour the milk into a large mixing bowl. Add the pudding mix and stir with a whisk for 1 full minute, or until smooth and creamy. Add the sherry and mix well.

2. Line the bottom of a trifle dish or a glass bowl with a third of the angel food cake; top with a third of the pudding mixture, then a third of the cherry filling. Repeat twice more to use all the angel food cake, pudding and cherry filling. Cover and refrigerate for at least 2 hours.

Makes 8 cups

↦ In a Flash!

Mix all ingredients together for a "country pudding."

↦ Spin Off

Puree leftover trifle and serve topped with toasted nuts for another dessert.

Almond Biscotti

Pictured on
page 325

This is a recipe I developed for the National Milk Producers' Light Milk and Cookie Break program a couple of years ago. These tasty Italian cookies are so delicious and so easy to make that I frequently prepare them for holiday and hostess gifts.

Each biscotti contains approximately:

Calories: 60
Fat: 2 g.
Cholesterol: 0 mg.
Sodium: 55 mg.

2	tablespoons finely chopped almonds
¼	cup sugar
1	tablespoon butter or corn-oil margarine, softened
2	egg whites, lightly beaten
1	teaspoon almond extract
1	cup unbleached all-purpose flour
½	teaspoon baking powder
⅛	teaspoon salt

1. Preheat the oven to 375°. Coat a 9″ × 5″ loaf pan with nonstick vegetable cooking spray.

2. Place the almonds in a baking pan and bake for about 7 to 8 minutes, or until they are a rich golden brown; watch carefully, as they burn easily.

3. In a medium bowl, combine the sugar and butter or margarine; mix well. Add the egg whites and almond extract; mix well.

4. In a large bowl, combine the flour, baking powder and salt; mix well. Add the egg white mixture and almonds. Mix well.

5. Spoon the dough into the prepared pan. Spread it evenly over the bottom of the pan by wetting your hands and pressing down on the dough. Bake for 15 minutes, or until a knife inserted in the center comes out clean.

6. Remove from the oven and unmold onto a cutting board. Let cool for 5 or 10 minutes, just until cool enough to handle. Cut into ½″ slices. Coat a baking sheet with nonstick spray or cover it with parchment paper. Lay the slices on their sides on the sheet. Bake for 5 minutes; turn the slices over and bake for 5 minutes, or until golden brown on both sides.

Makes 16 biscotti

↣ In a Flash!

Use already-toasted nuts.

↣ Spin Off

Crumble the biscotti as a topping for fruit salads, yogurt, frozen yogurt and ice milk.

Lemon Drop Cookies

These crunchy cookies have a wonderfully refreshing lemon flavor that is perfect after almost any type of meal. They can turn an ordinary fruit plate into a truly special dessert. They are also so unusual, so delicious and so very easy to make that they can quickly become habit forming! I often take them to parties as a host or hostess gift and always get asked for the recipe.

Each cookie contains approximately:

Calories: 48
Fat: 0 g.
Cholesterol: 13 mg.
Sodium: 25 mg.

Pictured on page 326

1   **egg**
½   **cup sugar**
1   **teaspoon grated lemon rind, yellow part only**
1   **teaspoon pure lemon extract**
½   **teaspoon baking powder**
⅔   **cup unbleached all-purpose flour**

1. Preheat the oven to 325°. Line a baking sheet with aluminum foil.

2. Place the egg in a medium bowl and whip until frothy. Add the sugar and mix until the sugar is completely dissolved. Beat in the lemon rind, lemon extract and baking powder. Slowly beat in the flour until you have a smooth mixture.

3. Drop the dough by tablespoonsful onto the baking sheet. Bake for about 14 minutes, or until the cookies start to color. Allow to cool completely on a wire rack before peeling the cookies off the foil.

Makes 16 cookies

↦ In a Flash!
Omit the lemon rind and add another ½ teaspoon lemon extract.

↦ Spin Off
Crumble cookies for a tasty topping on fruit salads or for the crust of a cheesecake.

Honey-Sesame Fruit Granola

*This tasty granola
is practically fat free
and high in fiber.
It can be served as
healthy candy or
just for a high-
energy, satisfying
snack. It takes only
a few minutes to put
together and keeps
for weeks in the
refrigerator. You can
also use other dried
fruits such as dates,
prunes and peaches.*

Each ¼-cup serving
contains
approximately:

Calories: 141
Fat: 1 g.
Cholesterol: 0 mg.
Sodium: 6 mg.

½	**cup frozen unsweetened apple juice concentrate, thawed**
½	**cup honey**
2	**tablespoons molasses**
1	**teaspoon ground cinnamon**
3	**cups puffed wheat or puffed rice cereal (or a combination of both)**
1½	**cups quick-cooking rolled oats**
½	**cup wheat bran**
½	**cup raisins**
4	**ounces dried apricots, finely chopped**
2	**tablespoons sesame seeds**

1. Preheat the oven to 275°. Coat a 13″ × 9″ baking dish with non-stick vegetable cooking spray.

2. In a large bowl, combine the apple juice concentrate, honey, molasses and cinnamon; mix well. Add the cereal, oats, bran, raisins and apricots; mix well.

3. Spoon the mixture into the prepared baking dish and press down firmly. Sprinkle the sesame seeds evenly over the top and press them in using your hands.

4. Bake for 50 minutes. Allow to cool on a wire rack. Crumble the granola and store, tightly covered, in the refrigerator.

Makes 4 cups

↔ In a Flash!
Use all raisins or currants to save the time it takes to chop the apricots.

↔ Spin Off
Use as a topping on fruit salads and on both regular and frozen yogurt.

Entertaining in a Timely Fashion

Entertaining is so much fun! And you can do it without spending a great deal of time. All it takes is a little planning.

For instance, when possible, shop for everything you need the day before your party. Plan a menu that you can prepare ahead of time so you are free to enjoy your guests. Set the table in advance of your party to eliminate some of the last-minute frustration of having too much to do and too little time to do it. Remember, as a host or hostess, you are not simply preparing a meal; you are entertaining the people you invited.

Most people I meet are well aware of the importance of good nutrition and try to eat in a healthy manner most of the time. That is, until they plan a party. Then all the stops are pulled because they wrongly think they can't please or impress their company with healthy, low-fat fare. My suggestion: When planning your next party menu, pretend you are going to be the guest. In other words, design a meal that you would like to be served if you were someone else's company. You will be amazed at the difference it will make in your menu planning and how appreciative your guests will be.

I have designed seven menus of varying types to help you get started. You can either follow them exactly or simply use them as guides to create your own. Ultimately, your personal touch is what makes your parties special.

Brunch

The word *brunch*, a contraction of the words breakfast and lunch, is generally used to describe a meal served later than breakfast but earlier than lunch. Traditionally, brunch is more popular as a meal shared by family and friends on Sunday than on any other day of the week.

This menu is perfect to serve when you are returning home from church, or any other early-morning activity, along with your guests. Everything can be prepared ahead of time so you don't have to spend much time away from your company.

Herbed Melon Soup (page 45)
Overnight Cheddar Cheese Strata (page 231)
Maple-Glazed Canadian Bacon (page 118)

Ladies' Luncheon

When you're hosting the ladies for lunch— whether it's for a bridge game, a birthday party or a bridal shower—this make-ahead menu will allow you time to enjoy your own lunch *and* impress your guests at the same time. It also adapts well for buffet service.

Sparkling Papaya Soup (page 44)
Savory Chicken Salad (page 58)
Lemon-Ginger Ice Milk (page 294)

Mexican Fiesta

Mexico's colorful culinary traditions began to evolve centuries ago, when the Spanish conquistadors first landed on Mexican shores. Since that time, the robust tastes and spicy aromas of this unique and flavorful cuisine have become popular all over the world. This quick and easy Mexican menu is sure to be a big hit with everyone attending your next fiesta.

Pickled Carrots (page 193)
Black Bean Dip (page 42) with baked tortilla chips
Tortilla Soup (page 126)
Fish Tacos (page 165)
Creamy Caramel Dip (page 276) with crisp apple slices

Asian Feast

Cooking is an ancient art in China. For over 3,000 years, the Chinese have been subtly blending flavors and textures. They place great importance on the color, fragrance, taste, form and nutritional benefits of the dishes served. The food is chopped into bite-size morsels that can be picked up with chopsticks.

In this menu, I have combined some of my favorite Chinese dishes, which are all fast, easy and inexpensive to make. Start your party by giving all of your guests chopsticks to eat with—you can always have forks handy for backup!

Egg Drop Soup (page 46)
Hot and Spicy Apple and Cabbage Salad (page 194)
Chicken Breast in Fragrant Sauce (page 241)
Stir-Fried Ginger Noodles (page 77)
Sesame Stir-Fried Asparagus (page 72)
Sticky Coconut Rice with Mango Sauce (page 291)

(Continued on page 327)

Blueberry Mousse with Raspberry Sauce (page 298)

Milk Chocolate–Raspberry Mousse (page 300)

Chocolate Mocha Cheesecake (page 302)

Fresh Peach Clafouti (page 305)

Fat-Free Fudgy Brownies (page 306)

Raspberry–Cream Cheese Brûlée (page 311)

Almond Biscotti (page 313)

Lemon Drop Cookies (page 314)

(Continued from page 318)

Italian Picnic

This rustic menu is perfect for any type of portable meal because it travels so well and can be prepared hours ahead. If you plan to go directly from work to the beach, the mountains or a local park, you can literally pack your picnic in the trunk of your car in the morning and have a relaxed al fresco dinner at the end of the day. You don't even really need a cooler, just a thermos for the soup. Don't forget to take along a can opener so you can add the tuna to the salad just before serving.

The recipes can easily be cut in half for a romantic lunch or dinner for two. Or you can expand them to accommodate any size crowd for a large picnic or tailgate party.

Italian Vegetable Soup (page 125)
Tuscan Tuna Salad (page 60)
Crusty Italian bread
Almond Biscotti (page 313)
Fresh fruit

Middle Eastern Medley

Middle Eastern cuisine is characterized by the tantalizing aroma of the many spices used in the food. In fact, no Middle Eastern kitchen can function without a spice grinder.

This Middle Eastern menu can be prepared in total before you leave the house in the morning and be ready to serve your dinner guests when you return at the end of the day. Another bonus—your house will smell heavenly *and* very Middle Eastern!

Hummus (page 41) with pita bread
Salad of Young Greens with Fennel Dressing (page 196)
Middle Eastern Lamb Stew in a Crock-Pot (page 258)
Honeyed Oranges (page 279)

Holiday

Holiday meals are traditionally served family-style, with all of the side dishes on the table in serving bowls. The turkey is usually carved at the table, allowing each guest to choose a favorite part of the bird.

This manner of serving makes the meal more relaxed and informal, and it doesn't matter if the food isn't "piping hot." In fact, food historians tell us that, in colonial times, all food was served closer to room temperature than hot. Keeping this in mind, cooking and serving this holiday meal should be easy and lots of fun.

Another bit of good news about this holiday meal is that, if you eat a serving of everything on the menu, the total calories add up to only 503, with just 12 grams of fat and 65 milligrams of cholesterol. What a gift for your family and friends!

Curried Waldorf Salad (page 195)
Turkey in a Bag (page 248)
Cranberry-Orange Ketchup (page 121)
Whole-Wheat Stuffing (page 216)
Herbed Green Beans (page 62)
Pumpkin Whip (page 287)

Time-Saving, Money-Saving Basics

Many of the following tips for cooking healthier and saving time and money do appear elsewhere in this book. Some are in the text chapters and others are sprinkled among the recipes. I've gathered them together here, in a separate section, so you can easily find whatever information you might need in order to revise your own favorite recipes to be healthier, faster, easier and even less expensive. And I've supplemented them with still more of my favorite techniques for maximizing flavor, minimizing fuss and paring unnecessary fat from recipes. They've served me well—I hope they'll do the same for you.

Enhance Flavor with Minimum Fat

The secret to enhancing the flavor of any dish is actually to boost the aroma. As I mentioned earlier in the book, the reason is that we taste only four things: sweetness, saltiness, sourness and bitterness. Everything else we "taste" is actually smell. The successful balancing of flavor is achieved by combining sweet, salty and sour tastes with the aroma of a dish's ingredients and especially its seasonings.

Many people say they can't taste food when they have a cold. The truth is that they can still taste just fine, but they can't smell. Even with a bad cold, you can determine whether something is sweet, salty, sour or bitter. But without seeing it, you can't tell whether it's a fruit or a vegetable, a piece of lamb or a slice of beef, because you can't smell it!

To achieve more flavor in low-fat recipes, you need to get the maximum amount of aroma out of every ingredient you use. Even though most fats don't have any aroma of their own, it's often fat that carries aroma. However, you can dramatically reduce the amount of fat used in cooking and still have truly delicious food by using the following suggestions for maximizing flavor.

Herbs and spices contain practically no calories and, when used liberally, can compensate for salt as well as fat. When you start using more herbs and spices in your cooking, you will be amazed at how much better everything tastes and how much your reputation as a creative cook is enhanced.

Chop or crush fresh herbs before adding them to any recipe. When using dried herbs that are not already powdered, always crush them using a mortar and pestle until you can smell them all over the kitchen. That releases their full aroma.

You can also greatly intensify the flavor of both whole and ground spices by browning them in a heavy pan or by roasting them in the oven. This technique is essential for many Asian and Indian dishes.

You can literally change the personality of a dish by just changing the herbs and spices used in it. For example, a simple chicken breast can be made to taste Italian with oregano and basil, Chinese with ginger and Chinese five-spice blend, Mexican with cumin and chili powder, southern with Cajun spices, Indian with curry powder, Scandinavian with dill or Moroccan with coriander and allspice. As you can see, the combinations are endless and fun to experiment with in your own cooking.

Marinating the ingredients to be cooked adds enormously to the final depth of flavor. Marinating is not just for fish, poultry and meats. Marinating fruits, vegetables and tofu enhances their flavor as well. A marinade can be as simple as plain lemon juice or as complex as a teriyaki or barbecue sauce. Many salad dressings make great marinades. Marinating can also help tenderize the tougher cuts of meat.

Browning or roasting meats and vegetables gives them a much richer flavor. You can do this either in a skillet on top of the stove or in a roasting pan in the oven. I like to keep roasted garlic and shallots in the refrigerator to add to soups, stews, casseroles and salads. When using a Crock-Pot or other slow-cooking method, browning the meat first greatly improves the flavor of the final dish.

Toasting nuts and seeds enhances their flavor so much that you can actually cut the amount almost in half and still end up with a tastier dish.

Sizzle garlic before adding other ingredients to the pan or before adding the garlic to sauces and salad dressings to intensify its flavor. Combine the garlic and a small amount of oil in a sauté pan and heat just until the garlic "sizzles."

Smoking is a technique that adds flavor not only to fish, poultry and meat but also to fruits and vegetables. You don't even need a smoker—you can use a wok or large pot with a tight-fitting lid. Line the pan with foil, add wood chips that have been soaked in water and place a rack over the chips. Cover, put over heat and allow the wood chips to start smoking. Place the items to be smoked on the rack and again cover tightly. Smoke until the taste is as strong as you desire. For even more flavor, add dried herbs and spices to the wood chips before heating them. Dried rosemary, cinnamon sticks and whole cloves are among my favorites.

Reduce the volume by simmering any liquid uncovered to intensify its flavor. Reduction sauces are used frequently in low-calorie cooking to achieve both a stronger taste and a thicker texture without adding fat.

Balance flavor with an acid to "sharpen" the flavor of something that tastes flat. You can do this with the addition of a very small amount of either citrus juice or vinegar. You can also use buttermilk or yogurt to replace a dairy ingredient.

Brighten flavor with hot ingredients like Tabasco sauce, chili oil, cayenne pepper or red-pepper flakes to stimulate the taste buds with what I call "painful pleasure." Hot additives are frequently used in many cuisines just to add this bite or sparkle to main dishes as well as condiments.

Use aromatic high-fat ingredients on top of dishes instead of mixing them in, so that their smell dominates. By doing this, the perception is always that you have used more than you really did. This technique works especially well with cheeses and nuts. With cheese, use only the highest quality, most aromatic types available, such as Parmigiano-Reggiano, Pecorino Romano or a very sharp Cheddar.

Make foods a day ahead of time and give the flavors a chance to "marry" overnight. Many dishes, such as curries, are much better when they are made the day before they are served.

Cook with Less Fat

Use nonstick cookware to prepare fish, poultry, meat and even pancakes without any oil at all. For even browning, give the food itself a spritz of nonstick vegetable spray. If you spray the pan instead, the spray has a tendency to bead up on a nonstick surface and prevent even browning.

Use nonstick vegetable spray instead of butter, margarine or oil in baking dishes to prevent sticking.

Glaze the skillet with stock to give color without using fat. Bring a small quantity of fat-free stock to a boil in a skillet or sauté pan and cook it until it has almost completely evaporated. Continue adding more stock until the pan has been thoroughly coated with a thin layer of glaze. Then add the ingredient to be cooked. This technique works particularly well for chicken breasts—by the time they are nicely browned, they are perfectly cooked.

Deglaze the skillet or roasting pan with water, stock, juice or wine to remove any tasty bits stuck to the bottom. Add the liquid to the pan and stir with a wooden spoon over heat to loosen the bits. Pour them and the liquid over whatever you've cooked.

Sweat onions by cooking them without any fat in a covered heavy pan over low heat for about 10 minutes, or until the onions are soft and translucent. Add a little water, if necessary, as the onions cook to prevent scorching. This is a great way to start making a classic sauce that usually calls for "heating the oil before adding the onions." Nobody will miss the fat!

Cook at a low temperature for a long period of time to allow flavors to marry. You can do this in a Crock-Pot or in an oven at a very low temperature. Either way, you'll create a rich-tasting dish with little or no fat in it.

Bake for a very short time in a very hot oven to crisp the outside of thinly sliced poultry, meat and fish without overcooking the inside. When "oven-frying" potatoes or onions, mist them first with a nonstick vegetable spray for a crisp texture.

Rapid roasting or baking, uncovered, at a very high oven temperature (500°) for a short period of time not only saves time but also improves both flavor and texture of thicker cuts of meat. It produces a shiny, crusted exterior with a still-tender interior. The best way to know when meat is done is to use a meat thermometer. For poultry, watch for the juices to run clear when you pierce the flesh with a sharp knife.

Slice fatty fish paper thin and either broil it or cook it in a hot non-stick skillet for 1 minute, or until it's opaque and begins to release its own fat. This is a superb way of cooking salmon, mackerel and other high-fat fish.

Remove Fat

Refrigerate soups, stews and sauces overnight. Fat that rises to the top will solidify and can be easily removed. If you are in a hurry, you can put the dish you wish to defat in the freezer for a shorter period of time.

Using a defatting pitcher, which has a low-placed spout, is the fastest method of removing fat from liquids. The fat rises to the top, allowing the fat-free liquid underneath to be poured out.

Damp paper towels can be used to remove fat from the surface of soups and stews. Drag them over the surface so floating fat can adhere to them.

Improve Texture with Minimum Fat

Texture can best be described as "mouth feel." It is also associated with the viscosity or "body" of things like salad dressings and gravies. Fat is often the ingredient that creates body, smooths out the texture and creates creaminess. So it is necessary to use other methods or ingredients for achieving this same smooth, creamy texture when using less fat or no fat in a recipe. Here are a few techniques that work especially well.

Thicken fat-free and low-fat dressings and sauces with gelatin. That makes it possible to achieve the same thick and slightly creamy texture usually associated with higher-fat dressings. You won't need much gelatin: One envelope, which is one scant tablespoon, will jell two cups of liquid—so just a pinch is usually enough to thicken a dressing or sauce.

Use dried fruit in fat-free sauces to add an enormous amount of flavor as well as a rich and creamy texture. Reconstitute the fruit in water, stock, wine or juice and then puree it. Use the puree in both cooked and uncooked dishes.

Substitutions for Fat

Substitute lower-fat ingredients for high-fat ones in recipes. Good examples are fat-free mayonnaise, nonfat cream cheese and reduced-fat cream soups.

Use two egg whites instead of one whole egg in almost all recipes. This is of particular importance to people who are on a low-cholesterol diet, because each egg yolk contains 213 milligrams of cholesterol.

Use liquid egg substitutes, which contain no cholesterol at all. A good rule of thumb is to use ¼ cup liquid egg substitute for each egg called for in a recipe.

Use tofu (soybean curd) as a flavor carrier by marinating it in stock, salad dressing or fruit juice. You can also puree tofu to extend volume in sauces and salad dressings, as I've done in the Herbed Mustard Sauce on page 37.

Use applesauce or pureed prunes to replace most of the fat called for in baked goods. This works well because the cellulose in apples and the pectin in prunes traps moisture in much the same way that fat does and therefore produces a moist texture.

Use cottage cheese to moisten low-fat meat loaf. When making meat loaf, pat half of the meat mixture in a pan. Take about 1 cup of cottage cheese and spoon or crumble it over the meat in an even layer. Top with the remaining meat.

Use the fat in the starch instead of in the sauce. You'll get a better textured, richer-tasting dish. For example, toss the pasta with a tablespoon of extra-virgin olive oil instead of adding oil to the sauce. Or add a little butter or margarine to the water or stock when cooking rice rather than putting it in sauce that you'll serve over the rice.

Tips on Presentation

Serving smaller portions of animal protein is healthier and less expensive. Replace the protein with larger portions of complex carbohydrates.

Butterfly fish, poultry and meats for quicker cooking and more plate coverage.

Pound poultry, meats and very firm fish into thin scallops (or paillards) for quicker cooking and more plate coverage.

Baking in parchment paper makes a dramatic plate presentation. And cleanup is quick and easy.

Tips for Saving Time

Keep a shopping list in your kitchen. Always keep it up-to-date on anything you're low on so that you never run out of products you use regularly, including dish soap, paper towels and coffee filters.

Make a weekly menu and add all ingredients to your shopping list so that you only have to shop once a week.

Shop regularly at the same market. You know where everything is, and you also know which brands they do and do not carry. If it's a small market, the cashiers get to know you, so you're able to cash a check if necessary.

Never shop the same day you are planning to entertain.

Call ahead to find unique or unusual items. You'll save yourself the time spent going from one market to another. This is particularly true for seasonal fruits and vegetables, items found only in health-food stores and foreign ingredients that may only be available in an Asian, Indian or Italian market.

Ask the butcher to bone, cube or slice poultry and meat for you. You can also ask to have skin removed from poultry if desired. Also, when buying seafood, ask the fishmonger to have your fish ready to use. This would include filleting whole fish or cracking and cleaning cooked shellfish such as crab and lobster.

Soak raw shrimp in white vinegar for 20 to 30 minutes before removing the shells. The shells will soften and can be much more easily removed. Rinse the shelled shrimp to get rid of the vinegar taste.

Start with a clean kitchen, including an empty dishwasher, to make clean-up much faster.

Clear the counter space necessary for preparation of any recipe before starting.

Arrange all ingredients needed for a recipe before you start to make it.

Prepare as much as possible a day or night in advance, such as cleaning, chopping and measuring.

Cooking vegetables in the same water with pasta eliminates the need for another pan and seasons the pasta at the same time. If the vegetables don't need to cook as long as the pasta, add them at the appropriate time.

Combine vegetables with rice and cook both at the same time.

Open both ends of tomato paste cans (or cans of any other thick substance) so you can easily push the food out.

Freeze fruit juice or leftover coffee in ice cube trays for quick coolers. To serve, just fill a glass with the cubes and add milk.

Keep a box of nonfat dry powdered milk in your kitchen. It's the next best thing to having your own cow! Whenever you run out of milk, you can simply make more. For a richer, thicker texture, add less water than the directions specify. After opening the box, store it in the refrigerator.

Smack garlic with a mallet and its peel will come right off. Or use a garlic press and you don't have to peel it!

Slam a head of lettuce on the countertop, core side down, to loosen the core for easy removal.

Double or triple recipes that freeze well and store them in the appropriate size containers for future meals. (Keep an adequate supply of containers for storing and freezing leftovers.)

Don't double recipes for baked goods. Instead, make two separate batches. That way, you won't overmix the batter and risk ruining whatever you're preparing.

For guaranteed no-lump sauces and gravy, combine the flour and liquid in a jar with a tight-fitting lid. Shake vigorously until the mixture is completely blended before adding it to hot ingredients.

Cook sweet potatoes in your waffle iron. It's an especially quick and easy way to make them. Just shred the sweet potatoes and put one cup in a hot waffle iron that has been sprayed with a nonstick vegetable cooking spray. Cook until the potatoes stop steaming, about 20 minutes. You can sprinkle them with ground cinnamon or nutmeg if desired.

Tips for Saving Money

Slice overly ripe bananas and store them in self-sealing bags in the freezer to use for frothy shakes and in baking. For a great shake, blend one cup of cold milk and a frozen sliced banana until completely smooth. This mixture is also wonderful as a cereal topping.

Bake bruised or overly ripe apples. Or use them for applesauce.

Use stale bread to make croutons and bread crumbs.

Buy all produce at a farmers' market when possible. Fruits and vegetables are not only less expensive but also fresher and tastier.

Buy staple products by the case.

Squeeze your own fresh fruit juice.

Make your own peanut butter. Just put peanuts in a food processor and turn it on. Blend to the consistency you like best. Store, covered, in the refrigerator.

Index

Note: <u>Underscored</u> page references indicate boxed text. **Boldface** references indicate photographs.

G

H

Halibut
    Italian Fish Dish, 234
    Italian Halibut Steaks, 100
Ham
    Ham and Cheese Calzone, **180**, 189
    Ham and Cheese Roll-Ups, 273
Harissa, **23**, 40–41
Hash
    Creamy Beef Hash, 115
    Turkey Hash, 112
Healthy cooking
    advantages of, 1–2
    timesaving recipes for, 4
Herbs. *See also individual herbs*
    for enhancing flavor, 330
    Grilled Swordfish on Herbed Couscous
        with Vegetable Minestrone, **158**,
        168–69
    Herbed Green Beans, 62
    Herbed Grilled Cheese Sandwiches, 43
    Herbed Lemon Chicken, 236
    Herbed Melon Soup, 45
    Herbed Mustard Sauce, 37
    Herbed Oven-Fried Chicken, 172
    Lamb Chops with Herbed Apricot
        Sauce, **178**, 186
    Mixed-Tomato Marinara Sauce with
        Herbed Couscous, **69**, 80–81
    Pickled Asparagus with Herbed Lemon
        Dressing, **29**, 53
Honey
    Baked Honey-Rosemary Lamb Shanks,
        260
    Honeyed Oranges, **264**, 279
    Honeyed Rice, 143
    Honeyed Yogurt Sauce, 37
    Honey-Mint Couscous, **67**, 74
    Honey-Mustard Chicken, 242
    Honey-Mustard Pecan Catfish, 96
    Honey-Sesame Fruit Granola, 315
    Warm Pear Slices in Honey-Pepper
        Sauce, **266**, 283

Horseradish
    Mashed Potatoes with Horseradish,
        151, 148
Hummus, **24**, 41

I

Ice milk
    Lemon-Ginger Ice Milk, **269**, 294
Italian-style dishes
    Antipasto Salad, **130**, 137
    Baked Italian Chicken, 240
    Fettuccine Alfredo, 79
    Ham and Cheese Calzone, **180**, 189
    Italian Fish Dish, 234
    Italian Halibut Steaks, 100
    Italian Spaghetti Sauce, 209
    Italian Vegetable Soup, 125
    Roasted Italian Chicken on Rotini, **228**,
        247
    Savory Polenta with Italian Salsa, 146–47
    Tuscan Tuna Salad, 60, **66**

K

Kabobs
    Salmon and Red Onion Kabobs, **157**, 167
Ketchup
    Cranberry-Orange Ketchup, **127**, 121
Kitchen equipment, 8–10
Kitchen organization, 5–10
Kitchen scale, 10
Kitchen scissors, 9
Kiwi
    Creamy Chilean Kiwi Dressing, 38
Knives, 8–9

L

Label reading, 13
Lamb
    Baked Honey-Rosemary Lamb Shanks,
        260
    fat content of, 31

Q

R

S